–The–
10-DAY
MBA

STEVEN SILBIGER

-The- 10-DAY MBA

A STEP-BY-STEP GUIDE TO MASTERING THE SKILLS TAUGHT IN TOP BUSINESS SCHOOLS

PIATKUS

I gratefully thank Rose Marie Morse and Sarah Zimmerman
of William Morrow for all their diligent efforts
to transform my MBA drafts into this book.

© 1993 Steven Alan Silbiger

All rights reserved

Permissions, constituting a continuation of the
copyright page, appear on page 377

First published in 1993 by
William Morrow and Company, New York

This edition published in 1994 by
Judy Piatkus (Publishers) Ltd of
5 Windmill Street, London W1P 1HF

The moral right of the author
has been asserted

*A catalogue record for this book is
available from the British Library*

ISBN 0 7499 1315 0

Printed and bound in Great Britain by
Butler & Tanner Ltd, Frome and London

CONTENTS

CONTENTS

INTRODUCTION

After I earned my MBA in May 1990, I had a chance to reflect on the two most exhausting and fulfilling years of my life. As I reviewed my course notes, I realized the basics of an American MBA education were quite simple and could be made understandable to a wider audience. In speaking to my friends, many of whom are doctors, lawyers, businesspeople, and aspiring MBAs, I found they were often curious to hear about what I had learned in business school. I have written this book to answer their questions. One can grasp the fundamentals of an MBA without losing two years' wages and incurring a $50,000 debt for tuition and expenses.

People from all over the world study at American business schools. They continue to enjoy a reputation as having spearheaded the revolution in business teaching. Prospective MBAs can use this book to see if a two-year investment is worth their while; those about to enter business school here or in the UK can get a *big* head start on the competition. It will give you an overview of the MBA course, and also serve as an excellent revision aid. Unfortunately, this book cannot provide you with the friendships and lifelong business contacts that you can develop at an elite school. However, it will give you knowledge of many of the skills that make MBAs successful.

The Ten-Day MBA summarizes the essentials of an American Top Ten MBA education. The mystique and the livelihood of the Top Ten business schools are predicated on making their curriculum appear as unique and complex as possible. Companies pay thousands of dollars to send their executives to drink from these hallowed fountains of knowledge for a few days. I spent two years of my life not only drinking from the fountain but also bathing and washing my clothes in it.

Which schools are included in the American Top Ten is a subject of considerable debate. The Top Ten actually refers to a group of fifteen nationally recognized schools that play musical chairs for Top Ten ranking. They distinguish themselves by long application forms, active alumni networks, long lists of recruiters, and the ability of their graduates to demand and receive outrageous starting salaries. The Top Ten schools require of candidates at least two years' work experience before admission. Experienced students can enrich class discussions and study groups. A great deal of my learning came from my classmates' work experiences.

The Top Ten schools do not necessarily offer the best teaching, facilities, or curriculum. Reputation plays a great part in their status. A variety of rating books are available that give the "inside" story on those reputations. According to the 1992 *Business Week* poll, "racking up the highest satisfaction scores from graduates are, in descending order, Dartmouth, Virginia, Northwestern, Cornell and Stanford." The recruiters' rankings, "on the other hand, are Northwestern, Wharton, Harvard, Chicago and Columbia."

The 1992 *Business Week* list of the best fifteen business schools in America includes Chicago, Columbia, Cornell (Johnson), Dartmouth (Tuck), Duke (Fuqua), Harvard, Indiana, Michigan, MIT (Sloan), North Carolina, Northwestern (Kellogg), NYU (Stern), Pennsylvania (Wharton), Stanford, Virginia (Darden).

My aim is to cut to the heart of the top MBA programs' subject matter clearly and concisely – the way only an MBA can, and the way academics would not dare. To cover the major concepts, I use examples and outlines and summarize wherever possible. I slice through the long-winded and self-serving academic readings that at times I had to trudge through. This book contains only the pearls of wisdom buried in my thirty-two binders of cases, course materials, and notes.

I have no vested interest in promoting any of the business theories presented in the book. Therefore, this book does not repeat the same idea over the course of two hundred pages as many popular business books have a tendency to do. I crystallize the most important concepts in brief passages so you can learn and remember them without losing interest.

From my interviews with graduates from Wharton, Harvard, Northwestern, and other top schools, I learned that all of their programs serve up the same MBA meal. Only the spices and presentations of the business banquets vary.

The basics of MBA knowledge in the United States fall into nine disciplines. Some schools have carefully crafted their own exalted names for each subject, but their unglorified names are:

Marketing   **Finance**
Ethics   **Operations**
Accounting   **Economics**
Organizational Behavior **Strategy**
Quantitative Analysis

The synthesis of knowledge from all of these disciplines is what makes the MBA valuable. In the case of a new product manager with an MBA, not only can she see her business challenges from a marketing perspective, but she can recognize and deal with the financial and manufacturing demands created by her new product. This coordinated, multidisciplinary approach is usually missing in undergraduate business curricula. By learning about all the MBA disciplines at once, in one book, you have the opportunity to synthesize MBA knowledge the way you would at the best schools.

When MBAs congregate, we tend to engage in "MBA babble." Our use of mystical abbreviations like NPV, SPC, and MBO is only a ruse to justify our lofty salaries and quick promotions. Please do not be intimidated. MBA jargon is easy to learn! As you read this book, you too will begin to think and talk like an American MBA (ideal if your work brings you into contact with American business people).

My goal is to make you familiar with the significant MBA tools and theories currently being taught at the leading business schools and to help you understand and develop the MBA mind-set. When you finish the ten days, please feel free to fill in your name on the diploma at the end of the book. It serves as evidence of your scholarship and you should proudly display it for all your friends to see.

MBA ABBREVIATION LEXICON

Abbreviation	Translation	Subject	Page
ADL	Arthur D. Little consulting group	S	334
AIDA	attention/interest/desire/action	M	22
BCG	Boston Consulting Group	S	331
CAPM	capital asset pricing model	F	202
CDF	cumulative distribution function	Q	183
COGS	cost of goods sold (UK equivalent: **COS** Cost of Sales)	A	81
CPM	critical path method of scheduling	OP	254
CPM	cost per thousand	M	51
EBIT	earnings before interest and taxes	F	237
EMV	expected monetary value	Q	161
EOQ	economic order quantity	OP	260
FASB	Financial Accounting Standards Board (UK equivalent: **FRS** Financial Reporting Standards)	A	79
FIFO	first in first out	A	84
FRICTO	flexibility, risk, income, control, timing, other	F	227
FSI	free standing insert	M	53
GAAP	generally accepted accounting principles	A	79

Abbreviation	Translation	Subject	Page
GDP	gross domestic product	E	287
GNP	gross national product	E	286
GRP	gross rating points	M	51
IPO	initial public offering	F	226
IRR	internal rate of return	Q	173
IT	information technology	OP	270
JIT	just-in-time inventory	OP	260
LBO	leveraged buyout	F	236
LCP	low cost producer	S	324
LDC	lesser developed country	E	–
LIFO	last in first out	A	79
M&A	mergers and acquisitions	F	235
MBO	management by objective	OB	137
MBWA	management by walking around	OB	137
MNC	multinational corporation	E	336
MRP	material requirements planning	OP	262
NNP	net national product	E	287
NPV	net present value	Q	171
PE	price earnings ratio	F	213
PLC	product life cycle	M	32
POP	point of purchase	M	54
QWL	quality of work life	OB	127
RIF	reduction in force (layoff)	OB	146
ROE	return on equity	A	111
SBU	strategic business unit	S	334
SEC	Securities and Exchange Commission	F	205
SKU	stock keeping unit	M	43
SMSA	Standard Metropolitan Statistical Area	M	28
SPC	statistical process control	OP	266
TRP	total rating points	M	51
TQM	total quality management	Q	–
WACC	weighted average cost of capital	F	228
YTM	yield to maturity	F	207

SUBJECT KEY: A–Accounting; E–Economics; F–Finance; M–Marketing; OP–Operations; OB–Organizational Behaviour; Q–Quantitative Analysis; S–Strategy

DAY 1

MARKETING

MARKETING TOPICS

The 7 Steps of Marketing Strategy Development
The Buying Process
Segmentation
Product Life Cycle
Perceptual Mapping
Margins
The Marketing Mix and the 4 P's
Positioning
Distribution Channels
Advertising
Promotions
Pricing
Marketing Economics

A scene from the boardroom of Acme Corporation:

DIRECTOR: Every time we do our annual review of our executives' salaries, I cringe when I think that we are paying more to Jim Mooney, our vice-president of marketing from Ohio State, than to our company's president, Hank Bufford from Harvard. I just don't understand it.
CHAIRMAN OF THE BOARD: What don't you understand? Without Jim's sales we wouldn't need a president — or anyone else for that matter!

Marketers see the world like the chairman of Acme. As renowned Professor Philip Kotler of the Kellogg School at Northwestern teaches, marketing comes first. Marketing integrates all the functions of a business and speaks directly to the customer through advertising, salespeople, and other marketing activities.

"HOLD ALL CALLS. I'LL BE DOWN IN ACCOUNTING FLEXING MY MUSCLES."

Marketing is a special blend of art and science. There is a great deal to be learned in marketing classes, but no amount of schooling can teach you the experience, the intuition, and the creativity to be a truly gifted marketer. That's why those with the gift are so highly paid. Formal education can only provide MBAs with a framework and a vocabulary to tackle marketing challenges. And that is the goal of this chapter and of the numerous expensive executive seminars conducted by the leading business schools.

The top schools prepare their students for executive marketing positions — in spite of the fact that their first jobs will likely be as lowly brand assistants at large food or soap companies. Therefore, the core curriculum stresses the development of full-fledged marketing strategies instead of the technical expertise needed on an entry-level job out of MBA school.

Numbers-oriented students tend to view marketing as one of the "soft" MBA disciplines. In fact, marketers use many quantitative or "scientific" techniques to develop and evaluate strategies. The "art" of marketing is trying to create and implement a winning marketing plan. There are literally an infinite number of possibilities that may work. McDonald's, Burger King, Wendy's, Hardee's, and White Castle successfully sell burgers, but they all do it in different ways. Because there are no "right" answers, marketing classes can provide students with either an opportunity to show their individual flair, or many hours of frustration as they try to come up with creative ideas. Marketing was my favorite subject. It was fun cooking up ideas for discussion. My B-school buddies still kid me about the time I proposed to the class that Frank Perdue introduce a gourmet chicken hot dog.

THE MARKETING STRATEGY PROCESS

The marketing process is a circular function. Marketing plans undergo many changes until all the parts are *internally consistent* and *mutually supportive* of the objectives. All aspects of a proposal need to work together to make sense. It is very easy to get one part right, but an internally consistent and mutually supportive marketing plan is a great accomplishment. It's a seven-part process.

1. Consumer Analysis
2. Market Analysis
3. Review of the Competition and Self
4. Review of the Distribution Channels
5. Development of a "Preliminary" Marketing Mix
6. Evaluation of the Economics
7. Revision and Extension of Steps 1–6 until a consistent plan emerges

Although there are seven steps, their order is not set in stone. Based on circumstances and your personal style, the order of the steps may be rearranged. This chapter could get bogged down in a morass of marketing theory, but to make it practical, I will outline the questions and areas that should be considered when developing a marketing plan. For expediency, I will concentrate on product marketing, but the same frameworks and vocabulary are also applicable to service marketing.

Marketing Strategy Development

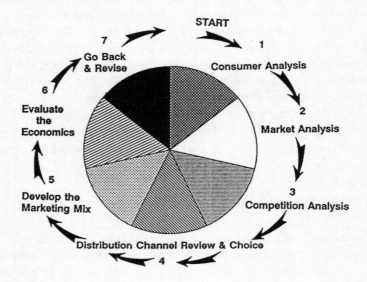

I will present the MBA models in the same seven-step order in which they are taught at the best schools. This chapter offers a generic structure to apply to whatever marketing issue you may encounter. I have not neglected to use the vocabulary taught at the schools, so you can pick up on the MBA jargon and speak like a real MBA marketer. Marketing is an area especially rich in specialized vocabulary. With the correct vocabulary, even your mediocre marketing ideas can appear as brilliant ones. That may sound funny, but that's the way ad agencies market *their* product, advertising.

1. CONSUMER ANALYSIS

Consumer Analysis → Market → Competition → Distribution → Marketing Mix → Economics → Revise

All marketing plans should begin with a look at the all-important "consumer" and his or her needs. People do not have the same needs or desires. The objective of consumer analysis is to identify *segments* or groups within a population with similar needs so that marketing efforts can be directly targeted to them. Starting anywhere else tends to restrict your thinking and all subsequent analysis. Several important questions must be asked to find that market which will unlock untold marketing riches:

What is the *need category*?
Who is buying and who is using the product?
What is the *buying process*?
Is what I'm selling a high- or low-involvement product?
How can I *segment* the market?

What is the need category? Who needs us and why?

What is the need or use that your product addresses? The question may seem unnecessary, but in answering it you may uncover a potential market for the product that was previously overlooked. That is why this question has to be addressed first, before you begin to pollute your mind with conventional thoughts. The people at Arm & Hammer baking soda have done a great deal of this type of analysis. They have made use of their powder in their own brand of tooth paste, air freshener, and carpet freshener. In addition, they profitably recommend their raw baking soda powder for hundreds of uses.

Who is buying vs. who is using the product?

Buyers many times are different from users. Women, for example, make the majority of purchases of men's underwear and socks. If an advertising campaign wanted to target the buyer of men's socks, it probably would be inappropriate to buy space in *Sports Illustrated*. Determining the buyer as well as the user provides the essential initial insights to create a marketing plan.

What is the buying process?

Once you have established the need, and who is making the purchases, you should try to form a hypothesis on *how* the product is bought. Marketing research is a prime source of information, but just as valid are your own observations, investigation, and intuition.

Understanding the *buying process* is critical because it will lead to the possible routes to reach buyers. The buying process includes all the steps that a person takes leading to a purchase. It is also called the *adoption process* and the *problem solving process* by some academics. Some researchers call it a Learn/Feel/Do process. Others call it *AIDA* for Attention/Interest/Desire/Action. I have read extensively on this topic and have boiled the theories down to five steps. For any particular product, the buying process can include one or all of the following steps:

Awareness → Information Search → Evaluate Alternatives → Purchase → Evaluate

In the instance of a soap purchase, the process would look like this:

Smell Body → What Should I Use? → Soap? → Ask Wife for Advice → Make Trip to the Store → Read Labels → Buy Dial Soap → Bathe → Smell Body for Odor → Buy Dial Soap Next Time

The Steps of the Buying Process Explained:

Awareness (Interest, Problem Recognition). "I might need something." At some point a person will realize a need, like the need to use soap. Advertising may trigger that need. Prestige products such as designer clothes and fragrances trigger desire. They meet emotional needs such as love and group acceptance. Head & Shoulders preys on the fear of a loss of love and group acceptance. You need to ask yourself, "How do consumers become aware of my product?" "Where are my targets likely to be exposed to my message?"

Information Search. "Sounds good, let me find out more about it." People involved in purchase decisions are confronted with information from a variety of sources: *Consumer Reports*, salespeople, specialty magazines, family, friends, and local experts. As a marketing manager, you want your target market to get as much favorable information as possible about your product when and where buyers make their buying decisions. For example, store displays play that role at the *point of purchase* (POP). Noxell's Clarion cosmetics has a little computer on the shelf in Kmart to assist buyers. For the same purpose, Estée Lauder has its Clinique ladies in department stores to do its talking.

Evaluate the Alternatives. Which one is best for me? This includes not only products within a category, but substitutes as well. When confronted with the high prices of automobiles, a college student may end up buying a motorcycle, a moped, or a bicycle. Depending on the importance of the product, consumers may seek additional information and advice. Car purchases often include a trip to the local mechanic or the neighborhood car buff. Placing positive information where your buyers are likely to look is one key to marketing success.

At this stage of the buying process the marketing manager would like to identify the *influencers* of his target's buying behavior. In the golf industry the club pro is a key influencer in the equipment-buying decision of golfers. If you can sell the pro, you can sell to the club's members.

Distribution is also crucial at the evaluation stage of the buying process. If a product is not readily available, a comparable substitute may be chosen just for convenience or immediacy of need. Coca-Cola and Pepsi's wide distribution make it tough for any new cola competitor to ever be any more than a fringe brand. Even if you crave Dr. Brown's Creme Soda, you probably will accept a Coke or a Pepsi when you're thirsty at the beach.

The Purchase Decision. This is the big sale. Even though the decision to buy could be "yes," in certain instances the first purchase is only a *trial*. *Adoption* of "new and improved" Bounty paper towels as your regular brand occurs only after a successful test with those tough spills. With many big-ticket items, such as ocean cruises and appliances, a trial is not possible. In those instances the decision process is more time-consuming and difficult to make because there is more risk involved. It is very important for the marketer to understand risk. Through the use of a number of marketing tools, such as advertising, knowledgeable salespeople, warranties, and printed materials, purchase risk can be reduced by offering the buyer information explaining what level of performance he can expect, as well as providing a basis of comparison with competing products.

Evaluate (Postpurchase Behavior). Did I make a mistake? This conclusion can be reached either on a physical level by testing the product's efficacy or on a psychological level by checking for peer approval. *Buyer's remorse* and *postpurchase dissonance* are terms to describe the period of confusion that often follows a purchase. Automobile advertising, for example, is not only targeted at potential buyers, but also at recent buyers to reassure them that they didn't screw up when they bought a Chrysler Voyager minivan instead of a Chevy Lumina APV.

In trying to understand the buying process, the first sparks of a marketing plan can be ignited into a tentative idea about advertising or promotion (to be considered later in Step 5 of the strategy development process).

Research Can Help to Understand the Buying Process. Consumer research is a major tool in helping make the buying process theory useful. Research can show a marketing director where he has succeeded and where his efforts need to be redirected. For example, if the marketing director of *The National*, a sports newspaper that failed in 1991, had conducted a survey that would have shown him that 50 percent of men were aware of the paper, but that only 1 percent had read it, that could have been useful. That finding could have led the director to increase his efforts to gain wider newsstand distribution and to give more more trial subscriptions. Research is valuable because it can be translated into tangible marketing actions. Before you embark on research, you *must* ask yourself:

"What specific question do I need answered?"

"How am I going to use the information once I have it?"

If you haven't thought through these two simple questions, you will probably waste your time and money. I can assure you that many marketing research companies will be glad to help you waste money.

Is the product a high- or a low-involvement product?

As the discussion of buyer behavior indicates, different products elicit different purchase behaviors because of their inherent importance to the buyer and user. If the consumer feels a high level of "risk" in buying a product, then it is considered a *high-involvement* product. There are several reasons for high-involvement purchase decisions:

High price
The need for the product's benefit (e.g., reliability, as in the case of a
   pacemaker)
The need for the product's psychological reward (e.g., status, love)

Stereos, clothing, cars, and professional services are examples of
high-involvement purchases. They are usually higher priced and at
times difficult to compare. Determining the differences between
alternatives makes high-involvement purchases difficult, especially
if the buyer is not an expert. Thus, the information search can be
quite extensive. When litigating a damage claim, for example, usually there is no second chance to take the case to trial. Therefore,
the choice of a lawyer is a high-involvement selection. With *low-
involvement* products the decision is simpler. For example, if a candy
bar isn't tasty, you can always pitch it and buy another one.

A helpful matrix on page 26 captures the possible behaviors resulting from the interaction of the levels of involvement and product
differences. By understanding the possible behaviors, you, as a marketer, may be able to take advantage of this knowledge to sell your
product.

This academic model does have real-world implications for action.
A high-involvement product, such as a Harley-Davidson motorcycle, would appear in the upper left-hand corner of the matrix. The
model would suggest that Harley's marketing efforts should be geared
toward demonstrating its technical superiority, but also include an
emotional appeal — "buy an American classic" — to engender loyalty.

The marketer's magic is at work when he or she transforms a
previously low-involvement product into a high-involvement one.
Athletic shoes are a prime example. Once just functional shoes for
gym class, sports shoes have become a status symbol for young
people and even the cause of murder on inner-city streets. The
conversion of a low-involvement product to a high-involvement
product can make a simple commodity product stand out against
an undifferentiated field of competitors. There are four generic
ways in which this can be accomplished.

CONSUMER BEHAVIOR MATRIX

	High Involvement	Low Involvement
Significant Differences	–Complex Process –Brand Loyalty	–Experiment –Random Behavior –Variety Seeking

Few Differences	–Anxiety (Dissonance)
	  Reduction
	–Baseless Beliefs
	  About the Product
		–Buy Cheapest One
		–Random Behavior
		–Baseless Loyalty
		–Inertia

Adapted from Henry Assael, *Consumer Behavior and Marketing Action*, 4th ed. (Boston: PWS-Kent Publishing Co., 1992), p. 100.

Link Product to a High-Involvement Issue. Linking Procter & Gamble's Puritan no-cholesterol cooking oil to a wife's fear of a husband's heart attack is a classic example of an advertising ploy.

Use Involving Advertising. If the advertising creates a *value-expressive* message about the product or service, then a product can become important. Such messages link values, such as social status and love, instead of promoting physical product attributes to differentiate the product from the competition. Pepsi tries to link being modern and youthful with its products by using singers in elaborate commercials to sell its soda.

Change the Importance of Product Benefits. Products as well as services provide a variety of benefits. If through marketing action a benefit can be raised to a heightened level of importance, buyers are likely to become more involved. The beer wars of the 1980s made calories an important competitive issue. An overlooked attribute — calories — made health-conscious drinkers more aware of their purchasing decisions, and consequently Miller Lite made out like a bandit.

Introduce Important Characteristic to Product. A marketer can also tinker with some of the elements of the product itself to distinguish it. When childproof caps were introduced on household cleaners, the involvement of parents in this purchase decision was heightened. The first products with protection caps stood out on the store shelves. But once all competitors copied the cap, new avenues of differentiation were needed and the purchase returned to its low-involvement status.

Truly low-involvement products often are that way because a minimum level of acceptable performance is required. A thumbtack, for example, does not have a very difficult job to perform. No matter what the brand, you can't go too wrong. If the cost of trial is low, such as for a pack of gum, involvement is difficult to stimulate.

Related to involvement is the level of purchase planning. Is the purchase planned or an impulse buy? High-involvement products are usually planned while impulse products are bought on the spur of the moment. If a purchase is planned, then a buyer is likely to seek information. If not, the proximity of the product to the need is very important. Snack foods are an example of impulse buying. Midday hunger leads to the nearest junk food.

Do I intend to segment the market? Why? How?

I skirted around this issue in the buyer behavior section, but the question "Who is our consumer?" is central to the marketing task. If you think you have something that is for everyone, then a *mass market* strategy is appropriate. If your product satisfies the masses, then feed it to them. If not, you must choose a *segment* or segments of the market to target. Segments are homogeneous groups of similar consumers with similar needs and desires. For instance, Coca-Cola uses a mass market approach to get everyone drinking the "real thing." Orangina, a specialty soda, appeals to a more narrowly defined market segment. It's priced higher and its bottle is shaped differently. Orangina appeals to a special segment of the soft drink market.

Segmentation of the market serves the following functions:

To identify segments large enough to serve profitably.
To identify segments that can be efficiently reached by marketing efforts.
To help develop marketing programs.

By having a definite segment in mind, you can effectively aim and efficiently execute your marketing activities to yield the most sales and profits. Without a target, you risk wasting marketing dollars on disinterested people. There are four major segmentation variables used in segmenting consumer markets:

- **Geographic**
- **Demographic**
- **Psychographic**
- **Behavioral**

Geographic Segmentation. Divides the market by country, state, region, county, and city. The federal census lists 310 *Standard Metropolitan Statistical Areas* (SMSAs) to define the major geographic population centers of the United States. Arbitron, a large media research firm, has defined a similar measure to capture the 210 major television markets of the country, called *Areas of Dominant Influence* (ADIs). A. C. Nielsen, a competitor, has a similar measure called *Designated Market Areas* (DMAs).

Demographic Segmentation. Divides a population based on the following measurable variables to reach a homogeneous group of people:

Age — different generations' different wants and needs.
Sex — gender use and buying patterns.
Income — the ability to purchase.
Marital Status — family needs.
Family Life Cycle — starting out, empty nesters, etc.
Education/Occupation — an indication of the sophistication of the consumer.
Ethnicity, Religion, and Race — particular tastes and preferences.

Psychographic Segmentation. Divides the market by psychological differences:

Life-style — activities, interests, and opinions.
Personality — conservative, risk-taking, status-seeking, compulsive, ambitious, authoritarian, gregarious. (People may have different hot buttons that advertising can try to trigger.)

Psychographic segmentation is difficult. Personality variables are tougher to identify and quantify than demographics, but they can be very valuable.

Behavioral Segmentation. Divides the market by observable purchase behaviors:

Usage — amount of use, manner of use, benefits sought.
Purchase Occasion — gift, vacation, seasonal, etc.
Brand Loyalty — loyalty to one product indicates receptiveness to others.
Responsiveness to Price and Promotion — some groups respond to special marketing efforts more than others. Housewives use more coupons than single professional women.

Marketers must not only select the "right" group of variables but also decide how many to use. The correct number of "useful" variables will identify the most accessible and receptive target, not the most specific. For example it is possible to describe a target segment for Corvettes as brown-haired, male, twenty-five to sixty-five years old, with income over $50,000. However, the ability to target just brown-haired men with effective advertising is limited and its usefulness would be dubious. Is brown hair a necessary segmentation variable? There are no magazines exclusively targeted to brown-haired males. Besides, blond and redheaded men may also be a reasonable market for Corvettes. You should use the following criteria to evaluate possible marketing segments:

Measurability — Can you identify the segment? Can you quantify its size?
Accessibility — Can you reach the segment through advertising, sales force or distributors, transportation, or warehousing?
Substantiality — Is the segment large enough to bother with? Is the segment shrinking, maturing, or is it a growing segment?
Profitability — Are there enough potential profits to make targeting it worthwhile?
Compatibility with Competition — Are your competitors interested in this segment? Are competitors currently investigating it or is it not worth their trouble?
Effectiveness — Does your company have the capabilities to adequately service this segment?
Defendability — Can you defend yourself against a competitor's attack?

With that theoretical background, here's a sample demographic profile of gourmet coffee buyers that marketers actually use:

Twenty-five to fifty-four years old
College educated
Professional or business executive employment
Childless households
Household incomes greater than $50,000

This "yuppie" market segment is measurable, accessible, large, and profitable. Consequently, many large coffee companies continue to target it.

Even in markets that appear hopeless, there may be a segment that others overlook. Xerox controlled 88 percent of the copier market in the 1970s. The majority of its sales came from large and medium-sized units. But by 1985, Xerox had lost more than half of its market share. What happened? Xerox ignored the small-copier market. Thousands of small companies with light copy needs had to run to the local copy shop every time they had a copy job. Canon, Sharp, and Ricoh seized this market by selling a smaller and less expensive copier. With a foothold in small copiers, the Japanese competitors proceeded to topple Xerox in the large-copier segment of the market.

Consumer analysis serves to "prime the pump" when you need to form a comprehensive marketing strategy. Do it first so as not to stifle your creativity with the quantitative analysis you will perform as part of the strategy development framework. On a first pass, you can make an "intuitive" choice of a target segment. After the other steps are completed it can be altered to fit an evolving marketing strategy.

2. MARKET ANALYSIS

Consumer → **Market Analysis** → Competition → Distribution → Marketing Mix → Economics → Revise

While segmentation analysis focuses on consumers as individuals, market analysis takes a broader view of potential consumers to include market sizes and trends. Market analysis also includes a review of the competitive and regulatory environment. By closely examining the market, a marketing manager can determine if the segment selected is worth the trouble of a targeted marketing effort. MBAs ask three important questions to evaluate a market:

What is the *relevant* market?
Where is the product in its *product life cycle*?
What are the *key competitive factors* in the industry?

What is the relevant market?

The easiest mistake to make is to believe that your *relevant* market includes the total sales of your product's category. In between the first and second years of my MBA education, I worked for an international trading company. I investigated the possibility of selling a Mexican gourmet ground coffee in U.S. grocery stores. It would have been misleading for me to assume that all coffee sales were in my relevant target market. Approximately $11 billion of coffee was sold in the United States in 1990. However, 60 percent of that total was sold in stores, while the other 40 percent was sold to the institutional markets, including restaurants and vending machines. That left me with a retail market of $6.6 billion.

But within that larger coffee market there were additional submarkets to investigate before arriving at my final relevant market. The gourmet coffee market accounted for $750 million, or 11 percent of the retail market's sales. Within the gourmet coffee market, only 60 percent of the coffees sold had no artificial flavorings. My Mexican coffee had no additives and the producer refused to artificially flavor his coffee. Therefore, my relevant market was further reduced to $450 million. But of that market slice, only 55 percent was sold in supermarkets. That left me with a $248 million market. *That* was my relevant market.

Once a market segment is identified, you have to ask if it is large and accessible enough to justify your marketing effort. If the answer to that question is no, then you have what is called a "makable" product, but not a "marketable" one. Only marketable products make money.

These questions are difficult to answer and involve marketing research. If it is a new product, the answers will not be readily available. Test markets may have to be used to obtain that information. This step may lead to further segment investigation.

The growth and decline of consumer segments within a market should also be noted. When the market is growing, future sales growth can come from new users or existing customers. If the pie is shrinking, any sales growth has to come out of your competitors' hide, and they'll fight you for market share! Following the demographic trends to attract a growing senior citizen market, Lederle Laboratory, the manufacturer of Centrum vitamins, made a very minor reformulation in 1990, and successfully introduced its "Silver" formula in 1990.

Where is the market in its product life cycle?

Markets can be characterized by the stage that they are at in their *product life cycles* (PLC). Instead of being merely a factor of time, the PLC describes how a product's sales grow as new segments become aware and begin buying it. Cellular phone service began in the early 1970s with fewer than ten thousand users. But it wasn't until the 1990s, when the prices dropped and many could afford a unit for their cars, that a multisegment market of over six million users emerged.

The PLC concept is important because the process of *diffusion* or adoption by the population has major implications for how a product is marketed. Each product develops its own unique PLC as it matures. Understanding the PLC can give you an MBA insight that your competitors may lack.

The four generic stages of the PLC and their implications for action are:

Stage 1: Introduction, "What is it?" Awareness and education are needed. If possible a trial is important. High advertising costs may be incurred to get the word out. Some vendors opt for an *exclusive distribution* of their products in a few select outlets at first. Initially companies make frequent product changes as customers' needs become known. The first buyers are called the *innovators*, followed by the *early adopters*. They freely take purchase risks because their personalities or pocketbooks allow them to do so. When companies introduce new products, managers must make difficult

The Product Life Cycle

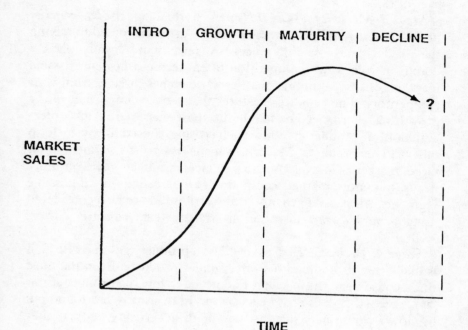

pricing decisions because there is frequently no basis for comparison. The level of initial prices and profits has great implications regarding the outcome of future battles with competitors as well as your ability to perform additional research and development (as with products like high-definition TV and digital audiotape).

Stage 2: Growth, "Where can I get it?" Education is still important, but at this stage competition is intensified. The *early majority* becomes interested. As more consumers become familiar with a product they examine the new models to decide *which* to buy, not *whether* they should buy. When buyers get to the store they start comparing features. To make the product more accessible, marketers often choose a *selective distribution* to gain a greater number and variety of outlets. At this stage it is important to boost your sales volume ahead of the competition in order to reduce costs through production and advertising efficiencies. This helps a company gain the competitive advantage in the next stage of the PLC (e.g., compact discs).

Stage 3: Maturity, "Why this one?" At this stage the *late majority* of the mass market buys. Because people are accustomed to buying the product and the differences are few, brand loyalty plays a dominant role. Price competition often becomes heated in stable markets because additional market share comes directly from your competitors. The product's features that were so important in the growth stage have become standardized. Because there is less differentiation on product attributes, advertising is used as a vehicle to differentiate products. Marketing managers try to segment their target market as much as possible to meet specific unmet consumer needs. In mature markets competitors are ferreting out all possible segments. All possible channels of distribution are also considered using a *mass market* distribution strategy (e.g., cassette players, VCRs).

Stage 4: Decline, "How much?" As a product ages in its PLC, it is likely that its competitors offer similar products. Even the most timid consumers, the *laggards*, find it safe to buy the product at this late stage. (If it does cause cancer, the FDA usually has found out by now.) Consumers turn a deaf ear to advertising because they know that all competing products are the same. At this stage many companies focus their efforts on reducing price if competition remains, or slowly increasing prices if the competitive field thins. Trade relations are key to staying on the retail shelf at this point, because without the excitement of novelty, distributors and retailers would rather allocate space to newer and potentially more profitable products. The effort to sell the trade is popularly called *relationship marketing* (e.g., black-and-white TVs, phonographs).

With some products the maturity phase does not necessarily mean death. Products can be reinvigorated after a period of maturity and a new growth phase can begin. Baseball trading cards underwent such a revival, encouraged by Topps Inc.'s marketing efforts in the 1980s.

In some cases, lingering death throes produce large profits for the last manufacturer. In the vacuum tube business, which supplies electronic tubes for old TVs, radios, and other equipment, Richardson Electronics is the survivor in an industry once dominated by

GE, RCA, Westinghouse, and Sylvania. Using an *end game strategy*, the remaining producers can extract large profits from customers since they have nowhere else to go for their replacement parts.

What are the key competitive factors within the industry?

The basis of competition in each industry or market tends to be different. It has a major impact on how a business attacks its market. There are five major *key competitive factors* that constitute the battleground in most industries:

- **Quality**
- **Price**
- **Advertising**
- **Research and Development**
- **Service**

In the fast food industry, for example, intensive advertising and promotion are key. In industries providing raw materials to others, price and service are key. In my investigation of the coffee industry, I found price and quality to be the basis of competition. When developing a marketing plan, you may want to try to change the basis of competition to one that favors your firm, but the key underlying competitive factors cannot be ignored.

3. ANALYSIS OF YOUR COMPANY VERSUS THE COMPETITION

Consumer → Market → **Competitive Analysis** → Distribution → Marketing Mix → Economics → Revise

By this stage the marketer has preliminarily chosen a consumer segment toward which to direct his efforts. Now, a plan to beat the competition must be developed. You need to look at yourself and at the competition with the same level objectivity. What are your advantages? (MBAs call them *core competencies*.) What are your weaknesses? How can your company capitalize on its strengths or exploit your competitors' weaknesses? The following questions help to flush that out.

What is your company good at and what is the competition good at?

- **Distribution** (Frito-Lay)
- **New Product Development and Introduction** (3M)
- **Advertising** (Absolut vodka)

Who are we in the marketplace?

- **Market Size and *Relative* Market Share**
- **Financial Position**
- **Historic Performance and Reputation**

What are our resources versus those of the competition?

- **People**
- **Technology, Research**
- **Sales Forces**
- **Cash**
- **Trade Relations**
- **Manufacturing**

Barriers to entry to new competitors in a market play an important role in assessing the competition. Barriers are conditions or hurdles that new competitors have to overcome before they can enter the market. The availability of cash and specialized knowledge are such barriers. The pharmaceutical industry, for example, is dominated by a few companies. To be a player, a company needs a large sales force, research labs, and a large bank account to pay for it all. Because of these barriers, most small companies team up with large ones if they have a promising new drug to peddle.

If in an industry the barriers to entry are low, the playing field becomes very crowded. Savvy marketers should plan for that eventuality by trying to form a marketing strategy that new competitors cannot easily copy. This is more fully discussed later in the book in the strategy chapter.

During my coffee investigation, I looked at what my company had to offer. It didn't have much. It didn't have any experience in the United States. We lacked distribution, advertising expertise, a reputation, and cash. The only thing my Mexican employer had to offer was quality packaged coffee. What could a small competitor do against Folger's and Maxwell House coffees? After much questioning, and feeling a little ill, I hoped that there might be a large food company that would like to enter into a joint venture. We would supply the coffee and the partner would do the distribution and marketing. We could *piggyback*, not unlike what small pharmaceutical companies do, recognizing that some profit is better than none.

What are the market shares of the industry players?

Many tracking services are available for consumer products such as Selling Areas Marketing Inc. (SAMI) and A. C. Nielsen. Checkout scanners and warehouse tracking collect supermarket sales data. However, for industrial products, such as manufacturing equipment, the information is less accessible. Trade associations are a good source.

The shift of share over time is extremely important. In the battle for "instant" coffee sales in the grocery store, for example, the top three competitors controlled 95 percent of the market in 1989, up 5 percent from 1986. They were Kraft General Foods (37 percent), Nestlé (34 percent), and Procter & Gamble (24 percent). Little was left for a new entrant.

Market share leverage is a key concept to consider when examining market shares within an industry. The companies with larger market shares relative to their competition usually enjoy higher profits. Larger competitors can produce more cheaply on a per-unit basis because they can spread their costs over more units. A smaller competitor cannot afford to spend as much on either research or more efficient equipment, because the smaller sales volume cannot support the burden. If I had been charged with a new instant coffee to sell, I would have had to reconsider entry into the declining instant-coffee market dominated by bigger, lower-cost competitors. Fortunately for my Mexican coffee's entry, in 1989 18 percent of the "ground" coffee market was controlled by smaller competitors. And that share had increased from 16 percent in 1986. This constituted a far more favorable environment for a new entrant such as my Mexican ground coffee.

How does my product perceptually map against the competition?

The *perceptual mapping* technique is a graphic way to view and compare your product against the competitors'. A commonly used grid is *price* and *quality*, but many others are possible and useful. Maps are another MBA technique to generate ideas for marketing for your product, and perceptual maps may highlight an unserved market segment by showing how the consumer perceives competing products, regardless of the physical reality of performance. Perceptions are paramount in marketing, just as they are in politics. In the paper towel industry, for example, towel strength and decorator appeal are very important. As an example, using my own judgment, I have created a "hypothetical" map on page 39. Notice that Bounty found itself a very profitable market segment by providing strength and a pretty pattern.

By visualizing how your product maps versus the competition, you may gain an insight into how to market your existing product, make product changes, or add additional products in a comprehensive marketing strategy.

If your company has many products within a category then you are said to have *depth* of line. In the paper towel market no one producer dominates the category. But over in the dog food aisle, Ralston's depth chokes the shelves with Dog Chow, Puppy Chow, HiPro, O.N.E., Lucky Dog, and at least six other brands.

If your company has many products in a variety of product classes, you are said to have *breadth* of product line. Kimberly-Clark has a wide breadth of paper products in several categories: Hi-Dri paper towels, Kleenex tissue, Kotex sanitary napkins, and Huggies and Pull-Ups diapers. Depth and breadth of product lines can be cleverly used in a *blocking strategy* to prevent competitors from gaining access to the channels of distribution. If they are not on the shelf, your competition can't make any sales.

In the dog food industry, competitors found other ways around Ralston to reach doggie owners. Iams sold $325 million of Eukanuba brand premium dog food in 1991 to breeders and specialty stores. In the same year Hill's Pet Products, a division of Colgate-Palmolive, pushed $560 million of Science Diet pet food through veterinarians' offices.

Perceptual Mapping
Paper Towel Brands (Hypothetical)

	Low	High
High	Brawny Northern Big N' Thirsty	*Ideal* Bounty
Strength		
Low	Coronet Marcal Hi-Dri	Scott Gala Viva

Decorator Appeal

4. REVIEW OF THE DISTRIBUTION CHANNELS

Consumer → Market → Competition → **Distribution Analysis** → Marketing Mix → Economics → Revise

Marketers speak of the avenues to the consumer as the *channels of distribution*. There are often many ways of reaching your customers, as described with dog food sales. Distribution channel analysis is critical, because the choice of channel influences the price you can charge, and, consequently, the profit margins that you may enjoy.

Three questions should be asked to provide you with a basis for your distribution decision:

How can my product reach the consumer?
How much do the players in each distribution channel profit?
Who holds the power in each distribution channel available?

How can my product reach the consumer?

In the case of many mail-order catalogs, there is a direct link between the marketer and the final consumer. A catalog manufacturer of clothing has a direct pulse on sales, returns, pricing, and consumer tastes. As manufacturers of grocery items, brand managers are distanced from the buyer. Cereal, for instance, must go through wholesalers and retailers before reaching the consumer. Those middlemen are called *channel intermediaries*. As a strategist, the marketing manager must outline all the paths to the consumer to develop a plan.

Commonly used channel intermediaries to the consumer are:

- **Wholesalers**
- **Distributors**
- **Sales Representatives**
- **Sales Forces**
- **Retailers**

How do the players in each distribution channel profit?

As I mentioned, it is very helpful to understand all the paths to the consumer in order to know all the possible ways to market your product. Take the time to draw them out on paper. A channel sketch can also give you the insight into the retail price that must be charged to make a profit.

Everyone who touches the merchandise takes a cut, which is called their *margin*. Participants in the distribution chain are said to "take margin" from the manufacturer. As a manufacturer of a product, you do not "give" the channel margin; there is no charity involved. Channel participants in most industries calculate their cut as a *markup on selling price*. Canadian and some U.S. drug firms use a markup on cost, but they are the exceptions. The *selling price* is not the ultimate *retail* price, but the price at which one intermediary sells goods to the next intermediary in the chain. The retail price is what a consumer pays.

Because of my experience in the coffee industry, I will use coffee retailing to demonstrate the economics of the channels of distribution. At each level of the chain, the intermediary buys the coffee from the previous level and takes a margin based on the sales price to the next level. The margin is *not* based on cost.

$$\text{Percent Markup on Selling Price (SP)} = \left(\frac{\$ \text{ Markup}}{\$ \text{ Selling Price}} \right) \times 100$$

This is how one dollar's worth of coffee beans, in my example, can reach the consumer at a price of six dollars. At each level, the channel participant adds value and incurs costs by either roasting, grinding, and packaging the coffee beans; promoting the brand; or distributing and shelving the packaged coffee for the consumer. I have outlined on page 42 what I estimated were the channel economics in 1989 for Maxwell House's gourmet Private Collection coffee.

At each level in the distribution channel, the participant performs its function, takes its margin, and sells to the next participant closer to the consumer. If a coffee processor, such as Kraft General Foods, believes that its gourmet Maxwell House Private Collection coffee brand must retail at $4.00 per pound rather than $6.00, then the economics of the chain must change. Let's work backward through the chain to see its effect on the prices charged at each level.

Selling Price × (1 − Markup %)
= The Preceding Distribution Level's Selling Price

Working backward through the distribution chain:

$4.00 Retail Price to Consumer ×   (1 − .23 Retail Markup) = $3.08
$3.08 Wholesaler Price to Retailer × (1 − .09 Wholesale Markup) = $2.80
$2.80 would be Kraft General Foods' (The Processor's) Price
  to Wholesalers

Channel of Distribution for Maxwell House's Private Collection Coffee with Channel Margins and Prices

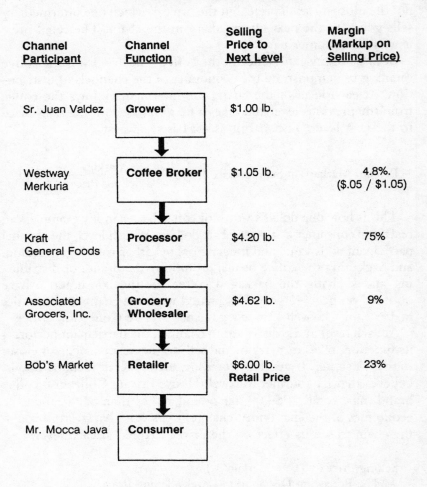

Channel Participant	Channel Function	Selling Price to Next Level	Margin (Markup on Selling Price)
Sr. Juan Valdez	Grower	$1.00 lb.	
Westway Merkuria	Coffee Broker	$1.05 lb.	4.8%. ($.05 / $1.05)
Kraft General Foods	Processor	$4.20 lb.	75%
Associated Grocers, Inc.	Grocery Wholesaler	$4.62 lb.	9%
Bob's Market	Retailer	$6.00 lb. Retail Price	23%
Mr. Mocca Java	Consumer		

At the $4.00 price, Kraft General Foods' brand manager must ask if $1.75 ($2.80 − $1.05) per pound is a sufficient margin to cover costs and provide an adequate profit. If the answer is no, the brand manager must reexamine the marketing plan's channel mathematics. Because marketing strategy is a circular process, another price, manufacturing process, or cost may have to be altered. Such changes could affect all the other elements of the plan.

The relative power of the channel participants can dictate pricing decisions based on the economics of the channel chosen. In Kraft General Foods' case, the brand manager could have opted for the lower $4.00 retail price in the grocery store. However, he chose $6.00 to yield his desired profits.

Kraft General Foods decided to use an alternative channel in addition to grocery stores. Kraft "bypassed" the grocery trade's middlemen and sold its Gevalia and Garraway coffee brands directly to coffee lovers by mail order at a price over $8.00 per pound. With most products there are usually a variety of ways to reach the consumer. Each channel has its own channel margin mathematics. By understanding the math you are better able to make a choice of channel.

Who has the power in the channels?

The question of channel power is very crucial in selecting where to sell. If your product is unique and in demand, then the manufacturer generally has the power to outline the terms of the relationship. If not, the channel's intermediaries will be able to dictate the terms to take as much margin as possible.

In the grocery trade, the power of the channel has shifted from the manufacturers to the supermarket chains. As smaller grocery chains consolidated into larger super chains in the 1980s, the larger chains' management realized that they held the prized real estate, "shelf space." Each *stock keeping unit* (SKU) on the shelf takes space. Each product must be tracked, shelved, and inventoried. (When Mazola cooking oil produces three sizes, it takes up three SKUs.) With a finite amount of store and warehouse space, the shelf real estate has become valuable, and retailers want to be paid for carrying each SKU. Marketers even diagram their shelves like architects in drawings called *planograms* and fight over best placement.

Packaged goods companies, large and small, must often pay *slotting fees* to the chains to reserve their "slots" on their shelves for both new and existing products. In the 1970s the packaged good giants could force their products on the trade. When there were many smaller grocery chains, Procter & Gamble and Kraft General Foods could play one chain against another by threatening to withhold their popular products. That is no longer the case.

Unfortunately, slotting fees can run into millions of dollars for a new product introduction. Therefore, in practice, slotting fees bar smaller competitors from selling in the supermarket. A maker of an excellent pizza in the Midwest that I knew failed to get off the ground because it could not afford the bribes necessary for space. Slotting fees are a "hot topic" in retailing. Feel free to interject this topic into MBA conversation as often as you like.

5. DEVELOPMENT OF THE MARKETING MIX

Consumer → Market → Competition → Distribution → **Plan the Marketing Mix** → Economics → Revise

Based on judgments developed in the analysis of the consumer, the market, the competition, and the distribution channels, the marketing manager must make a set of tangible decisions. MBAs call it the *action plan*. Marketing managers choose what *mix* of marketing efforts should be made. The mix is commonly referred to as the *Four P*'s of marketing.

The Marketing Mix

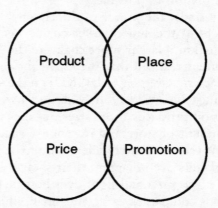

The development of the *marketing mix* is an evolutionary process whose goal is an *internally consistent and mutually supportive* plan. That cannot be overemphasized. Tinkering with one *P* in the mix generally means the marketing strategist must alter all the other *P*'s in some way, because one *P* affects the others.

Product   Place   Promotion   Price

Product Decisions

How does my product fit with my other products?
How will I differentiate my product?
How does the product life cycle affect my plans?

How does the product fit with my existing product line?

This question tries to identify areas of synergy among your products, or uncover a constraint on your activities. For example, if "The Dependability People" at Maytag added dishwashers to their line of clothes washers and dryers, the product, the customers, and the retailers for the dishwashers would be shared with their existing line. There would be a fit with this *line extension*. But if Maytag wanted to sell personal hair dryers, the fit would be questionable.

How will I differentiate my product?

Differentiation is a broad issue that includes any way that a marketer can distinguish his product from the field. Consequently there are many ways to do it.

- *Features* – Capabilities
- *Fit* – Tailoring
- *Styling* – Functional, visual
- *Reliability* – Warranties, return policies
- *Packaging* – Color, size, shape, protection
- *Sizes* – Clothing, appliances, computers, and luggage sizes
- *Service* – Timeliness, courtesy, accuracy
- *Brand Naming* – Labeling

If Ralph Lauren had used his real name, Ralph Lifshitz, he would have foregone the psychological benefits derived from his Ralph Lauren's Polo label on clothing, cologne, and bedding. Lifshitz somehow fails to convey the image of English aristocracy.

In many cases the so-called *brand equity* of one product can be transferred to new products using a *brand* or *line extension* strategy that differentiates it from the pack. Kraft General Foods has chosen to place the Jell-O brand name on its new pudding and ice cream treats. The Jell-O brand bestows upon the new products all the goodwill and brand recognition (brand equity) that Jell-O earned over decades. It would take many years of expensive advertising to establish the brand equity of the Jell-O brand. Accordingly, almost 70 percent of the twenty-four thousand new product introductions since 1987 were line and brand extensions. If stretched too far, a brand's equity can be diluted and its effectiveness with consumers devalued.

The choice of any one of these product differentiation techniques affects the entire marketing process, as it lays the groundwork for your promotional efforts. A product can be differentiated from the competition by creative advertising and promotion, even if competing products are physically identical.

Perceptual maps and positioning can help to differentiate the product. All the product attributes mentioned affect the *positioning* of a product in the marketplace. The marketer can always call upon his company's product engineers to develop a product's physical characteristics if the profits justify it. As my perceptual map of paper towels indicated, consumers have specific needs within a product class and they perceive each product differently. The marketer's job is to uniquely position the product (using a perceptual map as a guide if desired) to earn its place in the market. That place is often called a product's *niche* in the market. As pictured in the perceptual mapping of paper towels, James River's Brawny brand is positioned as the tough, durable towel for really dirty cleanups. Hopefully the brand manager will choose a niche that will yield the most sales and profits by targeting a market segment his product serves best. Positioning is inexorably tied to the market segment selected through your consumer and market analysis.

How does the product life cycle affect my plans?

Based on the point in the *product life cycle* (PLC), different aspects of the product become more important in the competitive battles. The previous discussion of the PLC noted that product features are extremely important to differentiate products in the growth phase, while branding is increasingly more important in the maturity phase. The emphasis on multiplay features on compact disc players, for example, currently indicates the growth phase of the PLC. In the mature cassette deck market, the battles over auto reverse and

Dolby noise reduction have already been played out. Whatever the choices for the product, product decisions will have a definite effect on the other *P*'s of the mix.

Product   **Place**   Promotion   Price

Place of Sale Decisions: Where to Sell?

In your review of the distribution channels, the goal was to determine what avenues exist and what margins are available. At this stage, having made product decisions and a choice of target market, the marketer has to choose an appropriate channel to fit with the product and the intended buyers.

What distribution strategy should I use?
On what basis should I choose a channel of distribution?

What type of distribution strategy should I select?

- *Exclusive* — Sell in only one outlet in each market
- *Selective* — Sell in only a few outlets in each market
- *Mass or Intensive* — Sell in as many outlets as possible

The place of sale affects the perception of your product. The choice of distribution is an evolving process that matches the product's intended diffusion along the product life cycle, as described in the market analysis passage. A distribution strategy can differentiate your product from the crowd. For example, if a new designer chooses to *exclusively* sell at Neiman Marcus, it gives a certain cachet to the product. Consumers tend to perceive certain attributes in a product, such as style, quality, and price, based on the point of sale. The same designer may choose to *selectively* sell in only better department stores to provide greater initial sales volume. The California marketer of car window sun shields had no such concern, and selected a *mass* distribution strategy. The company wanted to distribute the cardboard shade as widely and quickly as possible. That choice made sense since the shades, unlike designer clothing, did not have any status appeal and could be easily copied and manufactured.

Each of these distribution methods places certain responsibilities upon the manufacturer and the retailer. By choosing to be selective, the manufacturer may be "obligated" to provide high quality, good service, and possibly *cooperative payments* (co-ops) for promotional support. When manufacturers share the costs of advertising with retailers, that is called *cooperative advertising*.

In distribution relationships involving manufacturers' incentives, the retailer is also obligated. Retailers may be "obliged" to pay special attention to the product by giving it preferential placement, special promotion, display, and sales attention. If those obligations are not met, the contract is breached and the relationship can be severed. In Ralph Lauren's case he believed that his Polo clothing line was so unique that he became the first designer to demand separate boutique space in department stores. Ralph provided the image and the margins sought by retailers. The retailers were in turn obliged to provide Ralph Lauren with special placement and selling efforts.

Which channels of distribution to choose?

It depends . . . on a variety of factors. There is usually more than one choice. However, if a channel is integrated into a mutually supportive and internally consistent strategy, many choices can potentially be successful. Three factors should serve as a guide to make a selection.

Product Specifics — Another factor to consider is the level of attention needed for the sale. This is related to the level of complexity of the product, the newness, or the price. The product may indicate a need for your own sales force despite the costs. On the other hand, products such as candy and soft drinks are sold through a series of wholesalers and distributors before reaching the store shelves. These products are simple and do not require direct control by the manufacturer over the presentation and sale.

Need for Control — The ability to motivate the channels to carry your product effectively and appropriately enters into the placement decision. The further the manufacturer is removed from the consumer with distributors, wholesalers, and jobbers, the less control the manufacturer has over how a product is sold. Pharmaceutical companies usually have their own sales forces, also called *captive* sales forces, that are thoroughly trained to provide credible information to doctors. If Merck or Marion Merrell Dow had to rely on an independent sales force they would not have absolute control over their training or conduct in the field.

Margins Desired — The analysis of the channels of distribution helps to determine the potential profits available. Where are the margins taken at each level? Can your company deliver the product through the channels at a competitive price and still reserve enough margin for itself? Based on the available margins, channel decisions can be made. In the case of radar detectors, Cincinnati Microwave opted to sell directly to the public through magazine display advertising. They chose not to sell through electronics stores or other general merchandisers. Their management believed that the technological superiority of their Escorts and Passports would help the units sell themselves. Cincinnati Microwave chose to capture the entire retail margin and to cut out all the middlemen who typically distribute and sell electronics. Their strategy has been successful so far because they have maintained their product's technical edge.

Product   Place   **Promotion**   Price

Promotional Decisions

Promotion includes all the advertising and selling efforts of the marketing plan. Goal setting is paramount in developing a promotional campaign. You need to know the mission you want to accomplish before you can begin to draft or spend the promotion budget. The ultimate goal of promotion is to affect buyer behavior; therefore the desired behavior must be defined. Different products, at different stages of the PLC, with different levels of involvement and complexity, require different promotional efforts to perform different missions. The promotional mission chosen for your product must be consistent with the buying process outlined in your *consumer analysis*.

Buying Process	Promotional Mission
Awareness	Inform about product, prompt a need message
Interest	Provide compelling message, solve a need message
Trial	Motivate action

| **Repurchase** | Cue to buy, increase usage |
| **Loyalty** | Reinforce brand or image, special promotions |

Push or Pull Strategy? As with distribution, promotional efforts should be guided by a strategy. *Pull* strategies are those efforts that pull buyers to the outlets that carry your product. TV pitches that instruct viewers "to ask for Perdue chicken by name at your local grocer" *pull* consumers to the stores that carry it. Another important mission of promotion is to encourage the distribution channels to stock and sell a product to customers. Such efforts are a *push* strategy. Beer distributors, for instance, spend a great deal of their time trying to court bar owners to stock and promote their brew on tap. Most plans have an element of both push and pull strategies. In the beer industry they spend heavily to advertise the brand as well as to gain greater bar distribution.

To pull buyers to a store or to push the distribution channel to stock and sell, there are five general categories of promotional efforts:

Advertising
Personal Selling
Sales Promotion
Public Relations and Publicity
Direct Selling

Advertising. Advertising takes many forms: television, radio, outdoor (billboards), magazine, and newspaper. Two important things to keep in mind are your intended mission and the quantitative measurement of exposure required to accomplish it.

Please pay attention to the following measurement vocabulary. This is what you pay for when you buy advertising. The tendency for the uninitiated is to listen to the ad world's babble, not understand it, and buy their wares anyway. Buying advertising is just like buying marketing research — know what and why you are buying — buyer beware.

Reach and *frequency* are key quantitative measurements of media goals. Reach is the percentage of the target market who see and hear your promotion or advertisement. Frequency is the number of times they saw or heard it. Marketers refer to the number of times a person is exposed to a message as the total *impressions* made on that audience. Because of the buying behavior associated with different products, different mixes of reach and frequency are required to induce purchase. When multiplied, Reach × Frequency equals a measure called *gross rating points* (GRPs). Add the GRPs together and you get *total rating points* (TRPs). GRP and TRP are the measures by which radio, TV, and outdoor advertising is sold and purchased.

The desired demographics and segmentation variables of the audiences delivered also enter prominently into the equation. A TV station's regional golf program that delivers active, middle-aged golfing males with incomes over $100,000 in the Southwest could be efficiently used to advertise a variety of products. A TV program that attracts a muddled mix of demographic audiences is less valuable per audience member. Even if you have the right media vehicle, scheduling is key in reaching your target.

High GRPs do not guarantee sales. The message delivered is also a key determinant. When advertising people refer to the message, copy (wording), or layout of advertising, they call it the *creative*, a noun. Ad agency people who develop the ideas are called *creatives*.

Magazine and newspaper advertising is purchased based on the size and segmentation variables of their circulations. Magazines have a longer shelf life, but newspapers deliver a much more immediate and focused geographic readership which is best for sale promotions. Both of these print audiences are bought on a *cost per thousand* (CPM) readers basis. A comprehensive listing of media and mailing list prices is provided by SRDS (Standard Rate & Data Service), in a series of telephone book–sized volumes.

A competitive measure of media is *share of voice*. Using this measure, an advertiser can target a certain percentage of media spending by all competitors within a product category. Advertisers believe that to have an impact through the competitive *media clutter* and noise, the relative spending level is just as important as the absolute dollars spent.

Through the clutter, it would have been futile to run a TV ad to promote the tiny coffee brand that I managed during my summer internship. A small competitor had no chance against the likes of

Procter & Gamble, Kraft General Foods, and Nestlé, who together spent over $200 million in advertising in 1990. Any affordable ad would have been drowned out by the giants.

Remember, each medium has its strengths in reaching people. Some are more selective than others. Marketers want to reach their intended targets as efficiently as possible to induce the desired buying behavior.

Personal Selling. Marketers choose *personal selling* when they need to make direct contact with the buyer. A salesperson can personalize your message to fit the buyer's needs and situation, and can field objections and questions in this interactive process. This avenue is generally the most expensive element in any marketing mix because of the high cost of labor and commissions paid.

Managers of products that are new, complex, or expensive find that the benefits of personal selling often outweigh their high cost. Because some target markets are inaccessible by other media vehicles, personal selling is sometimes the only means to reach consumers. Water purification systems, pharmaceuticals, encyclopedias, copiers, and industrial products widely utilize personal selling in their marketing mixes.

Current theory holds that personal selling is a *problem-solving* and *consultation* process. Professor Derek A. Newton of the Darden School at the University of Virginia saw personal selling as having evolved over the years in four stages: Music Man, Animated Catalog, Magic Formula, and Problem Solver. Before World War I it was believed that the "Music Man" approach to selling was the key to success. It was the salesperson's personality that enabled him to charm his customer into buying. After World War I, the "Animated Catalog" was considered the right way to sell. Vacuum cleaner salespeople knew all the facts about their products, and their sales presentations were rehearsed catalog readings. During the 1930s the slick pitch or "magic formula" was thought to be the best sales approach. Encyclopedia sales reps would control the presentation and lead the customer down a "mapped-out road" to a "sure sale." Many books currently on the bookstore shelves claim they hold the "secret" of how to close a sale. Today, academics agree that personal selling still requires some element of pizzazz and cataloglike product knowledge, but sales forces must also have extensive knowledge of the prospect's needs and buying processes to be successful. Sales people should sell *benefits* that solve customers' problems, rather than simply peddling products.

Sales Promotion. Sales promotion is designed to elicit the desired behavior from the consumer, the sales force, and other channel participants. Sales promotions are designed to complement and reinforce other promotional efforts, especially advertising. Each type of promotion has its own associated vocabulary that you should be aware of. If you are not a marketer, knowing the vocabulary does not make you an expert, but it can sure help you to engage in intelligent marketing conversation, if need be. There are two types of promotions: those directed toward the consumer, and those directed at the distribution channels.

Consumer sales promotions techniques available are: coupons, refund offers, samples, premiums, and contests.

Coupons are a direct way to pass a price reduction on to consumers. As a manufacturer, if you give a retailer a discount in hopes that they will pass it along to consumers, you may be sadly disappointed. Marketers use coupons to encourage trial, brand switching, and brand loyalty. Grocery coupons are most often placed in a special coupon section of the Sunday paper called *freestanding inserts* (FSI). The leader in FSIs is Valassis Inserts, which prints almost half of the $100 billion in face value of coupon savings distributed annually in Sunday FSIs.

Refunds are generally used to accelerate the normal consumer purchase cycles. Refunds are usually used to increase the quantity or frequency of purchase by encouraging buyers to stock up. Battery manufacturers frequently use refund offers. Such offers have been cleverly used to stock up consumers just before a competitor's promotion or product introduction.

Samples are a high-cost way of introducing a new product. Sampling requires a cash investment to produce and stock the smaller-sized packages. Samples are properly used for products whose benefits are "sensory in nature" and cannot be communicated effectively by advertising. Sampling may also be effective for products that consumers would view as risky in switching to a new brand, or that may have a high probability of generating *word of mouth* (WOM) activity after use. Many new shampoos use free or low-cost samples since their benefits are sensory. Consumers are reluctant to risk four dollars to try a whole bottle. Sampling reduces the buyer's risk of trial.

Premiums are items offered at low or no cost to purchasers of a product. *Self-liquidating* premiums are those for which the price charged covers just costs. Hershey has periodically offered watches and Christmas ornaments as premiums. To get the goodies, chocolate lovers have to send in wrappers as proof of purchase. Mr. Bubble, the happy pink bubble bath man, is pictured on inexpensive T-shirts, beach towels, and sweatshirts that are printed on every box.

Contests and sweepstakes are a popular promotion and the most restricted legally, because they border on gambling. A very thorough analysis of the game rules and the laws must be conducted to avoid a disaster. State gambling laws must be investigated to ensure compliance. The game rules and odds of winning must also be scrutinized to ensure that the promotional budget will cover the forecasted costs. In 1984 McDonald's ran a summer Olympics medal game. Every time the United States won, game pieces could be redeemed for free food and other prizes. When the Communist bloc boycotted the games, the United States won most of the medals, and most of the game pieces became winners.

Trade-directed sales promotions tools include: sales contests, point of purchase displays, dealer incentives, trade shows, and in-store demonstrations.

There are many variations on the *point of purchase display (POP)*. To get them in the stores requires the cooperation of the trade. On the retail shelf a POP can be a *shelf talker*, a mini-billboard attached to the end of the shelf with a little ad used to attract attention. Freestanding aisle displays and built-in shelf displays are other forms of POP. When a display is at the end of an aisle it is referred to as an *end cap*. To get those prime spots, the manufacturer must entice the retailer. A marketer can do it by providing a high markup per item or a high turnover on lower-margin items.

Dealer and employee incentives — payments made to dealers for marketing support are called *spiffs*. They can take the form of slotting fees, case discounts, cash payments, free merchandise, or prizes. Spiffs enable the dealer to discount, promote, or justify carrying a product. A manufacturer can also give incentives to the dealer's employees to place store displays or award prizes for meeting sales targets.

Trade shows are a way to promote a new or existing product to the wholesalers, dealers, retailers, and distributors. This promotion tries to encourage the channel participants to carry your product. A fledgling start-up company making housewares, for example, would need to attend trade shows to develop the distribution contacts that might carry their products to retail. If you have no trade contacts, you have to develop them.

In-store demonstrations — trained experts from the manufacturer are extensively used to promote products that otherwise would not generate consumer interest or be accepted by the trade. Small kitchen gadget hucksters set up demonstration platforms to bring inconspicuous blades to life by creating "beautiful" plate garnishes with ordinary vegetables. The Clinique ladies in their white smocks perform a similar mission for their boxes of "natural" beauty at the cosmetics counter.

Whatever the sales promotion you may choose in a marketing mix, each element must have an explicit marketing mission to justify its cost in the marketing mix.

Public Relations and Publicity. Public relations (PR) is typically a promotional tool used to communicate to a broader audience. PR is intended to create a favorable climate for your product, not to directly sell it. The list of possible PR targets can include politicians as well as the communities in which a company operates. The PR message can be intended to create goodwill, correct a mistaken impression or factual situation, or to explain a firm's actions. Sponsorship of prestigious or charitable events or causes is often used to create a *halo effect* of positive feeling toward a corporation and its products. Hallmark Cards' sponsorship of television's *Hallmark Hall of Fame* aligned itself and its products with the attributes of quality, culture, and good citizenship.

Because the goals of PR are less defined than a sales target, the results are more difficult to measure. Opinion polls and legislative victories are often used to measure PR success.

Publicity, a form of public relations, is any *unpaid* form of mass media communication about a company or product. It can take the form of a news story or even the appearance of a product in the media. Publicity is a two-edged sword. It is judged as more credible by the public because it is not purchased; however, there is less control over the message. Press conferences, press releases, use by celebrities, and staged events are used to capture the media's attention. Using a PR agency allows you to tap into their media contacts to capture an audience and hopefully control the impression made about your company or products.

LEO CULLUM

" I HAVE CREDIBILITY, AND FOR THE RIGHT PRICE I COULD BRING IT TO THIS COMPANY. "

When tennis stars John McEnroe or Andre Agassi wear Nike shoes and sportswear at the U.S. Open, the TV can't help but flash Nike on the screen each time they serve and volley. This network time has great value. If the athletes make the national evening news or *Sports Illustrated*, which cost $40,000 per thirty seconds and $100,000 per page, respectively, the value of free media exposure can be great.

Accordingly PR executives track their effectiveness by measuring the value of the media time or space captured. Tracking services, such as Burrelle's press clipping service for print, report on their clients' PR and advertising media exposure across the country. Burrelle's can also track competitors in the same way. Although it is often overlooked in the marketing mix, publicity can often create a tremendous impact if skillfully and creatively orchestrated.

Direct Sales. Direct sales includes the realm of junk mail, catalogs, shopping networks, and long-format TV *infomercials*. Direct sales are big business. In 1987 mail order sales alone constituted nearly $100 billion in sales or 4 percent of all retail sales. Over 6,500 firms mailed out 12 billion catalogs that year and the numbers are still growing. In 1991 the leading home shopping network, QVC Network Inc., had $921 million in sales. The leading infomercial company, National Media Corp., racked up $102 million in revenues.

The nature of the direct mail game is to *segment, segment, segment*. Mailers target their market with a focused mailing list to directly reach those households with a compelling mail piece. Lists can be developed internally or purchased from vendors listed in SRDS's *Direct Mail List Rates and Data* directory. The more defined, affluent, and focused the list is on a desired demographic composition, the higher cost per thousand (CPM) names. The results are tracked by *rate of return* (ROR) and *dollar amount per order*. Because TV audiences lack a list's selectivity, TV sales pitches cannot be as directly targeted as direct mail.

The other component of both direct mail and TV selling is *fulfillment*. Fulfillment is the process of order entry, order processing, inventory management, mailing, and customer service. The dreams of those viewers of the Home Shopping Network who want to buy porcelain figurines must be fulfilled. The operation may be executed internally or subcontracted out to a *fulfillment house* which performs the duty for a per-order fee over certain volume minimums. It saves smaller companies the initial investment required to establish in-house fulfillment capabilities. Because direct selling is becoming such a large part of the economy, it should not be ignored as a possible channel to the consumer. A thorny issue connected with this selling method is the backlash against the "big brother" effect of having *very* personal information captured in mailing lists that churn out personalized pitches. This topic, like slotting fees, is a "hot" one for MBA chatter.

Each method of promotion — advertising, personal selling, sales promotions, public relations, and direct selling — can accomplish a separate mission depending on the product, the place of sale, and the price. The gifted marketer goes to his palette of promotional options and combines them in a coordinated promotional strategy to sell his product efficiently.

Product   Place   Promotion   **Price**

Pricing Decisions: What Should My Price Be?

The pricing decision, like the product decisions, can dramatically affect the marketing mix by suggesting a channel of distribution or an advertising strategy. The pricing itself can differentiate your product from the competition. Both the Yugo and the Rolls-Royce are differentiated at opposite ends of the automobile spectrum. There are many rationales behind pricing each product and service. Haven't you seen a pair of Nike cross-trainers for sale at $59.95 instead of $60 for some psychological advantage? Besides psychological pricing, there are eight major pricing methods and strategies suggested by research and case analyses.

Cost Plus. This is a simple method of taking your cost and adding a desired profit margin. Highway contractors often use this simple method; however, it is not the proper way to price.

Perceived Value to the Consumer. You can charge the customer the value provided, regardless of its cost. Replacement parts are a prime example — exorbitant prices are charged for a cheap but crucial custom nut or bolt. The owner of a fixture manufacturer confided to a group of my classmates during a school-sponsored plant visit that the majority of his company's profits were derived from the twenty-by-twenty-foot replacement-parts cage, not from the long assembly lines producing the fixtures. If the price charged for an item is commensurate with the benefits provided, then it will be considered a good *value* in the mind of the buyer. But remember, there are limits even in a monopolistic situation.

Skimming. Early in the introduction phase of the PLC, a company can opt to charge a high price and *skim* high margins from a new and novel product or service. The margins could be used to further R&D, as is done in high-tech industries, or to immediately reward the owners for fad product introductions. RCA used this strategy to charge high prices for color TVs when they were introduced in the 1960s.

Penetration. This pricing can be used in the introductory phase or later in the PLC. A *penetration* strategy would use a low price to gain market share; the goal is primarily to lower costs per unit by producing many units in hopes of eventually controlling a market as the low-cost producer. The specifics of this strategy are discussed later in the Strategy chapter's discussion of Japanese VCR production.

The Price/Quality Relationship. Because consumer perceptions are not necessarily based on just the physical attributes of a product, the "perceived" quality is often influenced by its price. Apparel, perfume, and jewelry are examples where the price itself affects the perception of product attributes. Consumers often *attribute* the characteristics of style and workmanship to a product just because of the high price charged.

Meet Competition. Strategists frequently decide to match or beat competitors' prices to gain or retain market share in a competitive market. This is especially the case in commodity products and services such as gasoline, steel, and airline tickets. The economics of pushing a product through the distribution chain, as explained in the discussion of distribution channels, has a great effect on what price a manufacturer can charge to sell his product to the distribution chain and still end up with a competitive retail price.

Meet Profit Goals Based on the Size of the Market. If a market is limited in size, then a price must be charged that will allow enough profit to justify the marketing and manufacturing effort. If the product cannot command a profitable price, then to lower costs either investigate other user markets or manufacturing improvements.

Price Based on the Price Elasticity of the Buyer. Price elasticity describes how a buyer's behavior changes due to a change in price. Buyers with *elastic* demand do not readily accept price hikes. Their demand is greater or smaller depending on the price. Buyers with *inelastic* demand behaviors don't care about price increases. They don't decrease their quantity or frequency of purchase depending on the price. Tobacco and crack cocaine smokers, for example, have absorbed many price increases and continue to buy because their addiction makes their demand inelastic to pressure to accept price increases. If elastic, buyers will not pay more than a given *price point* and will stop buying or buy much less based on the intensity of their desires, their personal disposable income, or their psychological price thresholds. Former New York City mayor Edward Koch proposed in the 1980s that the bridge tolls onto Manhattan Island be raised to ten dollars to reduce the city's gridlock traffic conditions. He believed that the majority of the driving public's demand would be elastic to such a price increase.

There are many avenues that may be taken with any given product. In the case of my gourmet packaged coffee, a distinctive coffee "product" may require a distinctive package, a higher "price," a targeted promotion, and a selective "place" for distribution. But what really tells the story is the economics. Can I do it and make money?

6. WHAT ARE THE ECONOMICS OF MY PLAN?

Consumer → Market → Competition → Distribution → Marketing Mix → **Determine the Economics** → Revise

This may be the last step of marketing analysis. This step may also send the marketing manager directly back to Go without collecting two hundred dollars. By that I mean that the consumer analysis may be exemplary, the marketing mix masterful, but it just doesn't make money. The costs may be too high, the market price too low. Perhaps unrealistically high sales volume may be needed to break even. In those sad cases the entire circular process of marketing strategy must be restarted in an effort to find a profitable solution. To determine whether you have created a plan that is both profitable and reasonable you must address several issues.

What are the costs?
What is the break even?
How long is the payback of my investment?

What are my costs? Fixed or variable?

The first cost question for a marketing manager should be, "Which of my costs are *variable* and which are *fixed*?" If this sounds like accounting, it is.

Variable costs are those which vary with the volume of products sold or manufactured. The costs of materials and labor are variable costs. As more units are sold or manufactured, the total costs of material and labor are higher. *Fixed costs* do not vary with volume even if no sales are made. As volume fluctuates neither rent nor supervisor salaries change — within a *relevant range*. By that I mean that if sales triple, a new factory may have to be leased, and thus fixed costs will go up. Promotional expenses such as advertising are also seen as a fixed cost of a marketing plan, because if the product is a flop the advertising dollars are already spent. They are considered *sunk costs* — after a TV ad airs, the dollars are "sunk" in the ocean of TV land. Total costs are a combination of both variable and fixed costs.

Total Costs = (Variable Costs Per Unit (VC) × Units Sold)
                 + Fixed Costs (FC)

They can also be shown graphically as follows:

Wooden End Table Production

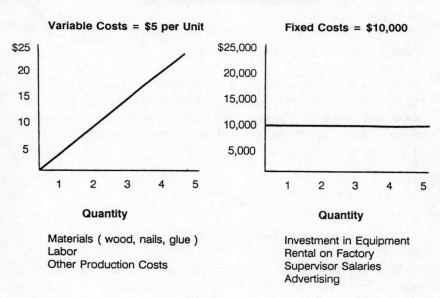

Variable Costs = $5 per Unit

Materials (wood, nails, glue)
Labor
Other Production Costs

Fixed Costs = $10,000

Investment in Equipment
Rental on Factory
Supervisor Salaries
Advertising

Fixed Costs + Variable Costs = Total Costs

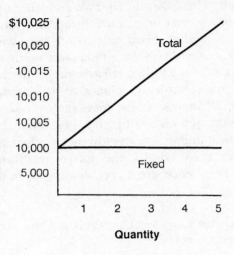

What can be seen in the graphs is that regardless of unit volume, the fixed costs remain constant. When units are actually produced, variable costs are added on top of the fixed costs to equal total costs.

What is my break even and is it reasonable?

Break even is the point at which the fixed costs are recovered from the sale of goods but no profit is made. Promotion and manufacturing are very expensive. A way must be found to recoup those investments. That's the whole point of marketing: to recover costs and make profits.

$$\text{Break Even Unit Volume} = \frac{\text{Fixed Costs}}{\text{Unit Contribution}}$$

(Unit Contribution = Your Selling Price − Variable Costs)

Using my data from the coffee industry, I have provided an example from the real world. I determined that the prices and costs of a proposed marketing plan for the Mexican gourmet coffee were:

	Cost	Cost Type
Retail Sales Price	$6.00 lb.	
Selling Price to Distributors	4.20 lb.	
Coffee Beans Cost	1.00 lb.	Variable
Roasting and Processing Cost	.44 lb.	Variable
Packaging Cost	.55 lb.	Variable
Shipping Cost	.25 lb.	Variable
Spiffs and Slotting Fees	50,000	Fixed
Production Equipment Rental	12,000	Fixed
Promotional Efforts	150,000	Fixed

The corresponding break-even volume was calculated:

$$\frac{(\$50,000 + \$12,000 + \$150,000)}{[\$4.20 - (1.00 + .44 + .55 + .25)]}$$

$$= 108,163 \text{ lbs. break-even (BE) volume}$$

And the *break-even dollar sales* were:

108,163 lbs. × $6.00 lb. = $648,978 break-even retail sales

The same equation can be used to calculate a *target volume* to yield a desired profit.

$$\text{Target Volume} = \frac{\text{(Fixed Costs + Profit)}}{\text{Unit Contribution}}$$

To return a $30,000 profit target, you just add the profit to the numerator with the fixed costs.

$$\frac{(\$212,000 + \mathbf{\$30,000})}{(\$4.20 - \$2.24)} = 123,469 \text{ lbs. target volume}$$

123,469 lbs × $6.00 = $740,814 target retail sales

One *very* important aspect of this analysis is that it does not include the costs that were "sunk" in the development of the product or the ad campaign if they have already been spent. The evaluation of the economics is always performed from the perspective of the present. There should not be any crying over spilled milk. You need to decide if you can make money on the proposed marketing spending in the future. For example, if the coffee blend was the product of millions of dollars of research, that would be irrelevant to the decision to whether I should spend additional money to market it. If I include the millions of research, it would be a definite "no go." However, with that money down the drain, it might be profitable to invest additional cash in a marketing effort.

The graphical representation of the marketing plan economics for the Mexican coffee looked like this:

Gourmet Coffee Marketing Plan Economics

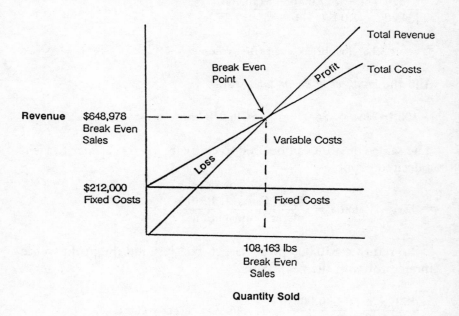

Quantity Sold

Is my break even reasonable in relation to my relevant market? Answering this question *must* be your next step. In the coffee example, $648,978 of break-even sales to retailers was a .26 percent share of the $248 million market for gourmet, nonflavored coffee sold through the supermarket channel as explained earlier in the chapter.

The targeted retail sales of $740,814 equaled only a .3 percent share of the relevant market. On that level, the plan appeared reasonable if I believed $150,000 of promotion and $50,000 of dealer incentives could have produced $740,814 in sales. Imagine that — I could have reached my goal with only a .3 percent share of the market!

Unfortunately, a small target share can easily lead you to believe that it is easy to obtain. How fierce was the fight for the grocers' shelf? If my coffee got on the shelf, somebody else's had to be kicked off. How would they react? Once in the supermarket, would my company have been willing to continue to support the coffee when a competitor went after my shelf space? In my case, the company was not willing yet to make that kind of long-term commitment to coffee.

What is the payback period on my investment?

This is another hurdle frequently used by companies to evaluate marketing projects when they have many to choose from. Companies want to know how long it will take just to get their investment back. Forget about profit. The payback formula is:

$$\frac{\text{Initial Investment}}{\text{Annual Profit}}$$

In the coffee example, the calculation would be:

$$\frac{\$212,000}{\$30,000} = 7 \text{ years}$$

If the yearly profit is not the same each year, there is no formula. The break-even point is where the plan returns the initial investment.

Seven years is a bit long for a risky venture. This may indicate that the whole marketing development process should start again. And unfortunately for me it did.

7. GO BACK AND REVISE THE PLAN

Consumer → Market → Competition → Distribution → Marketing Mix → Economics → **Revise the Plan**

At this stage of disappointment, I revisited the *marketing strategy development process* outlined at the beginning of this chapter. In circumstances such as those I faced, you must either tweak or discard your plans entirely. You may have something that can be salvaged . . . if you're lucky. You have to start by asking yourself tough questions. In the case of the coffee project I tormented myself with:

Should I target another segment?
Is the mail order distribution channel an option?
Should I not advertise and rely on a cheap price to move my product?

As these questions indicate, the marketing process is not easily defined or executed. It can be frustrating because there are no "right" answers. Consumer reactions cannot be easily predicted. It takes creativity, experience, skill, and intuition to develop a plan that makes sense and works together (*internally consistent and mutually supportive*). Marketing also requires close attention to the numbers to be successful. With this chapter you are armed with the MBA problem-solving structure and the MBA vocabulary to attack the marketing challenges that you may encounter. You haven't even paid a dollar in tuition, sat through a class, or anted up for an expensive executive seminar. Figure the break even on that investment!

I include the following notes that we all passed among ourselves at school to guide our case discussions and tests (open notes). These are the key questions that must be addressed by a comprehensive marketing strategy.

MARKETING STRATEGY OUTLINE

1. Consumer Analysis
- Makable or marketable product?
- Who's buying, who's using?
- What is the buying process?
- Who are the "Influencers"?
- How important is it to the consumer?
- Who needs it and why?
- What is the value to the end user?
- Is it a planned or impulse buy?

- What are the perceptions of our product?
- Does it meet their needs?

2. Market Analysis
- What is the market's nature? Size, growth, segments, geography, PLC
- Competitive factors? Quality, price, advertising, R&D, service
- What are the trends?

3. Competitive Analysis
- What is your company good at? Poor at?
- What is your position in the market? Size, share, reputation, historical performance
- What are your resources? Trade relations, sales force, cash, technology, patents, R&D
- Who is gaining or losing share?
- What do they do well?
- Compare your resources to theirs.
- What are the barriers to entry?
- What are your objectives and strategy?
- Any contingency plans?
- Short- and long-term plans and goals?

4. Marketing Mix
- Who is the target?
- *Product* — Fit with other products? Differentiation, PLC, perception, packaging, features
- *Place* — How best to reach segment, channel mathematics, draw channels.
- Exclusive, selective, intensive distribution? Fit with product?
- Who has the power?
- How to motivate the channels?
- *Promotion* — What is the buying process? How are $'s targeted to buying-process goals?
- Push or pull strategy?
- Media — type, measure, message
- Dealer incentives
- Consumer promos — coupons, contests
- *Price* — What strategy? Skim, penetrate?
- Seek volume or profits?
- Perceived value, cost-plus pricing?
- How does price relate to the market, size, product life cycle, competition?

5. Evaluate the Economics
- Break even in units

- Fixed Cost/(Selling – Variable Cost) Include fixed marketing and promo costs in fixed costs of the plan!
- Relate break even to relevant market
- What is the payback period? Exclude sunk costs!
- Are goals reasonable? attainable?

KEY MARKETING TAKEAWAYS

The 7 Steps of Market Strategy Development:
1. **Consumer analysis**
2. **Market analysis**
3. **Competitive analysis**
4. **Distribution channel analysis**
5. **Develop the marketing mix**
6. **Determine the economics**
7. **Revise**

Need Categories – All the possible uses of a product or service

The Buying Process – The stages of making a purchase

Product Involvement – The importance of a product to the consumer

Segmentation Variables – Ways to divide the population to find a profitable target

Relevant Market – The portion of the market that is interested in your product

Product Life Cycle – The birth-to-death (and possibly rebirth) life cycle of a product

Perceptual Mapping – A multivariable picture of a product and its competitors

Channel Margin Mathematics – Each level in the distribution takes a margin of the selling price it charges to the next level of distribution.

The Marketing Mix of the 4 P's – Product, place, promotion, and price

Distribution Strategies – Exclusive, selective, and mass market

Channel Power – Who in the distribution chain dictates the terms of the relationships

Advertising Measures – Reach, frequency, GRP, TRP, share of voice . . . Buy wisely.

Pricing Strategies – Cost plus, penetration, value pricing, skimming

Break Evens – The volume of sales needed to recover the fixed cost of a marketing plan

DAY 2

ETHICS

ETHICS TOPICS

Relativism
Stakeholder Analysis

Unlike most topics in the MBA curriculum, which have remained fairly consistent for decades, ethics is a new area in the MBA program. What appeared at first to be only a trendy elective course has now become institutionalized as part of the core MBA curriculum at Harvard, Wharton, and Darden. With the criminal convictions of insider traders in the 1980s, business schools are taking notice and jumping on the ethics bandwagon in the 1990s.

Ethical dilemmas make for a lively classroom discussion. It was revealing to see my fellow students deal with controversial topics. My "politically astute" classmates would play it safe and take the ethical high ground before teachers and peers. My more insecure classmates would not participate at all. Others would express just what they thought, no matter how politically "incorrect" it may have sounded. I fell into this last group. But I must admit, I took many unpopular positions just to liven up the class discussion. In any case, ethics is a good topic for speaker forums and great fodder for articles and dissertations. Since ethical problems often have no definitive answers, the area will remain fertile academic ground for years to come.

" WELL, THE DISCUSSION HAS APPARENTLY TURNED TO BASIC BUSINESS ETHICS, AND I MUST CONFESS TO BEING OUT OF MY DEPTH. "

The purpose of ethics in the MBA curriculum is not to make students model corporate citizens. Rather, the intention is to make students aware of the ethical implications of business decisions. Through casework and role playing, students confront ethical dilemmas similar to those they will face in the workplace.

The top business schools train their future champions of industry to deal with any challenge. You name the "hot" topic, we thrashed the issue out in class:

Environmental issues — pollution, toxic waste dumping, animal rights
Corporate restructuring — layoffs
Employee privacy issues — AIDS, drug testing
"Diversity" issues — race, ethnicity, gender, and sexual orientation
Sexual harassment
Conduct of multinational corporations (MNCs) — bribery
Other — antitrust actions, predatory pricing, insider trading

THE SOCIAL RESPONSIBILITY OF BUSINESS

Talk about ethics rests on the assumption that businesses ought to adhere to a socially responsible approach to decision making called the *social responsibility* approach. Proponents of this approach believe that corporations have societal obligations that go beyond maximizing profits. Business schools encourage students to adopt this "politically correct" philosophy. It is argued that because corporations are so powerful, they have an obligation to assume social responsibilities. Corporations should be managed for the benefit of their *stakeholders*: their customers, suppliers, employees, and local communities, as well as their owners. Corporate leaders bear a fiduciary responsibility to all stakeholders.

Flying in the face of the "politically correct" philosophy espoused at most institutions is a competing school of thought led by Milton Friedman of the University of Chicago. Friedman believes that business's sole duty is to make profits. "Businesses are in the business of maximizing shareholders' value by a prudent use of scarce organizational resources, as long as the activities of the business are within the letter of the law." In Friedman's view, it is up to government to determine what the laws should be. A profitable business benefits society by creating jobs, increasing the standard of living of its owners and its employees. Corporations pay the taxes that support government's social action. Although Friedman is exalted as one of the defenders of capitalism in economics courses, my school tended to discourage his views when it came to ethics class.

There are two major topics taught in the ethics curriculum: *relativism* and *stakeholder analysis*. Relativism examines why we often ignore ethics in our decision making, while stakeholder analysis provides a structure with which to confront ethical decisions.

RELATIVISM

The proponents of relativism hold that we can't decide on matters of right and wrong, or good and evil. Things are rarely black or white. There are so many shades of gray. Relativism proposes that ethics are "relative" to the personal, social, and cultural circumstance in which one finds oneself. Relativists are not torn by ethical dilemmas since they do not believe that truth can be discovered through soul searching. Professors teach relativism so that students may guard against it. To understand relativism, you need to recognize its four forms:

Naïve Relativism
Role Relativism
Social Group Relativism
Cultural Relativism

Naïve relativism holds that every person has his or her own standard that enables him or her to make choices. No one can make a moral judgment about another person's behavior. So many variables affect behavior that an outsider cannot possibly be privy to all the elements that went into making a decision. Therefore, an executive at Borden is not equipped to make a moral judgment regarding the actions of the chief executive officer (CEO) of Nestlé, whose corporation is possibly selling harmful baby formula in developing countries.

Role relativism distinguishes between our private selves and our public roles. These public roles call for a "special" morality which we separate from the individual making the choices. The president of a fishing company may personally dislike the incidental killing of dolphins in his company's tuna nets, but as an executive, he must not let his feelings interfere with the best interests of the company.

Social relativism is akin to naïve relativism. People refer to social norms to render ethical judgments. "Industry practices," "club rules," "professional codes of conduct," and "accepted practices" are the cop-outs of the social relativist. In the produce industry, it is "industry practice" to ignore child labor laws and employ small children to work in the field and miss school.

Cultural relativism holds that there is no universal moral code by which to judge another society's moral and ethical standards. If a whole culture holds certain beliefs, how can an outsider sit in judgment? "When in Rome ..." The concept of cultural relativism becomes more important as companies compete globally. Multinational corporations often follow local laws and customs that may violate ethical standards in their home countries. Discussions about apartheid revolve around issues of cultural relativism. Adopting a cultural relativist philosophy, a multinational corporation could justify its participation in South African gold and diamond mining activities despite the employment of "slave" labor in the mines.

In some instances U.S. corporations and citizens are barred from adopting the host country's business practices. In some countries it is ordinary business practice to pay bribes to get favorable treatment from businesses and government. The Foreign Corrupt Practices Act of 1977 outlaws overseas bribery.

The relativism concepts provide MBAs with an awareness of and a way to guard against inaction on ethical and moral issues. They provide a framework to go beyond currently held beliefs and patterns of behaviors. These concepts are also great conversational ammunition when MBAs get together on social occasions.

Other Ethical Frameworks. Relativism is not the only philosophical framework with which to approach ethical decisions. There is also *natural law, utilitarianism,* and *universalism.* Natural law serves as a guide to some who believe that the "right" thing to do is revealed in nature or the Bible. Utilitarianism holds that an action is justified if it provides the greatest benefit for the greatest number of people. Finally, universalism propounds that any action is condonable if the motive behind the action is good, since the results of a person's actions are so often not in his or her control.

STAKEHOLDER ANALYSIS

Although there are no magic formulas for solving ethical dilemmas, it is helpful to have a framework with which to organize your thoughts. *Stakeholder analysis* provides you with the tools for weighing various elements and reaching a decision.

As a first step a list should be made of all potentially affected parties, then there should be an evaluation of all the *harms* and *benefits* that a particular action will have on those involved. The next level of analysis ought to determine each of the affected parties' *rights* and *responsibilities.* Employees, for instance, have the right to a fair wage and safe working conditions, but they also have the responsibility to be productive for the company. In a typical stakeholder analysis the list of potentially affected parties might look like this:

The Decision Maker
Executives, board of directors
Customers — and the industry in which they operate
Shareholders, bondholders
Suppliers — and their industry
Employees — and their families
Government — federal, state, and local and their agencies
Special Interest Groups — industrial, consumer, environmental, political, unions
The Affected Community
The Environment — plants, animals, natural resources
Future Generations (an MBA favorite)
Competitors
Lawyers and the Courts

Obviously, the list could be much longer. At the analysis stage the list is narrowed to the significant players, then a situational analysis is performed, and eventually a decision is reached. In order, these are the steps:

1. Get the main cast of characters.
2. Determine the harms and benefits to each player.
3. Determine their rights and responsibilities.
4. Consider the relative power of each.
5. Consider the short- and long-term consequences of your decision alternatives.
6. Formulate contingency plans for alternate scenarios.
7. Make a judgment.

If you are interested in walking through the steps outlined above, take out a recent copy of *Time* or *Newsweek* and pick a topic with an ethical aspect. With a piece of paper, jot down the main characters along the top, then along the side, place the words "Harms and Benefits" first, and below that "Rights and Responsibilities." Now you have the framework with which to attack the moral dilemmas of the day — MBA style.

As an example, you might choose the debate regarding the need to preserve the habitat of the spotted owl by reducing logging on federal lands. The stakeholder analysis grid would look like this:

Spotted Owl Issue in a Stakeholder Framework

Stakeholders

	Lumber Companies	Loggers	Logging Communities	Owls & Trees
Harms & Benefits	• Higher Costs • Lower Profits, • Higher Value on Private Lands Owned	• Less Work More Free Time	• Lost Wages in Local Economy • Business Failures	• Survival
Rights & Responsibilities	• Value Maximization for Owners Within the Law	• Reasonably Exploit Natural Resources • Make a Living	• Reasonably Exploit Natural Resources	• Life

	Consuming Public	Politicians	Environmental Groups	EPA
Harms & Benefits	• Higher Costs • More Recreational Areas	• New Campaign Issue	• Power • Press Coverage	• Power & Influence
Rights & Responsibilities	• Benefit from Public Lands	• Public Good • Constituent Desires	• Free Speech	• Protect Environment • Regulate Industry

You may disagree with the way in which I have framed this issue, but with ethics there is no "right" way. People can approach a situation differently and feel other stakeholders need to be represented. In this situation, at the very least, a timber company executive ought to consider the stakeholders before clear cutting the owl's woods. With the tools of stakeholder analysis an MBA can tackle the issue of endangered owls as well as other ethical issues and make thoughtful and informed decisions.

KEY ETHICS TAKEAWAYS

Social Responsibility of Business — Concept that businesses are accountable to more than their owners

Relativism and Its Four Forms — Reasons to avoid making ethical decisions

Stakeholder Analysis — A framework considering who is affected by a business decision

DAY 3

ACCOUNTING

ACCOUNTING TOPICS

Accounting Rules
Accounting Concepts
The Financial Statements
Ratio Analysis
Managerial Accounting

Accounting is the language of business. Corporations need to communicate their results to the world. Their audience includes employees, investors, creditors, customers, suppliers, and communities. Within the company, accounting information provides a means to control, evaluate, and plan operations. Whatever the audience or function, accounting is *numbers*. Accountants (a-count-ants) "count the beans" so that business activity can be recorded, summarized, and analyzed. Accountants have been around from the beginning of time and professors don't let you forget it.

In biblical times the accountants kept track of how much grain was stored in the community's silos. How do you think King Solomon knew that there was only a thirty-day supply of grain during a drought? It was from the accountants. Throughout the ages accountants have kept track with their fingers, abacuses, and calculators. In modern times accounting has gone beyond the physical

" THE PHOENICIANS, OF COURSE, WERE THE FIRST ACCOUNTANTS. "

count of grain in storage. Accounting answers these basic questions about a business:

What does a company own?
How much does a company owe others?
How well did a company's operations perform?
How does the company get the cash to fund itself?

All corporate activities must eventually be measured in dollars, and that is where accounting comes in, like it or not. Although this area may appear tedious, you must have a working knowledge of accounting to function in the business world. Because knowledge is power, MBAs need to be literate in accounting to understand its function; more important, they must be able to ask for and use accounting information for decision-making purposes. Lawyers with accounting knowledge, for example, can interpret financial statements to get valuable information. In settlement negotiations, they become a force to be reckoned with. Because employee performance is often evaluated with accounting data, a knowledge of accounting is essential.

Having expert knowledge of complex accounting rules, however, is not the MBA's goal. Therefore, my aim here is to give you the basics, not to make you a CPA. Because every function of business, including finance, operations, and marketing, uses the numbers generated by the accountants, it is very important to grasp the fundamentals and read this chapter carefully.

GAAP RULES

Accounting has innumerable rules. You should not attempt to memorize them, but you should become sufficiently familiar with them to communicate with CPAs. Accounting rules set the standards so that financial reports of companies may be compared on an equal basis. Accounting's governing rules are called *Generally Accepted Accounting Principles* (GAAP). These "Gap" rules have been developed over the years and are analogous to the precedents in the legal profession.

As new areas of business activity develop, the *Financial Accounting Standards Board* (FASB) writes additional rules to deal with these situations. This body has generated over a hundred "Fasbee" rules over the years and accountants refer to them by number. For example, FASB 90 was issued in 1987 because of the problems of faulty nuclear plant construction. Electric utilities, such as WPPSS ("Whoops") in the Northwest, needed guidance on how to account for the abandonment of billions of dollars of unsafe and unnecessary plant facilities.

THE FUNDAMENTAL CONCEPTS OF ACCOUNTING

To understand accounting, before you get into the numbers you first must become familiar with the underlying concepts. The rules do not tell the whole story. The following seven concepts and vocabulary are not a set of laws, but rather a guiding set of policies that underlie all accounting rules and reporting.

The Entity
Cash and Accrual Accounting
Objectivity
Conservatism
Going Concern
Consistency
Materiality

The Entity

Accounting reports communicate the activities of a specific *entity*. The parameters covered by an accountant's report must be clear. A reporting entity can be a single grocery store, a production plant, an entire business, or a conglomerate. For example, General Mills prepares reports for each of its Red Lobster restaurants. It also reports on the entire chain of Red Lobster restaurants, as well as its restaurant group, which also includes the Olive Garden chain. Of course, there is an overall report for the whole corporation which includes Cheerios, Betty Crocker, Gold Medal flour, and Yoplait yogurt.

Cash Basis Versus Accrual Accounting

How the beans are being counted is very important. Using *cash basis* accounting, transactions are recorded only when cash changes hands. Very small businesses can get all the accounting information they need from their checking account register. If a store pays two years' rent in 1993, all the rent cost would be recorded as a cost in 1993, not over a period of two years. When a small machine shop purchases a power tool, its cost would be recorded when it was purchased, not over the useful life of the tool. Get the idea? Cash accounting tells you when and how much cash changed hands, but it doesn't try to match the costs of conducting business with their related sales.

Most companies of any significant size use the *accrual* accounting method. Accrual accounting recognizes the financial effect of an activity when the activity takes place without regard to the movement of cash. Kmart's rental costs are recorded each month with the benefits of occupancy. The cost of rivet guns at Boeing's aircraft factory is recorded over the useful life of the tools as workers use them on the factory floor. Due to the dollar magnitude of Boeing's purchases, cash accounting would distort its financial statements. Accrual accounting, as a consequence, raises two related issues, *allocation* and *matching*, because activity and cash movement most often do not occur at the same time.

Allocations to Accounting Periods. Because profit and loss statements reflect activities over a specific period of time, the period of recognition is *very* important. If IBM sold a large computer on credit to Ford Motor Company on December 31, 1991, accrual accounting would record the sale in 1991 when the binding contract was signed, not when Ford actually laid out the cash in 1992. The sale could be recorded at that point, because it was then that Ford became legally bound to take delivery of the computer. That was also the *period* in which IBM's accounting records would recognize the sale and its related costs and the profits. Ford, on the other hand, would recognize or *accrue* and *allocate* the cost of using the computer over its useful life.

Matching. Using the same logic as in allocation, sales made in one period are *matched* with their related selling costs or *cost of goods sold* (COGS) in the same accounting period. By matching sales dollars with their related costs, you can figure the profit a company has actually made. For example, when Safeway sells fresh produce on December 31, 1991, but doesn't pay the supplier's bill until 1992, accrual accounting will nevertheless record the costs related to those sales in 1991. Safeway's sales in 1991 caused the expense, and therefore, the sales should have the related costs allocated against them in the same year. Without established policies for *allocation* and *matching*, accountants could easily manipulate financial reports by choosing when to record sales or expenses in order to cover up or delay bad results.

Transaction Definition and Objectivity

Accounting records only contain transactions that have been "completed" and that have a "quantifiable" monetary value. Sales that have not been completed, but are thought of as "sure things," cannot be recorded. Even if a trustworthy salesman from Navistar (formerly International Harvester) swears that farmer Jones is a sure bet to buy a combine, the accountant would say no. For his accounting purposes, the sale has not taken place. Navistar has not delivered the machinery, nor has the farmer signed an enforceable contract.

Accountants also have an *objectivity* rule to guide them when in doubt. There must be *reasonable and verifiable* evidence to support the transaction, or else it does not get recorded.

For example, the goodwill generated by a public service campaign cannot be recorded on the books. What value could you put on it? Archer Daniels Midland (ADM) regularly runs TV propaganda telling consumers how cheap food is in America compared with the rest of the world. How could an accountant objectively put a dollar value on the "good feelings" directed toward the company in the hearts of grateful Americans or incumbent congressmen? Patents and inventions are also hard to value. If Du Pont purchases a patent on a new chemical from an inventor for $1,000,000, it would be recorded on the books at $1,000,000. The patent has quantifiable market value. However, if a Du Pont scientist developed a new process in the lab, the accountants could not record the innovation until it was sold. The accountant would need to have a contract and a canceled check to substantiate the entry in the books.

Accounting Conservatism and Historical Costs

When companies incur losses that are *probable* and that can *reasonably be estimated*, accountants record them, even if the losses have not actually been realized. When *gains* are expected, accountants postpone recording them until they actually are realized. If in 1986 the management of International Paper Company anticipated a big profit in 1988 on the sale of their Manhattan corporate headquarters, they could not record their profit until 1988. Their move to Memphis was uncertain. Management could have changed their minds, or the real estate market could have tumbled. But for the sake of argument, let's assume that International Paper discovered in 1986 that in 1988 it would have to clean a toxic waste pool beneath its building. Management would have to hire a consultant to estimate the cost of cleanup and record that cost in 1986. In this way, the financial statement readers would be warned of dark clouds looming over the horizon in 1988. Accounting *conservatism* governs the preparation of financial statements. When in doubt, be conservative. Accounting records contain only measurable and verifiable properties, debts, sales, and costs.

Conservatism also dictates that transactions be recorded at their *historical costs*. International Paper's New York headquarters appreciated in value during the real estate boom of the 1980s, and yet this gain could not be recognized, even if the company had paid the Indians a few trinkets for it in the 1600s. The records continue to value the real estate at the cost of the beads given to Indians in exchange for the property. In the accountant's mind, the value of the building may decline by the time it's sold.

If the value of an asset falls below the recorded cost, that's another story. Conservatism dictates that the loss be recognized *today*. To do otherwise could mislead the reader of a financial statement to believe that the assets represented are at least worth their historical cost.

The value of goods held in inventory is also stated at historical cost. Even if prices change, the *objective* price is that which the business paid historically. There must be verifiable purchase orders and bills to support the cost. For instance, if Ginn's Office Supplies carries notepaper produced by International Paper on its books, it would value the paper at cost. Even if reorder costs for the same inventory had gone up, the cost of the merchandise on hand would remain at Ginn's historical cost on the books.

Going Concern

Financial statements describe businesses as *operating* entities. The values assigned to items in the accounting records assume that the business is a *going concern*. Accountants presume that companies will continue to operate in the foreseeable future, therefore, the values assigned in the financial statements are not "fire sale" prices. They use historical costs, as you already know. Steel rolling equipment, for example, is expensive to purchase. It may have great value to an ongoing manufacturing company such as US Steel, but put up for sale at a bankruptcy auction, its value would be pennies on the dollar. Used industrial equipment has limited value to outsiders. Accordingly, accounting records use historical costs assuming that the company is using its machinery productively.

Consistency

The *consistency* concept is crucial to readers of financial statements. Accounting rules demand that an entity use the same accounting rules year after year. That enables an analyst to compare past with current results. This rule, like the others presented earlier, tries to minimize the temptations of accounting monkey business that businessmen like to engage in to cover up bad results.

The consistency rule insists that companies value their inventory the same way from year to year. The major methods available are a *FIFO* (First In First Out) or *LIFO* (Last In First Out) basis. Using FIFO, the oldest purchase costs of goods are recognized as costs "first," leaving the most recently purchased cost of goods in the value of inventory held for sale. Using LIFO, the "last" costs of goods are recognized as costs first, leaving the oldest costs in the value of inventory. The accounting method is independent of the physical movement of inventory. It is just an *accounting method*. As you might imagine, if you could change accounting methods at will, a crafty accountant could manipulate the financial statements from year to year. Consistency requires that the same accounting method be used from year to year.

As an example of FIFO and LIFO methods, consider a coin dealer who has only two identical gold coins in his showcase. One he bought in 1965 for $50, and the other he purchased recently in 1989 for $500. A numismatist comes to his shop and buys one of the coins for $1,000. Using FIFO, the shop owner would record a sale of $1,000, a cost of $50, and a resulting profit of $950 in his accounting records. His remaining inventory would reflect one coin at a historical cost of $500. The cost of the first coin purchased was the first to be recorded as a cost of goods sold. Using the alternate LIFO method, the owner would record a cost of $500, and a profit of only $500. His inventory records would show a coin with a value of $50. The last cost was used first. Which coin was actually sold, the 1965 or the 1989 acquisition, does not matter. It's only an accounting method. But the method chosen dramatically affects the way a company calculates profits and values inventory. That *does* matter.

If a change of accounting method is necessary for a "substantial" reason, the financial statements must state the reason in the *Footnotes* located at the end of the report. The footnotes must state the change and its justification. The footnote must also state how the change affected the profits and asset values that year. You can run, but you cannot hide from the accountants.

Materiality

An important caveat of financial statements is that they are *not* exact to the penny, even though you would expect that tenacious accountants would produce such reports. In fact, they are only *materially* correct so that a reader can get a *fairly stated* view of where an entity stands. Financial statements give a materially accurate picture so that a reasonable person can make informed decisions based on the report. For a small soda fountain's financial statements, a one-hundred-dollar error may materially distort the records, while a ten-dollar error may not. In contrast, huge multinational companies like Coca-Cola may have million-dollar errors in their reports and not materially distort the picture for decision making.

By now you can begin to develop an insight into how accountants think about businesses and possibly why they are, for the most part, conservative even as people. I found the cartoon on page 86 on the bulletin board at Arthur Andersen & Co., one of the Big Six international accounting firms, where I worked as a CPA for three years and had conservativism burnt into my psyche. I still wear white button-down collared shirts out of habit.

THE FINANCIAL STATEMENTS

MBAs are not trained to key transactions into a computer; rather they are schooled to interpret the information that accountants generate. The financial statements are the summary of all the individual transactions recorded during a period of time. Financial statements are the final product of the accounting function. They give interested users the opportunity to see what went on in a neat summary. To know a company, you must be able to read and understand three major financial statements:

Drawing by Leo Cullum (©) 1985
The New Yorker Magazine, Inc.

The Balance Sheet
The Income Statement
The Statement of Cash Flows

The Balance Sheet

Definitions. To set the stage you need to know the basic vocabulary of the *balance sheet*. The balance sheet presents the *assets* owned by a company, the *liabilities* owed to others, and the accumulated investment of its owners. The balance sheet shows these *balances* as of a specific date. It is a snapshot of a company's holdings at a given point in time. The balance sheet is the foundation for all accounting records, and you must be familiar with it. The following are the components of balance sheets.

Assets are the resources that the company possesses for the future benefit of the business.

- **Cash**
- **Inventory**
- **Customers receivables** — *accounts receivable*
- **Equipment**
- **Buildings**

Liabilities are dollar-specific obligations to repay borrowing, debts, and other obligations to provide goods or services to others.

- **Bank debt**
- **Amounts owed to suppliers** — *accounts payable*
- **Prepaid accounts or advances from customers to deliver goods and services**
- **Taxes owed**
- **Wages owed to employees**

Owners' equity is the accumulated dollar measure of the owners' investment in the company. Their investment can be either in the form of cash, other assets, or the reinvestment of earnings of the company.

- **Common stock** — *investment by owners*
- **Additional paid-in capital** — *investment by owners*
- **Retained earnings** — *reinvestment of earnings by owners*

The Fundamental Accounting Equation

As the name implies, the balance sheet is a "balance" sheet. The fundamental equation that rules over accounting balance is:

Assets (A) = Liabilities (L) + Owners' Equity (OE)

What you own (assets) equals the total of what you borrowed (liabilities) and what you have invested (equity) to pay for it. This equation or "identity" explains *everything* that happens in the accounting records of a company over time. Remember it!

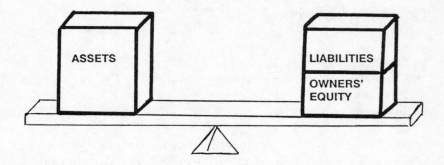

Examples of the "Balancing" Act

Using the example of a new local supermarket called Bob's Market, I will give you three examples of how the balancing act works.

1. When the market opened up for business, Bob purchased a cash register. Assets increased on the left side of the scale, while bank debt, a liability, was also increased on the right to pay for it. The asset increase was balanced by an increase in liability.
2. When Bob invested some of his own money and attracted some of his father's in order to open the market, equity increased on the right side of the scale, and cash, an asset, increased on the left to balance the transaction.
3. When the store becomes successful, it will hopefully be able to pay off its bank debt for the register (liabilities reduced on the right). The cash, an asset, would be reduced, thus balancing the transaction on the left.

All transactions adhere to this balancing concept. There is no way to affect one side of the balance sheet without a balancing entry. The accounting records are therefore said to be in "balance" when the assets equal the liabilities and owners' equity (A = L + OE). If the records do not balance, an accountant has made a mistake.

The Accounting Process: The Double Entry System

As you may have heard, accountants make *journal entries* in their books to record each of a business's individual transactions. Accountants call their books the *general ledger*. Using the same balancing concept shown by accounting's *fundamental equation*, asset additions are placed on the left side, called a *debit*. Liabilities and owners' equity additions are placed on the right side, called a *credit*. In all cases, journal entries have at least two lines of data, a debit and a credit. Entries to reduce assets are placed on the right, a credit, and reductions of liabilities and equity are placed on the left, a debit. Because of this right side/left side method, the manual record keeping of each account's transactions resembles a "T," and consequently these records are called "T" accounts.

Rules for Entries into Accounts

Asset Accounts		Liability Accounts	
		Debit	Credit
		Decrease	Increase
Debit	Credit	**Owners' Equity Accounts**	
Increase	Decrease	Debit	Credit
		Decrease	Increase

To illustrate, at the beginning of the year Bob and his father issued themselves 1,000 shares of stock for their initial investment of $15,000 in their store. The journal entry to record the transaction looked like this:

Balance Sheet Journal Entry #1

Account Title	(Type)	Debit	Credit	Effect
Cash	(Asset)	15,000		increase
Common Stock	(OE)		15,000	increase

Similarly a repayment of a debt would be *journalized* as:

Balance Sheet Journal Entry #2

Account Title	(Type)	Debit	Credit	Effect
Bank Debt	(Liability)	15,000		decrease
Cash	(Asset)		15,000	decrease

Because each entry to the records balances, at the end of a period of time, the entire balance sheet that summarizes the individual "accounts" and their net ending balances also balances (A = L + OE).

A Balance Sheet Example

Let's continue with the local grocery store example and see what balances appeared during its first year of operation.

Bob's Market
Fairway, Kansas
Balance Sheet
as of December 31, 1992
(the first year of operation)

Assets		*Liabilities*	
Current Assets		**Current Liabilities**	
Cash	$ 5,000	Accounts Payable	$80,000
Accounts Receivable	10,000	Wages Payable	5,000
Store Inventory	100,000	Taxes Payable	2,000
Total Current Assets	$115,000	Total Current Liabilities	$87,000
Long-term (Noncurrent) Assets		**Long-term (Noncurrent) Debts**	
Store Equipment	$30,000	Bank Debt	$10,000
less one year's		Total Liabilities	$97,000
Accumulated			
Depreciation	(3,000)		
Net Long-term Assets	$27,000	*Owners' Equity*	
		Common Stock issued	$15,000
		(1,000 shares outstanding)	
		Retained Earnings	30,000
		Total Owners' Equity	$45,000
		Total Liabilities and	
Total Assets	**$142,000**	**Owners' Equity**	**$142,000**

Bob's statement resembles the typical balance sheet of many retail and manufacturing firms. Three things are worth noting. *The total of assets equals the total of liabilities and owners' equity.* Second, the *assets are on the left* and the *liabilities and OE are on the right*, just like the journal entries of debits and credits. The third noteworthy item is that the balance sheet is as of a *point certain in time*, December 31, 1992, a specific date. Even though a business is the result of buying and selling over time, the balance sheet is only a "snapshot" of what the company's resources and obligations are at a stated time.

Liquidity: Current and Long-term Classifications

An important aspect of the balance sheet statement is that the assets and liabilities are listed in order of their *liquidity*, from most liquid to least. Liquidity means the ability of an asset to be converted to cash. Cash, Accounts Receivables from customers, and Inventory are labeled *current* and are listed first since they are easily transferred and converted into cash within the next operating period, typically in one year (i.e., they are liquid). Equipment is not very easily sold, therefore it is classified as *fixed*, *long-term*, or a *noncurrent* asset (NCA) and listed below the current items. Check out Bob's balance sheet to verify the placement of these items.

On the liabilities side, the accounts payable to suppliers, wages payable to employees, and taxes payable are current liabilities. They are short-term obligations that will have to be paid within a year. The bank debt is *long-term* or a *noncurrent* liability (NCL) because it will be paid off over a period of years.

Working Capital

A commonly used term in accounting as well as finance is *working capital*. It refers to the assets and liabilities that a company constantly "works with" as part of its daily business. They are also the most *liquid* assets, giving a financial statement reader a clue to a firm's solvency. Consequently, working capital items are the current assets *and* liabilities of the firm. *Net working capital*, a measure of solvency, is the total of current assets less the total of current liabilities.

Current Assets − Current Liabilities = Net Working Capital

At Bob's Market net working capital amounts to $28,000 ($115,000 − $87,000). That's Bob's excess of liquid assets to make good on its current obligations. From a banker's vantage point, a grocer with a large amount of net working capital may be considered a good credit risk because the business can make its debt payments. Conversely, it could also show a corporate raider or operations analyst that the store owner is mismanaging his inventory by holding too many goods on the shelves or too much cash in the registers. An astute operator would reduce inventory levels and the cash on hand to more efficient levels and pocket the difference as a dividend. The proper amount of working capital depends on the industry.

How Owners' Equity Fits In

Owners' equity represents the long-term obligation of a company to its owners. Companies are obligated to pay the owners a return on their investment based on the success of the firm. OE does not carry a set rate of interest or maturity like a bank loan, so it is segregated below the liabilities. Owners are paid only after all other debt payments are made. An owner's return is dependent on the success of the company. If debt repayments cannot be made, the firm can be forced into bankruptcy. The inability to pay a dividend to investors has no such penalty. If the company is highly profitable, the owners win. If not, they can lose all of their investment. That's the risk of ownership.

By reversing algebraically our accounting identity from $A = L + OE$ to $OE = A - L$, you can see that OE is the "residual" interest of the firm, assets less liabilities. OE is also called *net worth*, as it is the "net" value after all other obligations. In the case of Donald Trump, the notorious real estate magnate of the 1980s, he may have owned billions of dollars of property, but his net worth reportedly became zero in 1990 as his debts became even larger than the value of his properties in New York City and Atlantic City.

Owners' equity is increased by conducting business. Businesses buy and sell and provide and receive services. Hopefully after a period of time, the company has increased its wealth with those activities. If the net assets increased over time then it must have increased its OE.

The OE captions on the balance sheet can be affected in two ways. Investors can contribute more funds or they may elect that the company "retain" its profits. The line "Retained Earnings" is on the balance sheet for that purpose. If owners want to take out earnings they may elect to receive *dividends*. Dividends reduce their accumulated retained earnings.

Accountants sometimes prepare the *Statement of Owners' Equity* with the financial statements if the information is useful. These detailed statements outline the owners' investments, their stock transactions, and the dividends paid to them during the year. These transactions affect the owners' equity captions on the balance sheet. The Statement of Owners' Equity, also called the *Statement of Changes Shareholders' Equity*, is considered a minor statement. However, it may be very important for companies that have a great deal of owner activity. Large companies always produce this statement because it reveals many transactions that interest the public. Take a moment and go back to Bob's balance sheet and review its presentation before you move on to the income statement.

The Income Statement

As the balance sheet shows *balances* as of a specific date, the income statement shows the "flow" of activity and transactions over a specific "period" of time. That period may be a month, a quarter, or a year. There are *revenues* from sales and *expenses* relating to those revenues. When revenues and expenses are properly *matched* using *accrual accounting*, the difference is "income."

Revenue − Expenses = Income

An Income Statement Example. Let's look at the income statement of Bob's Market to see how his operation performed during his first year of business.

Bob's Market
Fairway, Kansas
Income Statement
for the Year Ending December 31, 1992

Sales to Customers	$5,200,000
Cost of Goods Sold	3,900,000
Gross Margin	**$1,300,000**

Less Selling, General, and Administrative Expenses:

Payroll	$1,000,000	
Rent	150,000	
Utilities	75,000	
Advertising	18,000	
Allocated Cost of Store Equipment (Depreciation)	3,000	
All Other	$10,000	
		$1,256,000

Operating Income (EBIT)	**$44,000**
Less Interest Expense	1,000
Income Before Taxes	**$43,000**
Less Federal and State Income Taxes	13,000
Net Income	**$30,000**
Net Income Per Share ($30,000 / 1,000 shares)	30.00

Income Statement Terminology

As with the balance sheet, the income statement has several note-worthy features. In the income statement, the classifications of expenses are extremely important because different types of income are calculated. Each offers a particular insight about Bob's operating results. Please refer to Bob's income statement as you read through this terminology section.

Gross Margin. The top part of the income statement calculates *gross margin*.

Gross Margin =
Sales − The "Direct" Cost of the Goods or Services Sold

At this point, the reader can determine if the company is making a profit without considering the burden of corporate expenses. At Bob's Market gross margin was his sales less the cost of goods sold (COGS). COGS includes the cost of groceries and all costs "directly" related to making the groceries salable, such as the cost of shipment from the wholesaler. In a manufacturing company it includes the costs of production, materials, and labor. In a simple retail situation like Bob's, COGS is calculated by this formula:

Beginning Inventory + New Purchases − Ending Inventory
= Cost of Goods Sold

If a business has a negative gross margin, either costs are out of control, or the pricing structure of the industry does not afford the company a profit. A small electronics manufacturer would encounter this situation if it tried to compete with the Japanese video recorder manufacturers, Sony, Hitachi, and Panasonic. A small U.S. manufacturer could not be as efficient and could not charge a higher price to cover its higher costs of production.

Operating Profit. The next part of the income statement relates to the *operating profit* of the company, the earnings before interest and taxes (EBIT). The further we move down the income statement, the more expenses that are deducted. At the operating level of profit measurement, all the other corporate expenses *directly* related to the revenue process are deducted. In Bob's case he has employee wages, rent, utilities, advertising, and many other smaller items.

Accrual accounting dictates that the *allocated cost of fixed assets,* also called *depreciation,* be charged to earnings. Using the principle of *matching,* the cost of providing the company's products is matched with its related revenues of the period. Accountants divide the cost of equipment, tools, buildings, and other fixed assets by their *useful lives* to estimate the cost of using up assets needed in the revenue-generating process. In Bob's case, he spent $30,000 for shelves, carts, and cash registers. Because he estimated that they will last 10 years, Bob's income statement will show an expense of $3,000 ($30,000/10) each year *to match and allocate* the cost of using those assets with the period of sales benefited.

"Other Expenses" is a catchall category for items not large enough to justify a separate line on the income statement. On Bob's income statement it includes fixing those annoying stuck wheels on his shopping carts and the losses on bad checks.

Net Income. Below the *operational* level of profit, items not directly linked to operations are deducted to calculate income. The first is the interest expense for the period. A case can be made that corporate borrowing is used to support the operation. However, the method of financing the company is separate from the operating activities of the business. Accountants do not include interest in operating income, because companies in similar businesses may have been funded by using differing proportions of bank borrowing and investors' money. Investors' dividends are not deducted. Owners pay dividends out of the net income at the bottom of the statement.

If interest were to be included in *operating income*, similar companies could have vastly differing operating incomes just by the way they funded their cash needs. A company under a different management could fund all its cash needs by additional investments from its owners. These funds would incur no interest charges, and, therefore, the company's operating income would be higher. If the same company borrowed for all its needs, its operating income would be reduced by the interest expenses. By segregating interest expenses, the operating income reflects only the costs of "operating" the company, rather than "financing" it.

Using the same logic that excluded interest from operating income, tax expenses are segregated to leave operating income free of nonoperating expenses. Different tax strategies can result in greatly different tax expenses. Because taxes are often the product of a skilled tax accountant's pen instead of operating results, tax expenses are put below operating results as a separate deduction, leaving *net income* as the *final* measure of income. Net income is the bottom-line profit of the company and it is the figure that is reported in the media as the measure of success or failure.

How Income Statement Journal Entries Are Made

In keeping with their age-old duty to count the beans, accountants make *journal entries* to the company's books to tally up net income during the year. Net income is the result of subtracting the expenses from the sales made during a defined period of time. Net income is also the net increase in assets for the same period of time. Journal entries keep track of the total of all the revenues and expenses as well as their corresponding increases and decreases in assets. Accountants make the entries for the income statement at the same time as they prepare the balance sheet.

During the year, running totals are accumulated for each revenue and expense to calculate the final net income figure for the entire year. At year's end when the final tally is completed and net income is calculated, the running totals of revenues and expenses are set to zero for the new year and the difference or net income or loss is recorded on the balance sheet as retained earnings. That accounting year, at times called a *fiscal year*, can begin in any month. It does not have to start in January.

The journal entries look the same as those that you have seen used for the balance sheet. To track the income statement, *revenues* are recorded as *credits* (on the right side) and *expenses* are recorded as *debits* (on the left).

Income statement entries are combined with balance sheet entries. A sale means that the business received something of value, an asset, in exchange for something else of value, an expense. At Bob's grocery store, sales meant that an inflow of cash came in exchange for grocery inventory. Bob's accountant made weekly entries to record his sales and their costs in the following way:

Income Statement Journal Entry #1

Account Title	(Type)	Debit	Credit	Effect
Cash	(Asset)	100,000		increase
Sales Revenue	(Income Statement)		100,000	increase

Similarly the accountant recorded the cost of those sales:

Income Statement Journal Entry #2

Account Title	(Type)	Debit	Credit	Effect
Cost of Goods Sold	(Income Statement)	95,000		decrease
Inventory	(Asset)		95,000	decrease

To illustrate a full year's income statement entries, assume that those two entries were the only sales and costs for the entire year. The net income for the year would have been the net of the total sales revenues of $100,000 less the total COGS of $95,000, or $5,000. That net income figure also mimicked the change in net assets recorded by those same entries. Cash increased $100,000 and groceries decreased $95,000, a net of $5,000.

At year's end the net increase of assets of $5,000 equals the net income for the year. Bob would have recorded that net change on the balance sheet as an increase to retained earnings. He would also *close out* or set to zero all the revenue and expense accounts for the year in preparation for recording the next year's activity in the following entry:

Income Statement Year End Close Out Entry

Account Title	(Type)	Debit	Credit	Effect
Sales Revenue	(Income Statement)	100,000		reversal
Cost of Goods Sold	(Income Statement)		95,000	reversal
Retained Earnings	(Owners' Equity on the Balance Sheet)		5,000	increase

Notice that the journal entry balances. The income statement entries reversed themselves, leaving the net income addition to retained earnings on the balance sheet. Where sales of $100,000 were entered on the right during the year, they are cleared at year end with a $100,000 entry on the left. The balance sheet's asset, liability, and owner's equity balances are permanent running totals that are carried forward to the next accounting year. There you have it. In a page you've witnessed an abbreviated version of an entire year's accounting cycle and hours of MBA classroom consternation.

The Income Statement's Link to the Balance Sheet

From Bob's actual income statement, the reader can see that the store had a marginally profitable year. He had a *net income* of $30,000. What is even more important than just the calculations of income is the understanding of how the income statement relates to the balance sheet. The income statement is the result of many activities during the year. Assets and liabilities are affected upward and downward during the year through many individual transactions. At year's end, the net assets of the firm, as totaled by the balance sheet, had changed because of operating activities. The net income, as calculated by the income statement, tells the story of the year's operations by showing *how* that change in net assets occurred. Because it was Bob's first year, retained earnings equaled $30,000, the first year's net income. In succeeding years it will be affected by the next year's earnings and dividends.

The Statement of Cash Flows

The Importance of Cash

As the saying goes, "Cash is king." Without the green a business cannot function. For example, let's take a look at Leonard, Inc., who sold package printing equipment to the food companies that supplied Bob's Market. If Leonard, Inc., sold three printing presses to Ralston Purina at $5 million each and earned $2 million on each, Leonard's income statement would show $6 million in profits. However, Leonard manufactured the equipment during the summer and Ralston paid for it in the fall when it was delivered. The factory employees wouldn't be too happy if their July paychecks bounced while the company waited for the cash in October.

Because the cash is critical for operations, and most important in order to stay out of bankruptcy, the FASB wrote rule No. 95 mandating that all financial statements include the *Statement of Cash Flows* or *Cash Flow Statement*. Remember those FASB rules that I mentioned accountants make to address current business concerns? Because knowing the "sources" and "uses" of cash is paramount for a business, the addition of the statement of cash flows has been widely seen as a great improvement by the financial community.

The inability to manage a company's cash needs is often the primary cause of the demise of many "profitable" enterprises. Many companies that measured their success by their net income have had a rude awakening when confronted with cash shortages and angry creditors. This is just what happened to Chrysler in 1979 when it went hat in hand to the federal government for a bailout.

Investors myopically looking at the income statement for a measure of health can be deceived. For example, McDonnell Douglas, the defense contractor, had healthy earnings in 1990 that masked an underlying corporate illness. *Forbes* reported it to its readers:

On the surface, things don't look so bad for McDonnell Douglas. It will probably report over $10 a share in earnings in 1990, versus $5.72 last year. But even a cursory glance examination of the numbers shows that earnings are shaky, if not ephemeral. Start with cash flow. It was negative $35 million by the third quarter of 1991 . . . and the bleeding of cash could accelerate. . . .

The leveraged buyout (LBO) phenomenon of the 1980s used the principles of cash flow as its tool. A raider's ability to repay the money borrowed to acquire a target company was based in large part on the cash flow generating ability of the acquisition. Much of that information lies in the statement of cash flows. In 1989 Kohlberg Kravis Roberts (KKR) bought RJR Nabisco in the largest leveraged buyout ever with $26.4 billion in debt financing based on the cash-generating ability of the company to pay off the debt.

The Cash Flow Statement's Link to the Balance Sheet

The cash flow statement also follows the balancing act principle of accounting. I will present the accounting math first so that you may understand the logic of what, at first glance, can be a confusing statement. With the math out of the way, the cash flow statement example can be readily understood. The equations that follow are not included to impress, merely to inform.

Using the golden *fundamental accounting equation* we have:

$$A = L + OE$$
Assets = Liabilities + Owners' Equity

Because assets and liabilities are composed of both current (short-term) and noncurrent (long-term) items, the equation can be expanded:

$$CA + NCA = CL + NCL + OE$$

Current Assets + Noncurrent Assets = Current Liabilities + Noncurrent Liabilities + Owners' Equity

To further break it down, the *current asset* class can be shown as its individual components:

(Cash + Accounts Receivable (AR) + Inventory (INV)) + NCA
= CL + NCL + OE

Rearranging the equation algebraically, we can isolate cash:

Cash = CL + NCL + OE − AR − INV − NCA

As revealed by the equation, an increase in a current liability (CL) on the right of the equals sign would mean an increase in cash on the left. Increasing your debts to suppliers frees up a business's cash for other purposes. Conversely an increase in an asset such as Inventory would mean a decrease in cash. It makes sense; buying inventory requires cash. Adding or subtracting on one side of the equals sign affects the total on the other side of the equation.

My study group at business school found cash flow statements to be the most confusing of the major topics in accounting. But if the former Peace Corps volunteer in my study group with no business training caught on, I have full confidence in your ability to pick it up also. With the preceding as foundation, I will illustrate the importance of the cash flow statement and use Bob's Market as an example to finish off the cash flow lesson.

The Uses for the Cash Flow Statement

The cash flow statement is a management tool to help avoid liquidity problems. Both the income statement and the balance sheet are used to form the cash flow picture of a company. The statement answers the following important questions:

What is the relationship between cash flow and earnings?
How are dividends financed?
How are debts paid off?
How is the cash generated by operations used?
Are management's stated financial policies reflected in the cash flow?

By using a statement of cash flows, managers can plan and manage their cash sources and needs from three types of business activities:

Operations Activities
Investing Activities
Financing Activities

These activities are shown clearly in the cash flow statements.

A Cash Flow Statement Example

Let's look at Bob's Market as a springboard from my theoretical discussion and get into an actual cash flow statement.

Bob's Market
Statement of Cash Flows
For the Year Ending December 31, 1992

Operating Activities:
Net Income $30,000

Add Back Expenses Not Using Cash:
Depreciation (Allocated Cost of Store Equipment)   3,000
                                                                 $33,000

Adjust for Changes in Working Capital:
Increase and Decreases During the Year

   Current Assets:
   Customer Receivables   (Increase) Decrease $(10,000)
   Store Inventory   (Increase) Decrease   (100,000)

   Current Liabilities:
   Vendor Payable   Increase (Decrease)   80,000
   Wages Payable   Increase (Decrease)   5,000
   Taxes Payable   Increase (Decrease)   2,000
                                                                $(23,000)

Cash Flow from Operating Activities $10,000

Investing Activities:

Purchase of Store Equipment	$(30,000)	
Cash Flow from Investing Activities		$(30,000)

Financing Activities:

Proceeds from Bank Borrowing	$10,000	
Sale of Stock to Owners	15,000	
Payment of Dividends to Owners	0	
Cash Flow from Financing Activities		$25,000

Increase in Cash for the Year	$5,000
Cash at Beginning of Year	0
Cash at End of Year	$5,000

It is easy to get too wrapped up in the numbers and not really grasp the logic behind the preparation of the statement. Therefore, let's look at each entry separately and explain the logic behind it. The MBA's accounting education focuses on the logic behind the numbers, while undergraduate programs focus primarily on the accounting mechanics to turn out CPAs, not MBA managers.

Please refer to Bob's cash flow statement during the following discussion.

Operating Activities

In the *Operating Activities* section, accountants calculate the cash generated from the day-to-day operating activities of a business. The income statement showed "accounting profit" of $30,000 for Bob, but it did not show how much *cash* was used or generated by his operations. As I explained earlier, most companies use *accrual basis accounting*, as Bob has, to determine his net income. The cash flow statement converts that accrual basis net income to a cash basis. To do that the net income has to be adjusted in two ways to get back to a cash basis.

Step 1. Adjust Net Income for Noncash Expenses. The first step to determine the flow of cash is to adjust the net income from the income statement. Operating items that did not use cash, but were deducted in the income statement as an expense, must be added back. *Depreciation*, as explained in the income statement section, does not actually take the company's cash "out the door." Only when Bob purchased the carts, registers, and displays was cash used. But over the life of these assets, depreciation is only an "accounting cost" that *matches* the original cash expenditure for these assets with the sales they benefit. Therefore, depreciation must be added back. It is not a use of cash. The purchases of the assets themselves are included later in the *Investing Activities* section.

Step 2. Adjust Net Income for Changes in Working Capital. Net income must also be adjusted for the changes in current assets and current liabilities that *operational activities* affected during the year. By adjusting net income for working capital increases and decreases, we can determine the effect on cash by using the fundamental accounting equation.

When Bob increased his current assets, such as his shelf inventory, he used cash because it took cash to buy groceries. This is shown as subtractions on the cash flow statement. When he extended credit to his customers, it delayed his receipt of cash, thus "using" cash that the store could have been using for other purposes. This is also shown as a subtraction on the statement. Conversely, reductions in inventory, i.e., sales, would have increased Bob's cash. If receivables had declined, i.e., customers' payments, cash would have been generated. *Point of Learning:* Increases in current assets use cash while decreases in current assets produce cash.

Current liabilities changes have the opposite effect on cash. In Bob's case his vendors advanced him $80,000. When Bob ran up a large debt with his vendors and employees, this meant that credit was extended to him, which in turn freed his cash for other purposes. In a sense, cash was created. If Bob had reduced his liabilities, that would have meant that he had made payments to reduce his debts, reducing cash. *Point of Learning:* Increases in current liabilities increase cash while decreases use up cash.

To calculate the net changes for the year, simply subtract the beginning of the period's balances of current assets and liabilities from the ending balances items. Because it was Bob's first year (and to make it simple), the beginning balances were all zero and the ending balances are equal to the account increases for the year. The increases in current assets are "uses" and the increases in current liabilities are "sources" of cash.

Convince yourself that Bob's cash flow statement is correct. Refer to his cash flow statement. Look back at the income statement to verify the net income. Review the balance sheet to check that the changes in the working capital items (CA + CL) equal the changes shown on the cash flow statement. It all fits together!

Investing Activities

As the title explains, this area of the cash flow statement deals with cash use and generation by long-term "investments" by the company. Accordingly, the investment activities section reflects the cash effects of transactions in *long-term* (noncurrent) assets on the balance sheet. When a company buys or sells a long-term asset like a building or piece of equipment, the cash relating to the transaction is reflected in the *Investing Activities* section of the cash flow statement. In Bob's case, he invested $30,000 in store equipment as shown on his statement. If he had sold the equipment, the cash received would have been reflected. Review the balance sheet to verify how the change in his long-term assets was reflected in the investing section of the cash flow statement.

Financing Activities

There are two ways a company can finance itself. Either managers borrow money or they raise money from investors. Borrowing would be reflected in changes in the long-term liabilities section of the balance sheet. The participation by investors would be reflected in changes in the owners' equity accounts of the balance sheet.

Bob borrowed $10,000 from the bank, which increased Cash. On the balance sheet, "Bank Debt" increased from $0 to $10,000 and it was reflected as a source of cash. When the store repays the debt, it will be reflected as a use of cash in the *Financing Activities* section.

Referring back to Bob's Market's balance sheet, the owners' equity accounts are on the right side. The balance sheet shows that investors contributed $15,000 cash to start the business. That is shown on the balance sheet as "Common Stock" issued, and it is also reflected on the cash flow statement as a source of cash.

As we have already learned, the other component of the owners' equity section is *retained earnings* (RE). As explained, there will be changes in RE when net income is added during the year and if *dividends* are paid out to investors. Bob and his father elected to continue to "finance" the business by having the company "retain" its earnings. The financing section, accordingly, does not show any dividend payments. If the owners elected to pay a dividend it would have been shown as a use.

After a year of operations Bob had $5,000 more than when he started. With his cash flow statement he can understand how it happened!

Once prepared, what does the cash flow statement mean?

Take a step back, or else you can get lost in the mechanics. This cash flow statement shows the net change in cash for the year. It appears at the bottom of the statement. Take a look. It sounds simple, but some newly minted CPAs I worked with at Arthur Andersen & Co. never really understood that fact as they labored to prepare the report's details. You do. *Where* the changes in cash took place is of real importance to MBAs.

> Was the company a seemingly profitable company, but must borrow heavily just to stay alive?
>
> Did the company's operations throw off cash, even though it may be just marginally profitable according to the income statement?

Those are samples of the important questions that neither the balance sheet nor the income statement can tell a reader. That is why the cash flow statement exists.

When a company is healthy, operating activities will generate cash. That message is delivered by the net income adjusted for changes in working capital. That is the *Operating Activities* section's function.

Does the company require a great investment in fixed assets such as new equipment or technology? Is the company selling off its assets to fill an insatiable cash drain from operations? That type of information lies in the *Investment Activities* section.

Dying businesses stay alive by cannibalizing their assets to fund their unprofitable operations. Pan American Airlines withered in 1991 when it sold its coveted European routes to its competitors to raise cash. Pan Am died in 1992.

Did the company borrow heavily or has the company gone to investors to fund its operational or investing activities? The *Financing Activities* section tells that important story. In Bob's case he borrowed from the bank and invested his own money.

Whatever the sources and uses of cash, the statement of cash flows tells a great deal about a business's health. To many financial analysts, it is the most important statement of all.

ACCOUNTING'S BIG PICTURE

A knowledgeable person can always get back to the fundamental equation of accounting to make sense of any jumble of numbers making up any of the financial statements of a company: *Assets = Liabilities + Owners' Equity*.

With the statement of cash flows it was demonstrated that the changes during the year in the cash balance had to result from changes in assets, liabilities, and owners' equity. The assets and liabilities changes came from the balance sheet. The owners' equity changes were the result of changes in net income, provided in detail by the income statement. *The three basic financial statements are inextricably tied together*.

The fundamental accounting equation, the balance sheet, and each of the many journal entries made during the year *always* balance. That fundamental property allows for changes in any piece of the accounting puzzle to be explained by changes in the other parts. By grasping this basic concept of the interrelationships of the financial statements, you have learned the essence of accounting. Congratulations!

READING THE FINANCIAL STATEMENTS USING RATIOS

With an understanding of how accountants create their financial statements, let me add some tools to interpret them: *ratios*. Absolute numbers in a financial statement in and of themselves often are of limited significance. The real information can be found in an analysis of the relationship of one number to another or of one company to another in the same industry — using ratios. In the grocery game, profits are usually low in relation to sales, so grocers must sell in large volume to make any real profit. A jewelry store survives on slower-paced sales but higher profits per item. That is why ratios are used to compare performances among companies within an industry and against a company's own historical performance.

There are four major categories of ratios:

Liquidity measures: How much is on hand that can be converted to cash to pay the bills?

Capitalization measures: Is a company heavily burdened with debt? Are its investors financing the company? How is the company funding itself?

Activity measures: How actively are the firm's assets being deployed? (MBAs *deploy* assets, rather than just use them.)

Profitability measures: How profitable is a company in relation to the assets and the sales that made its profits possible?

There are literally hundreds of possible ratios, but most have their origin in eight basic ratios from the four categories listed above. Using Bob's financial statements, I have calculated these eight ratios for his operation and have placed them below each of the ratio explanations.

Liquidity Ratios

1. Current Ratio = Current Assets / Current Liabilities

Can the company pay its bills comfortably? A ratio greater than 1 shows liquidity. It shows that there is leeway in the current assets available to pay for current liabilities.

$$\left(\frac{\$115,000}{\$87,000} = 1.32 \right)$$

Capitalization Ratios

2. Financial Leverage = (Total Liabilities + Owner's Equity) / OE

$$\left(\frac{\$142,000}{\$45,000} = 3.155 \right)$$

When a company assumes a larger proportion of debt than the amount invested by its owners, it is said to be *leveraged*. In a profitable company, by using a higher level of debt, the return is much higher because a smaller amount appears in the denominator of the ratio. The "same" amount of earnings is divided by a smaller equity base. Ratios of greater than 2 show an extensive use of debt. I will explain leverage more fully when discussing the profitability ratios.

3. Long-term Debt to Capital = Long-term Debt / (Liabilities + OE)

$$\left(\frac{\$10,000}{\$142,000} = .07 = 7\% \right)$$

Because debt payments are fixed obligations that *must* be paid while dividends to investors are not, the level of debt is a very important measure of a company's riskiness. A ratio of greater than 50 percent shows a high level of debt. Depending on the timing and stability of a firm's cash flows, 50 percent could be considered very risky. Stable electric utilities have predictable sales and cash flows; therefore, ratios over 50 percent are commonplace. Investment analysts on Wall Street consider those debt levels conservative.

Activity Ratios

4. Asset Turnover per Period = Sales / Total Assets

$$\left(\frac{\$5,200,000}{\$142,000} = 36.6 \text{ turns} \right)$$

This ratio tells the reader how actively the firm uses all of its assets. The firm that can generate more sales with a given set of assets is said to have managed its assets efficiently. Ratios are industry-specific. Thirty-six is a high turnover of assets for most industries, but for an antique shop a turnover of three may be considered very high. One-of-a-kind antiques sit waiting for the right collector to come along. In the grocery trade 36.6 turns per year is normal because the shelf inventory of a supermarket is sold about every week. The produce, milk, and toilet paper inventory turn over several times a week, while the exotic spices take much longer to sell.

5. Inventory Turns per Period = Cost of Goods Sold / Average Inventory Held During the Period

(A simple way to calculate "Average Inventory" is by adding the beginning and ending inventory balances, then dividing by two.)

$$\left(\frac{\$3,900,000}{\$100,000} = 39 \text{ turns per year} \right)$$

6. Days Sales in Inventory = Ending Inventory / (Cost of Goods Sold / 365)

$$\left(\frac{\$100,000}{(\$3,900,000 \, / \, 365)} = 9.36 \text{ days} \right)$$

These two *activity* ratios show how actively a company's inventory is being deployed. Is inventory sitting around collecting dust or is it being sold as soon as it hits the shelf? In a high-turnover business, like the grocery trade, there are many turns of inventory during a year and only a few days of inventory on hand. Most grocery items are perishable and purchased frequently.

Profitability Ratios

7. Return on Sales (ROS) = Net Income / Sales

$$\left(\frac{\$30,000}{\$5,200,000} = .005769 = .58\% \right)$$

"Return" ratios are very easy to calculate and investment analysts use them frequently. They calculate the return on just about any part of the balance sheet and income statement. Another common one is the return on assets (ROA).

8. *Return on Equity (ROE)* = *Net Income / Owners' Equity*

$$\left(\frac{\$30,000}{\$45,000} = .6667 = 67\% \right)$$

The mix of debt and equity can dramatically affect the ratios. If a company has a high level of debt and a small amount of equity, the return on equity (ROE) can be tremendously affected. That is called *financial leverage*, the term that I mentioned before in discussing capitalization ratios. To illustrate the point, Bob and his father could have decided to leave very little equity in the company in 1992. They could have taken all of the $30,000 of net income made in 1992 out of the company as dividends and borrowed for their future cash needs. If that had happened, the balance sheet would have reflected a long-term debt balance of $40,000 ($10,000 + $30,000) and only $15,000 ($45,000 − $30,000) in equity. The resulting *debt to equity ratio* would increase from 7 percent to 28 percent and the *return on equity* would have increased from 67 percent to 200 percent ($30,000/$15,000). As shown, ratios can be greatly affected by the financial leverage used. The choice of a lower equity level can "leverage" the ROE to extremely high levels.

ROE ratio is a widely accepted yardstick to measure success. In *Forbes*'s "Annual Report of American Industry," companies with the greater ROEs were ranked higher than many of their more profitable counterparts simply because of their financing choices. If management's goal is to achieve a higher profitability ratio through leverage, there is a risk cost. Higher debt levels require higher interest payments that a company may not be able to service if operations do poorly. The corporate failures in the 1990s of Revco Drugs, Southland's 7-Eleven, and Federated Department Stores were cases in which management risked bankruptcy with high leverage and lost.

The Du Pont Chart

Academics have a tendency to give imposing names to simple concepts. Your MBA vocabulary would not be complete without including the *Du Pont Chart*. The chart shows how several of the most important financial statement ratios are related to one another by displaying their components.

The Du Pont Chart

Profit Margin		Asset Turnover		Return on Assets (ROA)
$\dfrac{\text{Net Income}}{\text{Sales}}$	X	$\dfrac{\text{Sales}}{\text{Total Assets}}$	=	$\dfrac{\text{Net Income}}{\text{Total Assets}}$
Return on Assets		Financial Leverage		Return on Equity (ROE)
$\dfrac{\text{Net Income}}{\text{Total Assets}}$	X	$\dfrac{\text{Total Assets}}{\text{Owners' Equity}}$	=	$\dfrac{\text{Net Income}}{\text{Owners' Equity}}$

By charting the interrelationships among ratios, one can see that changes in a component of one ratio affect the other ratios. The ratios share the same inputs. For example, when Total Assets is reduced, both the Asset Turnover and Return on Assets ratios increase because Total Assets are included in the calculation of both of those ratios as a denominator. Conversely, a reduction of Total Assets (equal to total liabilities and owners' equity) increases Financial Leverage as it is used in that ratio's numerator.

Ratios are Industry-Specific

Profitability is, as in the case of all other ratios, very industry-specific. Every industry has a profit level depending on the physical demands of the industry. Heavy manufacturers such as steel makers have a *return on assets* (ROA) of less than 10 percent. They have large steel mills and a great deal of factory equipment. Service businesses such as profitable head hunting firms may have ROAs over 100 percent. The only assets they need are cash, office furniture, and customer receivables. Their real asset is their staff's talent in pursuing and persuading, which cannot be quantified on the balance sheet.

Profitability also depends on the level of competition. In the grocery business, intense competition keeps the *return on sales* to a very low 1 percent. During Bob's first year he had a .58 percent return, which was below the industry average. Considering that it was his first year, any profit should be commended.

Any part of the financial statements can be compared to another with a ratio of some sort. Any calculator can divide one number by another. Only those ratios that can provide some insight into a business's performance are valuable. The true value of ratios is seen when one firm's ratios are compared to those of another in the same industry, or to that firm's historical performance. Alternatively the "attractiveness" of various industries as business opportunities may be explored by comparing their averages. Each firm and industry has its own key operating statistics that are meaningful.

For industry-specific references on all these ratios, Robert Morris Associates publishes its *Annual Statement Studies*. This valuable reference book, available in most libraries, includes financial and operating ratios for over 300 manufacturers, wholesalers, retailers, services, contractors, and finance companies.

MANAGERIAL ACCOUNTING

Managerial accounting, like ratio analysis, uses accounting data to manage and analyze operations. Managerial accounting focuses on operations. Instead of ratios managerial accounting uses *standards*, *budgets*, and *variances* to run the business and explain operational results. The object of managerial accounting is to budget a company's activities for a period of time, and then to explain why the actual results "varied" from the projections. In most manufacturing settings, monthly budgeting and analysis are the norm so that management can take *timely* action.

To establish a yardstick for measuring performance, the factory team must set *standards* for comparison. This requires the input from more than just the accountants. In automobile manufacturing, the production manager establishes what she believes should be the standard costs for materials, labor, and other expenses. Industrial engineers help by performing studies to obtain the data. Factory managers work with sales managers to *budget* production volumes to meet forecasted demand and also to maintain assembly line efficiency. Sales managers set standard prices and quantities for their products. Using those standards as a yardstick, managerial accountants analyze actual results to explain the *variances* from those budgets and standards the company's team developed. Once completed, variance analysis highlights the source of positive or negative results for management decision making.

Price and Volume Variances

There are two basic types of variances, *price and volume variances*. As with financial statement ratios, they are derived from simple mathematical formulas.

Sales Price Variances. The *price variance* tells the manager how much of the difference between budgeted sales revenue and actual sales revenues is due to changes in sales price changes.

(Actual Sales Price − Standard Sales Price) × (Actual Quantity Sold) = Sales Price Variance

Sales Volume Variances. The *volume variance* isolates the dollar effect of a different unit volume from what was budgeted assuming no price changes.

(Standard Sales Price) × (Actual Quantity Sold − Standard Quantity Sold) = Sales Volume Variance

Using a hypothetical example, General Motors planned to sell 10,000 Chevy Lumina minivans in July 1991 at a price of $15,000 each for a total of $150 million in sales. In August the analyst received accounting data showing that sales were actually $280 million in July. GM actually sold 20,000 Luminas at an average price of $14,000 due to a $1,000 rebate program. The total variance of sales was $130 million. (10,000 × $15,000) − (20,000 × $14,000). How did that occur? Variances told the story.

The variance solely due to price, the *price variance*, was a negative $20 million (($14,000 − $15,000) × 20,000 units). But because 10,000 more units were sold than planned, the *volume variance* was a very positive $150 million ((20,000 − 10,000 units) × $15,000). The two variances (−$20 + $150 = +$130) equaled the total variance from the total sales budget ($280 − $150 = +$130). The variance analysis told the GM executive in charge of the Lumina model that the overall increase in sales was primarily due to a larger sales volume, rather than to a price increase. Conversely, the small negative price variance due to a rebate was more than made up by a stronger sales volume. When you add together the price and the volume variances they equal the "total" monthly sales variance from budget. The variance analysis enabled the Lumina executive to explain why his results hit his division's targets.

Purchase Price, Efficiency, and Volume Variances

Using the same two basic formulas, *sales price and sales volume variances*, production departments also calculate variances for management control.

Purchases and usage of production materials have *purchase price variances*.

Purchase Price Variance = (Standard Price − Actual Price) × (Actual Quantity Purchased or Used)

The amount of materials and labor used to produce products may also differ from the standard amount. Similar to sales volume variances, these differences are called *efficiency variances*. Shoe workers, for example, can be more efficient by using more leather from a hide than planned. Chemically dependent workers on the assembly line in Detroit could take more labor hours than planned to produce their cars.

Material or Labor Efficiency Variance = (Standard Use Quantity − Actual Usage Quantity) × (Standard Cost of Material or Labor)

Using the Lumina again as an example, the production foreman had budgeted in July that each Lumina made should use a standard 8 gallons of paint at a cost of $10 per gallon. It actually took 7 gallons at a cost of $12 per gallon for the 20,000 minivans that were produced. The accountant calculated the following variances for the Lumina executive:

Material Price Variance = ($10 − $12 price per gallon) × (20,000 units × 7 gal.) = −$280,000 negative paint price variance

This was the effect of paying more per gallon than planned. Instead of scratching his head, the GM executive could use this information to confront his purchasing agent and demand that he negotiate a better deal the following month.

Material Efficiency Variance = (8 gal. − 7 gal.) × (20,000 units) × $10 per gallon = $200,000 positive variance

This was the effect of using less paint than planned.

As with ratios, there is an infinite number of variances that can be cooked up to keep a department of accounting analysts busy from now until the next century. There are basically only two types of variances: *price* and *volume* variances. When you hear the words "managerial accounting," think *variances*.

ACCOUNTING OVERVIEW

I hope you have not struggled too hard through this chapter, but in a few pages I have tried to give you the essentials of accounting from both my CPA background and the MBA curriculum. If the material in this chapter was totally new for you, most probably you have not absorbed it completely. You should have remembered that:

- **Assets = Liabilities + Owners' Equity**
- **There are three basic and interdependent financial statements: Balance Sheet, Income Statement, Cash Flow Statement.**
- **Accounting records and statements *always* balance.**
- **The statements can be interpreted by using Ratios.**
- **Operating results can be analyzed and managed using Variances.**

That's the accounting game in a nutshell. At MBA school accounting struck the most fear in the hearts of the liberal arts undergraduates. This chapter has given you, in a tidy predigested form, what kept them up late at night.

KEY ACCOUNTING TAKEAWAYS

Cash Basis Accounting — The method of recording transactions only when cash changes hands

Accrual Basis Accounting — The method of recording transactions that matches revenues and expenses regardless of cash flow movements

The Balance Sheet — The listing of what a company owns and owes at a point in time

The Fundamental Accounting Equation — Assets = Liabilities + Owners' Equity

Net Working Capital — Short-term assets less short-term liabilities

The Income Statement — The summary of profit-generating activities during a period of time

Gross Margin — Revenues less the direct cost of goods sold

The Statement of Cash Flows — The summary of how a company generates and uses its cash during a period of time

Depreciation — The cost of using equipment allocated over its useful life

The 8 Basic Ratios for Financial Statement Analysis — A method of analyzing statements and comparing them to industry standards

Price and Volume Variances — A method of explaining operational results by isolating the effects of price and volume differences from budgeted amounts

DAY 4

ORGANIZATIONAL BEHAVIOR

ORGANIZATIONAL BEHAVIOR TOPICS

Problem Solving Model
Psychology Lesson
Motivation
Leadership
Creativity
On-the-Job Office Procedure
Power
The Organizational Model and Structures
Systems Theory
Organizational Evolution and Revolution
Resistance to Change

NEW MBA GRADUATE: I have the answer! My Lotus spreadsheet says that we should reorganize the company by geographic region rather than by product. We could save at least three million dollars a year by cutting unnecessary staff and travel. We hypothetically implemented a similar plan at the Brandon Lee Company in a class discussion. It worked real well.

BOSS: Sounds great. You've been with the company seven months and you want to do a radical reorganization. I assume you already assembled a roster of redundant employees?

NEW MBA GRADUATE: Well, I've not thought it through *that* far yet.

Organizational Behavior (OB) classes attempt to teach MBAs how to deal with the human challenges in the workplace. Quantitative skills may provide the magic theoretical pill in the classroom, but OB tries to instill in young MBA turks the human sensitivity to apply their MBA skills in the real world.

Many organizational theories are not unlike what you can find in books about self-awareness and sensitivity training at the local B. Dalton or Waldenbooks. The reason for the similarity is that many of those books are written by the very same professors who pro-pound the academic theories that appear in MBA curricula. The difference is that faddish books about the "new" corporate rejuvena-tion theory or the "one-second manager" make more money than articles that appear in obscure academic journals.

Organizational behavior, the "touchy feelie" subject, is often where MBAs show their true colors. Sexism, prejudice, and greed rear their ugly heads in classes when seemingly open-minded stu-dents attempt to cope with the cases at hand. Regardless, the classes are a welcome relief to overworked MBAs. There is no need for intricate quantitative analysis or extensive reading. As with other MBA subjects, knowing the vocabulary and using it at the right moments goes a long way in establishing credibility on the job.

What is taught in the OB classes, if internalized, are the lessons that well may be the most influential in the careers of MBAs. With-out people skills, MBAs are equipped with the power tools but are without the electric cord to use them.

THE OB PROBLEM SOLVING MODEL

Just as marketing offers seven steps to marketing strategy develop-ment, OB provides a three-step technique to solve organizational problems.

Problem Definition
Analysis
Action Planning

Problem Definition

The first step to solving an organizational problem is to know the source of the difficulty. Real problems are often masked by symptoms. It is easy to be misled into solving the symptoms instead of their cause. Unless the cause is dealt with, fresh headaches will undoubtedly arise. MBAs are taught several analytical techniques to aid in flushing out the sources of trouble.

Want Got Gaps. There is a problem when a gap or "deviation" exists between what a manager thinks "ought" to be occurring and what is "actually" occurring. Defining the problem entails viewing situations from the perspectives of all the participants and outlining their *Want Got Gaps.*

In the wake of a failure to introduce a critical new computer technology, a large service organization hired a new vice-president, Hank Helpful, to lead the computer department out of its trouble. In his judgment the problem was caused by interdepartmental rivalries. He felt that the computer department was isolated and always at odds with the rest of the company. Hank saw the gap as follows:

I Want → Gap ← I Got

Interdepartmental → Gap ← Isolated Departmental
    Cooperation   Islands

The VP felt that other gaps existed as well. The computer department believed it lacked the respect of the operational arm of the company. The people in the department felt that they were being treated as second-class citizens. Both perceptions were true. But the other sales and operating departments had their own gaps. They wanted timely computer services at an affordable cost.

In many instances, organizational problems are less easily diagnosed. Often managers do not know exactly what the gap is. Is there a gap at all? A manager's perceptions can cloud what is "actually" happening. That is often the cause of trouble in the first place.

The Level of Problems. When you know what gaps exist, it is then important to understand the ways in which they affect the organization. Problems can affect a company in three ways:

- **Within or between certain people**
- **Within or between groups**
- **Within the whole organization**

In the case of the computer department described above, the problem existed at all three of these levels. Each level had to be addressed to successfully "solve" it. The hard feelings between individuals occurred at a *personal* level. The interdepartmental squabbling was an *intergroup* problem. The company's failure to adopt competitive new technologies occurred at the *organizational* level.

Source Problems and Causal Chains. The goal of an effective MBA is to find the most important problems and solve those first. Those are called the *source problems*. Eliminate the source, eliminate the *symptoms*. Source problems, such as the lack of respect for the computer department, caused a multitude of other problems.

A graphical method used to get at source problems is to draw a *causal chain*. Using a causal chain, the company's interdepartmental problem would look like this:

Contributing Problems → Source Problem → Business Problem

Lack of Interaction: →   Lack of Respect → Project Failures
Personality Differences   for Techies

Analysis

After defining the gaps and using causal chains, the MBA is taught to link the problems to their causes. In addition to drawing causal chains, during this analytical step you try to *understand* the causes. Why do they exist? What environmental factors play a role? By asking these types of questions you can begin to confront which causes can be corrected through management action. If one problem is insurmountable, different solutions have to be tried. In the example above, firing uncooperative people was an option for the vice-president. Sensitivity training and interdepartmental discussions were other possibilities. As in a marketing plan, there are many possible avenues for action available to achieve a successful resolution to a problem.

Action Planning

MBAs are taught to be decisive and *proactive* — a frequently used MBA adjective. After a thorough analysis, MBAs should be able to formulate a plan. The *action plan* has six important steps.

1. Set Specific Goals.
2. Define Activities, Resources Needed, Responsibilities.
3. Set a Timetable for Action.
4. Forecast Outcomes, Develop Contingencies.
5. Formulate a Detailed Plan of Action *in Time Sequence*.
6. Implement, Supervise Execution, and Evaluate Based on Goals in Step One.

As you can imagine, solving problems MBA-style is not simple. It requires time and effort. To add to your MBA vocabulary, you should refer to your menu of possible actions as *action levers*. This sounds very forceful and progressive. An action lever may be a reward, a control, or a planning system.

The idea behind OB is to train MBAs to avoid tactical errors because they failed to take into consideration the people involved. With a framework to tackle challenges, the MBA curriculum inculcates in its students the theories and methods of the day so that they can use them.

INDIVIDUAL AND ORGANIZATIONAL LEVEL OB TOPICS

The previous discussion covered the frameworks used to analyze a problem and implement a solution. The next sections deal with the topics that provide the background for that process. The MBA curriculum logically starts with the theories and topics that deal with the individual, then builds to larger organizational issues that become progressively complex with the addition of more people. Along the way, students are asked to apply their newly acquired skills to analyze and plan solutions to increasingly complex and challenging case situations.

The MBA Psychology Lesson: The APCFP Model

In the effort to gain an insight into why people act the way they do at work, the MBA curriculum includes some form of the *APCFP model* pictured here. This model attempts to explain the cognitive process of linking external events to employee behavior. *Assumptions* affect the *perceptions* people have. Those perceptions affect the *conclusions*. And those conclusions prompt *feelings*. Ultimately those feelings drive *behaviors* that managers observe. By trying to understand this process, MBAs may have a chance to influence positive behaviors in themselves as well as in their coworkers. The model looks like this:

The APCFB Psychology Model

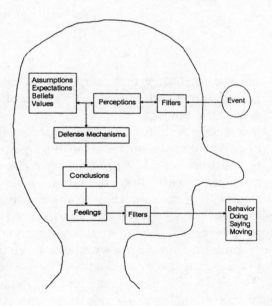

"Why People Behave the Way They Do," Case UVA-OB-183, Figure 5, Copyright © 1986 by the Darden Graduate Business School Foundation, Charlottesville, Virginia.

Given an analytical tool, MBAs are made to believe that they can understand anything. However, confounding forces within people prevent perfect communication and understanding. We all see through *filters* that often prevent us from perceiving events accurately. Filters also prevent us from acting out our true desires. We all have internal *defense mechanisms* that act as additional filters to protect us from psychological damage. They also prevent an accurate psychological reading of other people. For example, if an insecure supervisor has a poor aptitude for numbers, then by way of defense, he may find fault with an analyst's technical presentation. That would help him avoid confronting his own ineptitude with numbers.

MBAs have a chance to affect *assumptions*, the beliefs we hold about the way the world or other people or ourselves *should* or *ought to* be. These assumptions make up our value system. Listed in order of ease of accessibility, assumptions include:

Expectations
Beliefs
Values

Expectations and to some extent *beliefs* can be changed through clear management intent and action. *Values* are deeply held assumptions that may be altered, if at all, only in time.

When a manager is able to tap into the values of subordinates, then real productivity may result. Personally, I place a high value on creativity and freedom. When my manager taps into that well inside me, he elicits my best work. For example, when my boss seeks an insightful marketing analysis, he presents me with an opportunity to express my creativity. Our goals are said to be *congruent* or equivalent because we are both aiming at the same thing. The desired behavior is produced. *Goal congruence* among the individuals of an organization makes the group productive. "Goal congruence" is a popular MBA phrase — it sounds great, and it is in fact meaningful.

Let's take the example of a strategic planning manager. He wanted to tap his team's creativity in developing plans to compete in an evolving marketplace. In the past, he had done all the creative work himself. His staff members were simply used to crunch numbers. To elicit a change in their behavior, he had to learn to tolerate the trial and error that are part of the creative process. Because staff failures in the past had been met with firings and ridicule, the team understandably would be slow to comply with his wishes. The staff's assumptions stood in the way. To effect the desired change, he needed to build trust by rewarding creative behavior on a consistent basis.

The bottom line is that understanding a bit of psychology is useful if you wish to motivate people.

Expectancy Theory of Motivation

Motivation is an elusive animal that all organizations want to capture. *Expectancy* theory outlines the factors that produce motivation with individuals. Managers, staff, and even you can use expectancy theory to attempt to understand employees' behavior.

Motivation = Expectation of Work will lead to Performance ×
Expectation Performance will lead to Reward ×
Value of Reward

This equation may be helpful in isolating the source of a problem. Each of the equation's components can explain some aspect of motivation. If a marketing manager of a declining make of automobile has been losing market share to a better-manufactured and better-promoted competitor, he might feel that no matter what he did he would fail. That naturally would decrease his motivation. If the company never rewarded superior performance, that would also lead to discontent. And finally, if the reward were simply a set of keys to the executive washroom, then a manager might think of working elsewhere.

Three academic heavyweights, Hertzberg, Maslow, and McClelland, believe that behavior is motivated by the urge to satisfy needs. Fred Hertzberg posits that motivation will be enhanced by maximizing the motivators or *satisfiers* on the job and minimizing the *dissatisfiers* or maintenance factors. A promotion or an award can be a satisfier. Maintenance factors don't necessarily bring happiness, but they are expected. A safe place to work and a living wage are typical maintenance factors. Abraham Maslow sees employee motivation as a function of meeting an employee's *hierarchy of needs*. The hierarchy is frequently depicted as a pyramid. The need for food and water is at the bottom of the pyramid, followed by the *need for safety*, the *need to belong*, and the *need for status*, while *self-actualization needs* are seen as the highest order of needs. These needs are met when a person experiences a sense of personal growth and self-fulfillment by accomplishing a challenging goal.

Finally, David McClelland proposes that people have three basic needs, the *need for achievement*, the *need for power*, and the *need for affiliation*. Whatever the theory, managers must recognize the needs of employees.

Job Design

Another way to understand and affect employee motivation is to investigate the way a job is designed. Each job has certain *core job dimensions* that describe the duties performed. These duties lead to *critical psychological states* within employees that result in a variety of *outcomes*. Outcomes are the visible manifestations of work performance, while psychological states are hidden in the hearts and minds of people. If the human element is ignored, then quality and efficiency will suffer.

If the MBA is confronted with a personnel problem, it may be the result of job design. A close study of the core job dimensions can often yield great benefits without significant costs. For example, at a Lockheed parts factory in Los Angeles, unskilled minorities were hired and trained to assemble parts for jumbo jets fabricated at another factory. The employees were unmotivated and the quality of their output was poor. In talking with the men workers, the managers realized that the work had no meaning to them. They did not understand what they were producing. To fix that the workers were taken to the aircraft assembly plant to see where their parts were installed. They also met those who were inconvenienced when they received a defective product. Realizing the relevance of their work, the employees became more productive and part defects decreased. Their previously pointless assembly task acquired significance, and they responded by performing better. The end result was a happier work force that took pride in a job well done. The MBA term for

Job Design Model

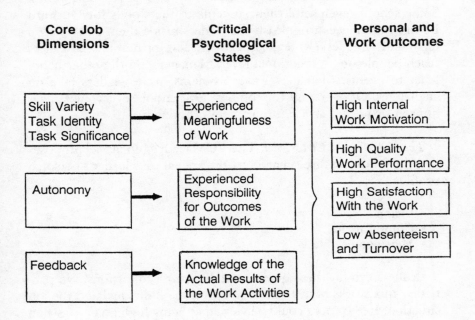

Core Job Dimensions	Critical Psychological States	Personal and Work Outcomes
Skill Variety Task Identity Task Significance	Experienced Meaningfulness of Work	High Internal Work Motivation
Autonomy	Experienced Responsibility for Outcomes of the Work	High Quality Work Performance
		High Satisfaction With the Work
Feedback	Knowledge of the Actual Results of the Work Activities	Low Absenteeism and Turnover

Adapted from "Introduction to Job Design," by Professor William Zierden, Case UVA-OB-91R, Figure 1. Copyright © 1975 by the Darden Graduate Business School Foundation, Charlottesville, Virginia.

such employee happiness is *quality of work life* (QWL). When employees are given the chance to be all that they can be, the word MBAs use to describe this is *empowerment*. You can hardly pick up a business book today without tripping over that word.

MBA Personality Traits

Business schools teach young women and men business skills, but they also try to motivate their students to maximize their own potential. In that vein, MBAs are taught to be innovative leaders.

Leadership. The top MBA schools claim to be incubators for the business leaders of tomorrow. In this pursuit organizational behavior classes probe the subject of leadership and its responsibilities. Some schools even send their students to the woods for Outward Bound experiences to unleash the leaders inside them and develop team skills. Leaders shape goals. Leaders develop new ideas. Leaders reach people on an emotional level. Managers, on the other hand, react to events. Managers solve problems, while leaders take on challenges. Of course, at the top business schools, everyone fancies himself or herself as a future captain of industry.

The Leadership VCM Model. The VCM leadership model proposes that the following three characteristics are part of a leader's personal profile:

- **Vision**
- **Commitment**
- **Management Skills**

Leaders exhibit these qualities in differing proportions. No particular mix works best. It all depends on the individual and the job situation. Lee Iacocca could be viewed as being high on *vision* when he saw the potential for the Ford Mustang in the 1960s. He also saw hope for Chrysler in its dark days in the late 1970s. In the accounting profession vision is not as critical, whereas *management* skills and *commitment* to long hours are the keys to success.

Leadership Patterns. There are as many ways to lead the troops as there are people. Leadership styles lie on a spectrum from *boss-centered* to *subordinate-centered*. In the 1960s executives raced to be tested to see where they fell on the spectrum. Based on a *managerial grid*, they could be classified a "dictator" or a "wimp." Some bosses use their authority directly to press their people into action. They do the thinking, and the staff does the legwork. Others give their people the freedom to use their own wits to organize and accomplish tasks. The boss's function is to give general direction. Which leadership style a leader chooses is regulated by three basic forces:

Leadership Styles
Vision, Commitment, and Management

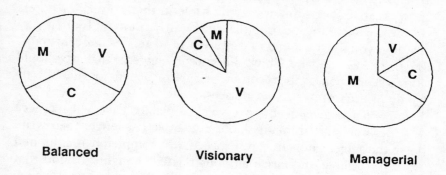

Balanced   Visionary   Managerial

Adapted from "Survey of Managerial Style," by Professor James Clawson, Case UVA-OB-358, p. 14. Copyright © 1988 by the Darden Graduate Business School Foundation, Charlottesville, Virginia.

- **The forces within the manager**
- **The forces within the subordinates**
- **The forces of the situation**

If the leaders do not have confidence in their subordinates, they cannot delegate tasks. If a staff doesn't have the ability to work unsupervised, full delegation of authority is inappropriate. When the staff has a clear understanding of the business situation and how to address it, it's best to delegate authority.

It is very important for a leader to understand his or her own personality traits. As you might imagine, a leader's insecurities may lead to an authoritarian style, regardless of what the situation may dictate. That is why self-awareness is important; it will enable you to avoid inappropriate management styles.

"My faults and my virtues are the same. . . . Nothing is ever enough. I must check everything. It causes me problems—people think I don't trust anyone. But I must know what's going on."
— Giorgio Armani, *Forbes*, October 28, 1991

Creativity. Not only are MBAs schooled to understand leadership, they are taught to become leaders by tapping their own creativity. Because *vision* is an element in the VCM pie, MBAs ought to nurture their own creativity. Everyone has *idea-friendly times* when they are most creative. For some it may be while in the shower, for others on the porcelain throne or in the car. Creative thought is often very fleeting; you must be able to capture it in its tender, nascent stage. *What a Great Idea* by Chick Thompson suggests that we should always keep a pen, a tape recorder, or a grease pencil (for the shower) handy in each of our *friendly* places.

The *mind mapping* technique is also available. Take a blank piece of paper and start thinking about a creative challenge, then write down the subject and circle it. Proceed, in a completely uninhibited style, to scribble and circle all your related thoughts around that subject's key words and connect them like the spokes on a wheel. Each of the spokes should have spokes around them, and so on. No thought is too stupid! After it's all done, something may emerge from the jumble of free association. I've used the technique to think up titles, promotional copy, and project solutions for this book. Try it — you have nothing to lose.

An abbreviated mind mapping session to develop the name for this book looked like this:

Mind Mapping for a Book Title

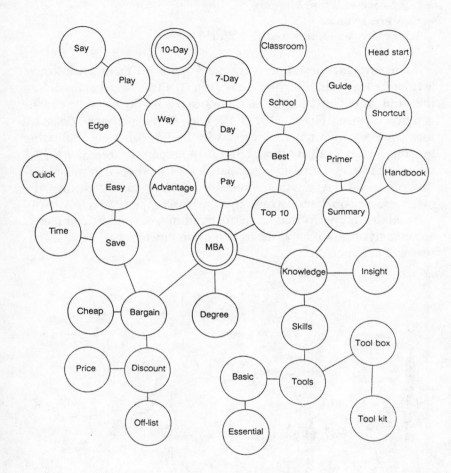

Type A and B Behaviors. OB professors have introduced the concept of behavior typing into the curriculum as an added tool for personal understanding. Since most MBAs attending the Top Ten schools were admitted because their Type A personalities helped them to the top of their college classes, it seems appropriate that they should understand that aspect of themselves. *Type A behavior* was originally identified in 1959 by two cardiologists, Meyer Friedman and Ray Roseman. They noticed that patients with severe coronary heart disease were often characterized by:

- **A Competitive Need for Achievement**
- **A Sense of Time Urgency**
- **Aggressiveness**
- **Hostility to Others and the World**

Additional manifestations of Type A behavior include explosive, accelerated speech, interruption of others, a fast-paced approach to life, and impatience. Type A's always try to do more than one activity at once. That's what those Day-Timer planner books are for. Type A's are often dissatisfied with life, showing a free-floating hostility. They evaluate their self-worth based on external achievements. One sure symptom is competition with others in noncompetitive situations. A classmate reported such a case: "During the interview season I was struck by a pizza company executive who boasted that his performance on the treadmill, during the company's annual physical, was superior to that of his coworkers." That executive was a Type A.

On the opposite side of the spectrum, there are the Type B's who enjoy life and are more relaxed. Some Type B's also sneak into business schools. Most individuals fall in the continuum between the two poles. Hopefully, by recognizing the Type A signs, MBA hard chargers may be able to head off a heart attack by exercising some control over their behavior. If not, behavior typing can make good bar conversation for MBAs heading for coronary oblivion.

MBA Office Procedures

The OB faculty, besides making students aware of their potential and shortcomings, tried to teach us some practical interpersonal skills that would help us to succeed on the job.

Active Listening. One of the most valuable skills is to be able to *really* listen. *Active listening* helps you to gain a clear *perception* of situations so that you can effectively deal with them. It differs from conversation in three ways:

- **You Respond to Information and Don't Lead.**
- **You Respond to Personal Information and Don't Give Advice.**
- **You Identify the Interviewee's Feelings as Well as the Content.**

An active listener cedes control of the conversation to the other party. Given enough leeway, true motivations, feelings, and beliefs can come forth. After the active listening session runs its course, you can start to talk and act like an MBA know-it-all again.

Performance Appraisals. One of the most mismanaged tools for organizational improvement is the performance appraisal. Rating forms are sometimes used very effectively for timely feedback and personal development. However, most of the time it is a task that is delayed until the appraisal really has lost all usefulness. *Effective* appraisals ought to have three types of goals:

Organizational
Feedback and Evaluation
Coaching and Development

Organizational goals aim to ensure proper conduct and levels of performance, placement, promotion, and pay. The *feedback and evaluation* aspects provide both employees and employers with a formal process and documentation of performance. *Coaching and development* should ultimately be the primary goals of an appraisal. How can we improve, rather than punish, unsatisfactory performance? Working together, the boss and the subordinate should agree on specific targets and timetables for improvement. These plans for the future lay the groundwork for a follow-up.

The problem is that managers tend to avoid this evaluation process. Subordinates are defensive. The appraisal must be timely; both participants must be prepared. The boss should foster an open climate of real communication (both ways) and make the purpose of the appraisal clear. As simple as the appraisal can be, it is seldom done right.

In addition to the potential for improvement, appraisals provide employers the SYA (save your ass) documentation to legally fire an employee. Without documentation a disgruntled worker could sue the company for lack of just cause.

Reprimands. Sometimes an MBA will be called on to lower the boom. In line with my class discussions, the MBA should reprimand a subordinate using the following five steps.

1. **Check out the facts first.** Ask yourself if you caused the problem.
2. **Give warning that you need to talk about the problem.**
3. **Pause and express your displeasure.** Tell it exactly as you see it. Yelling is counterproductive.
4. **Display a caring attitude.** "I did not approve of your behavior, but you are still okay." "Let's learn from this and put it behind us." The idea is to do it firmly, clearly, and move on to new business.

"A good manager can balance his reprimands with praise."

Managing Your Boss. MBAs are not always bosses. Most start out as lowly analysts, planners, and associates. Ironically, these are the positions that operations classes characterize as corporate fat, ripe for trimming. Even if MBAs find themselves in more senior managerial jobs, it's a safe bet that they will have a boss to deal with. Even presidents have to deal with chairmen!

Management of the relationship *upward* is as important as managing your relationship below. That's why I've included it in this book. To give the MBA an edge, the curriculum includes a session on how to *manage your boss*. "Managing Your Boss" appeared in the *Harvard Business Review* in January 1980. It was written by John Gabarro and John Kotter and it captures the subject well.

"The first step to success on the job is to understand bosses and their context, including:

- **Their stated and unstated goals and objectives**
- **The pressures on them**
- **Their strengths, weaknesses, blind spots**
- **Their preferred work styles**

"The second step is to be introspective and assess yourself and your needs, including:

- **Your own strengths and weaknesses**
- **Your personal style**
- **Your predisposition toward dependence on or resistance to authority figures**

"The third step is to incorporate the first two steps and develop and maintain a relationship that:

- **Fits both your needs and styles**
- **Is characterized by mutual expectations**
- **Keeps your boss informed—bosses hate surprises!**
- **Is based on dependability and honesty**
- **Selectively uses your boss's time and resources"***

Simply by asking a few questions at the start of the relationship, you can avoid making major political blunders in the future. Some

*Reprinted by permission of *Harvard Business Review*, "Managing Your Boss" by John J. Gabarro and John P. Kotter (Jan./Feb. 1980). Copyright © 1979 by the President and Fellows of Harvard College; all rights reserved.

bosses like a formal relationship, memos, and meetings with agendas. Others prefer informal notes and frequent unstructured meetings. Smart MBAs take the initiative to ask their bosses how they would prefer to communicate rather than guess. Careers often hang in the balance. I still keep Gabarro and Kotter's article at my desk as a reminder to manage my boss.

Understanding Power on the Job. If MBAs want power, then they ought to know more about what they seek. There are actually five types of power:

Coercive
Reward
Referent
Legitimate
Expert

Coercive power is based on fear. Failure to comply with a request could result in some form of punishment. A person with coercive power can influence or directly fire, demote, or transfer an employee. At a firehouse, the chief has the power to assign shifts. If you get on the chief's bad side, it could mean you work holidays.

Reward power is based upon the expectation of receiving praise, recognition, or income. It's the opposite of coercive power.

Referent power is derived from being a person whom other people admire regardless of formal job status. These people are said to have charisma to inspire and to attract followers. Star salespeople have this role in sales organizations.

Legitimate power is due to the formal status held in the organizational hierarchy. Those with this type of power can use it to reward, to ax, and to influence the lives of others in the organization. A shift foreman has the power to assign duties on an assembly line.

Expert power comes from one's own skill, knowledge, or experience. People with expert power have the ability to manipulate others. This is without regard to their position in the company. Often it is a lowly computer technician who may have the power to bring a senior executive to his cubbyhole. The boss must crawl for assistance. Crafty technicians fix it so that they alone have the ability to tap into the data base. This preserves their expert power. It's a manager's job to cross-train people to prevent the birth of such little generals in their organizations.

In the political gamesmanship of corporations, it is important for MBAs to recognize all the people in the organization with the power to influence their lives.

MBO and MBWA. MBO and MBWA are frequently used abbreviations in MBA babble. MBO means *management by objective*. It is a management style popularized by management guru Peter Drucker in the 1950s. Bosses delegate tasks by "negotiating a contract of goals" with their subordinates without dictating a detailed road map for implementation. MBO managers focus on the result, not the activity. At Frito-Lay, for example, a vice-president might set a sales target for her regional sales managers. The managers decide what tactics and strategy are needed to meet the objective.

The MBO style is appropriate when your staff is competent. Chief executives of multinational corporations (MNCs) use MBO for their country managers abroad. Their bosses in the United States often have little knowledge of what is required for success in those international markets. MBO is appropriate in situations where you wish to build employees' management skills and tap their creativity and initiative. The drawback to MBO is the time needed to adequately negotiate and document the process. Therefore, MBO should be used in appropriate situations.

MBWA, *management by walking around*, was a theory expounded at Hewlett-Packard, the computer giant. HP executives were encouraged to be out of their offices working on building relationships, motivating, and keeping in direct touch with the activities of the company. MBWA is a simple concept, but it has become part of an MBA's portfolio of management theories.

ORGANIZATIONAL LEVEL TOPICS

With a psychology lesson and a set of MBA office procedures to work with, the OB courses take a "bigger picture" look at organizations. With a larger scope also come grander theories and the vocabulary to accompany them.

The Basic Organizational Model

To understand an organization, you have to consider all of its components. Organizations are networks of related parts. Each element works together to support efficient operations. The new MBA buzzword for it all is *organizational architecture*.

The Basic Organizational Model

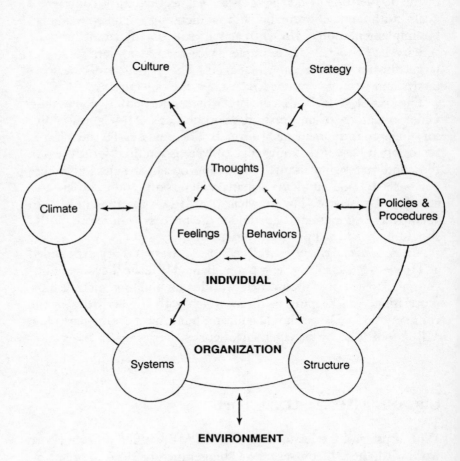

A noteworthy feature of the diagram is that the individual is at the center. The reason for this is that organizations are made not of brick and mortar but of people. Organizations affect those individuals. The theories in the previous sections focused on the individual. In the following sections the macro-view of the organization is explored in MBA terms.

As shown in the diagram, there are six elements that define organizations. Some are self-explanatory, but others have special MBA significance that you should be aware of.

Strategy. Strategy describes an explicit or implicit plan for success in the marketplace. When an airline decides to lure customers with either lower prices or better service, that is a corporate strategy. (Later in the book, I devote an entire chapter to this truly MBA topic.)

Policies and Procedures. Policies are formal rules that, in all but small companies, are captured in a handbook, while *procedures* are the observable ways in which a company conducts business. Vacation and benefits are policies that are codified. Routine tasks such as how waste paper should be separated for recycling may not be committed to paper. It's a procedure that is understood.

Organizational Structures. Structure vocabulary is a lexicon that no MBA can be without. It is a frequent subject of discussion in corporate meetings and is also an important tool for managing organizational behavior. Structures describe the hierarchy of authority and accountability in an organization. These "formal" relationships are frequently diagrammed in *organization charts*. Most companies use some mix of structures to accomplish their goals. People who are directly involved in producing or marketing the firm's products or services are called *line* employees. The others who advise, serve, and support the line are called *staff* employees. Line and staff employees can be organized along the following lines:

Functional
Product
Customer
Geographic
Divisional
Matrix
Amorphous

Functional. The functional form divides work by tasks, e.g., advertising, accounting, finance, and sales. These departments report to the senior executives.

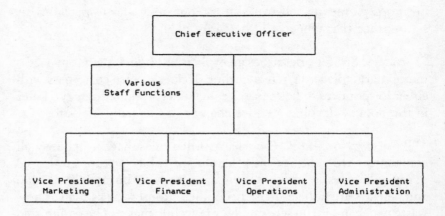

"Organizational Structure," written by Professor James Clawson, Case UVA-OB-361, Figures 1–8, Copyright © 1988 by the Darden Graduate Business School Foundation, Charlottesville, Virginia.

Product. The product structure groups all functions necessary to deliver a specific product. Product managers manage individual products as smaller businesses within a company. Black & Decker, for example, is divided into separate units responsible for power tools, small appliances, and accessories.

Customer. The customer structure focuses on — you guessed it — the customer. Activities, such as production and marketing, are grouped with other functions to satisfy specific customer needs. The customer structure is common in service industries. Banks often divide responsibility by customer type. For instance, some loan officers are specially trained to serve business clients, while others are trained to serve individuals. Each has "expert" knowledge to deal with his customers' specific needs.

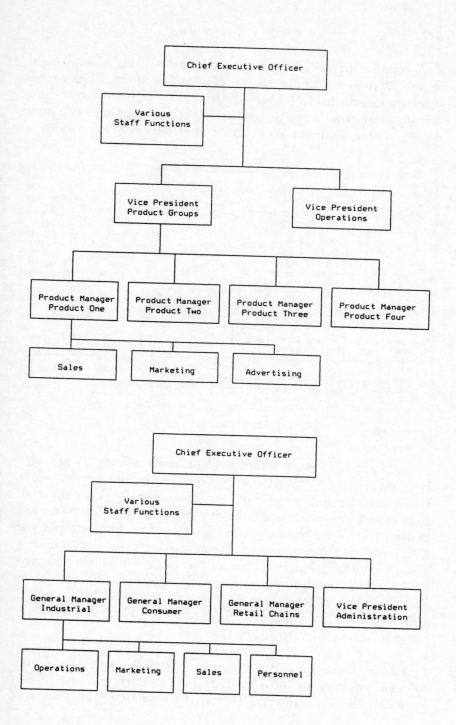

Geographic. In this arrangement work is divided by location. Geographic structures cut across customers and products. Regional offices are established to manage the business. At Nutri/System Inc., the diet program company, operations were divided into two divisions in 1990, East and West, that comprised over twenty cities.

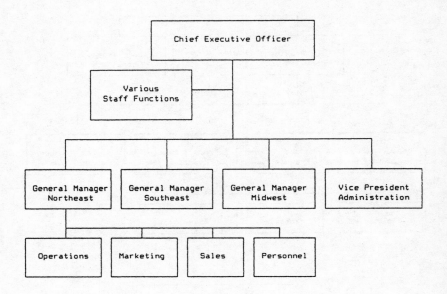

Divisional. Divisions are independent businesses operating under the umbrella of a parent corporation. Unlike the previous four structures, divisions run somewhat autonomously. They do it all themselves, from marketing to buying raw materials. However, most divisions use the parent company for financing. For example, the Philip Morris Companies includes Miller Brewing, Kraft General Foods, and Philip Morris Tobacco. These three businesses are centrally owned but separately operated. Within each of the divisions there may be other organizational substructures. For example, Miller may use the geographic form and Kraft General Foods may use a product structure (chart, page 143).

Matrix. The matrix structure departs from the principle of *unity of command*: only one boss for each employee. Here there are two or more lines of authority. The matrix is common in businesses

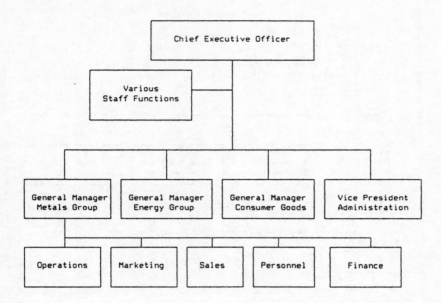

involved in large, complex projects that require highly specialized skills. In this structure, both the product and the functional structures coexist. Employees report to both a project manager in charge of their assigned product and a functional manager who controls specific activities such as manufacturing, finance, and marketing. As you might expect, this organizational form can be confusing. It requires a staff that is flexible and professional. The defense and computer industries often opt for the matrix structure to handle large development projects (top chart, page 144).

Amorphous. This is my personal favorite. The amorphous structure is no formal structure at all. It's the free bird. In these companies highly motivated and productive managers create and dissolve reporting relationships as the task at hand requires. In these companies, the structure incrementally grows as events dictate. Digital Equipment Corporation is said to have grown with an amorphous structure (bottom chart, page 144).

Hybrid. These entities are composed of a mix of operational structures. Most companies fall into this category. General Electric has

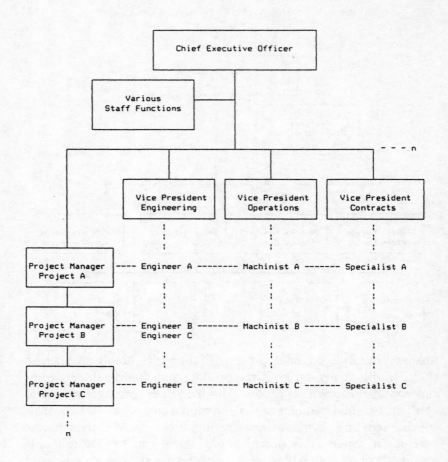

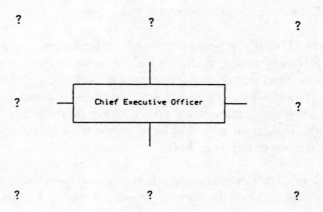

a divisional corporate structure that includes the NBC television network, GE Lighting, GE Capital, and GE Aerospace. But within each division, there are geographic manufacturing organizations, matrix research staffs, and customer sales grouped organizations. In the example below a single business is organized in a functional/ product hybrid. The brand managers control their products and marketing, but they do not have complete control over the financing or operations of the business.

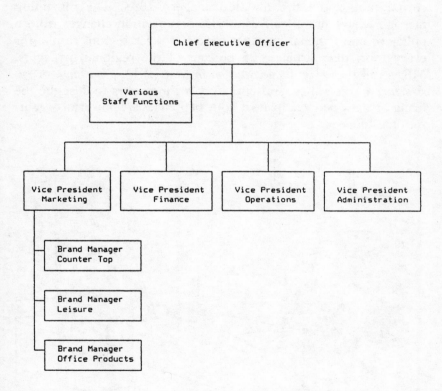

The choice of structure dramatically affects the operations of a company. There needs to be a *fit* between the business activities required and the corporate apparatus set up to produce and deliver the service.

Managers should select a structure that reflects their goals and strategy. The structure that is set up enables individuals to interact in ways that will best achieve goals. Informal reporting relationships form spontaneously and these fail to be represented in the organizational charts kept by the personnel department. Recognizing both the formal and informal structures is crucial in executing a successful *action plan*.

An important issue related to reporting relationships is the *span of control*. The span describes the number of people who report to a manager. During restructuring, downsizing, and recessions this topic becomes popular. Using a decreased span of control, large corporations often fire middle-manager MBAs. The remaining managers have more staff. If a sales organization changes from a policy of one regional manager for every three regions to one for every four, that displaces 25 percent of the regional managers. MBAs call these layoffs a *reduction in force* (RIF), *demassing*, or *restructuring*. It's a nice, antiseptic way for managers to describe the firing of many people. Span-of-control policies are powerful organizational tools.

" YOU'RE FIRED, NEVINS, BUT WE'VE
ENJOYED YOUR BEING HERE AND HAVE SOME LOVELY PARTING GIFTS FOR YOU. "

Systems. Each organization develops *systems* for allocating, controlling, and monitoring money, things, and people. Systems also perform informational activities by gathering information and channeling it to interested users. Systems fall into one of six categories:

Money Allocation, Control, and Monitoring — accounting, investment, and budgeting systems

Object Allocation, Control, and Monitoring — inventory and production systems

People Allocation, Control, and Monitoring — human resource planning, employee data and appraisals

Future Anticipation — strategic planning, marketing-sales planning, business development functions

People Reward and Incentives — compensation schemes, bonus plans, profit-sharing plans

Integrative — mixes of the first five. In well-managed companies, integrated systems forecast sales, which in turn dictates production schedules required to meet that need.

It is crucial to understand the systems of an organization, because they are the tools for change. Systems provide both a means and, at times, a barrier to corporate change.

Climate is a nebulous term that refers to the emotional state of an organization's members. Many companies hire expensive consultants to perform satisfaction studies to determine the "climate" of their organization so that improvements can be made. In service industries where people are the most valuable assets, such as law firms, investment banking houses, and consulting practices, the climate of the firm plays an important role in determining service quality.

Culture is another hazy term. Culture is the mix of behaviors, thoughts, beliefs, symbols, and artifacts that are conveyed to people throughout an organization over time. It may extend to such silly things as an unwritten rule that all men must wear white pinpoint oxford shirts or corporate lapel pins. Culture may include a belief about desired employee conduct. "Senior executives must always work past six o'clock." "It's important to look busy at all times." A main criterion for recruiting is often the perceived "fit" of interviewees with the organization. If a person does not appear to "fit" into the corporate culture, then he or she in many recruiters' eyes probably will not be an effective employee.

The six elements of an organization (strategy, policies, structure, systems, climate, and culture) dynamically affect one another. Each element interacts with the environment as a business strives toward its goals. The *problem definition/action planning* process requires that a manager look at all six elements of the organization model to determine which *action levers* will exist to implement positive change. If the environment changes, the organizational elements must adapt. MBAs like to refer to companies that can change as *learning organizations*.

Organizations that are stuck in the same old pattern of thinking and acting are said to be trapped by their *paradigms* or mindset. High-priced consultants often counsel stagnant companies on how to break their old paradigms so that they can change and succeed. Use the word *paradigm* several times in a conversation tomorrow, and you're one step closer to becoming a *Ten-Day MBA*.

The Human Talent Flow Pyramid

The structure of a firm dictates not only how employees are grouped but also how they can advance in a firm. At each progressive stage the individual assumes more authority. People either leave, get fired, or are promoted. A handy MBA tool to track this flow of human capital is a pyramid diagram.

By tracking the flows of people in and out of an organization, we can clearly identify turnover problems, skill deficiencies, and entrenched management. The diagram helps to point out graphically the "leakages" and "blockages" of people flows within the organization. Employees enter all levels of the organization as depicted at the left and move up within the pyramid. If there is little movement from one level to another, this blockage may cause many people to become frustrated and leave to the right of the pyramid, a leakage. Discrimination issues such as "glass ceilings" for women and minority promotions can be analyzed using this pictorial technique.

Systems Theory and Organizational Analysis

Systems theory is a concept that likens organizations to living organisms. Just as animals have their endocrine, digestive, and nervous

The Human Talent Flow Pyramid

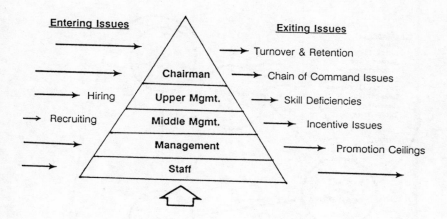

systems, academics propose that organizational bodies have similar *subsystems* that enable them to live. When diagrammed, an organization looks like a paramecium.

The *management subsystem* is the organ that sets the goals, plans, and controls, similar to the brain. This is the role of executives.

The *adaptive subsystem* acts as a firm's eyes to monitor the environment. The system also makes sure that the firm's products and services are appropriate in a changing environment to ensure survival. Information gathered from market researchers, customer service representatives, and salespeople makes a company adaptive.

The *boundary spanning in subsystem* is the mouth. It controls the intake of the organization's food. In a company, this subsystem includes recruiting people, buying raw materials, and raising money.

The bowels of the company are the *production subsystems*. It converts the inputs into goods and services. In a manufacturing company, these are the factories.

The bowels lead to the *boundary spanning out subsystem*. The marketing crew helps the company produce its products and services. The personnel department deals with the outplacement of employees who have not met company standards. And finally, the public

Systems Theory

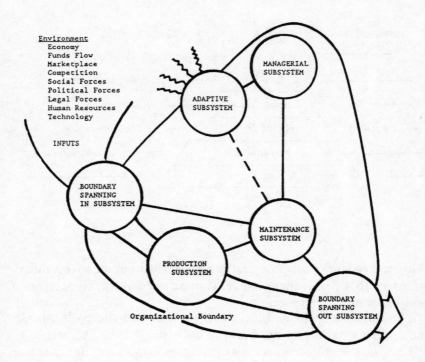

"Systems Theory and Organizational Analysis," by Professor James Clawson, Case UVA-OB-214, Figure 1, Copyright © 1983 by the Darden Graduate Business School Foundation, Charlottesville, Virginia.

relations department tries to put a good face on the company's actions.

Once the animal is breathing and functioning properly, the *maintenance subsystem* tries to keep the other subsystems working efficiently together. This cerebellum maintains a balance in the organization by coordinating all the movements of the body. Examples of the maintenance subsystems include employee incentives and company newsletters.

Systems theory provides yet another way of analyzing an organization to gauge its health or to make a change in its life-style.

Evolution and Revolution as Organizations Grow

Larry E. Greiner of the Harvard Business School wrote a noteworthy article with this title in the *Harvard Business Review* in July 1972, describing the growing pains that organizations go through.

Greiner proposed that organizations exhibit five predictable stages of growth called *evolutions* and five periods of crises called *revolutions*. His theory is readily applicable to many organizations. The growth pattern consists of tightening and loosening of management reins in response to changes within the organization and the environment.

The evolution/revolution pattern, as shown by Apple Computer, is an excellent way to put a company's history into MBA perspective. Apple Computer sprang forth from the *creativity* of Steven Jobs and Stephen Wozniak. Beginning in 1976, these two entrepreneurs were on a freight train of rapid growth until the company became so unwieldy that it almost jumped the tracks in 1983. Apple was faced with the *leadership crisis* of a growth company that didn't have anyone who could efficiently run its day-to-day operations. Jobs was a lofty visionary making speeches, while Wozniak was the magic technician.

The company started to run out of gas as its creative fuel ran low. Apple II sales slumped and the new Lisa computer failed. John Sculley (Wharton MBA '63) was brought in from Pepsi-Cola to give the company *direction*. Sculley reorganized Apple and cut costs in its bloated headquarters. Steve Jobs and his followers demanded more *autonomy* to develop a new breakthrough product and Sculley gave it to them. The *delegation* resulted in the creation of the Macintosh.

The Mac created another explosive growth period. However, Jobs could not work in a growing corporate bureaucracy, and he started a new company called NeXT. In 1989 the aging Mac faced fierce competition, and as profits declined in 1990, a new Apple crisis of *control* was brewing. Michael Spindler was appointed as

Evolution and Revolution of Organizations

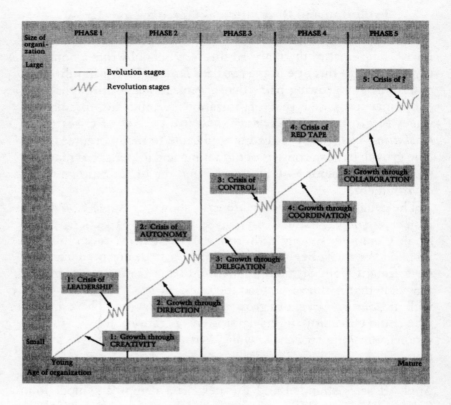

chief operating officer to assist Sculley as chairman to take control and return the company to increasing profitability. By 1992 they had succeeded.

Choosing Strategies for Change

In addition to all the theory about the mind and corporate body, MBAs receive practical guidance for taking action in difficult situations. Even if an action plan is "perfect," there is always resistance to change. Even those well-thought-out plans such as the one the new MBA proposed to his boss at the beginning of this chapter may run up against a wall. Fortunately, John P. Kotter and Leonard A. Schlesinger formulated a tidy model to assist MBAs in their article "Choosing Strategies for Change" in the *Harvard Business Review* of March 1979. The appropriate course of action all depends on the situation.

Situation → Action Needed for Change

Company Lacks Information → Education and Communication Tactics

In a stodgily run manufacturing company in Salt Lake City, the employees were kept in the dark about corporate profitability. Judging by the expensive cars of the owner, they assumed that all was well. Unfortunately, the company was losing money and layoffs would be inevitable unless productivity rose. In this situation, the employees would need to be informed about the true condition of the company before they gave their full cooperation to work more efficiently.

You Need Information and You Have Little Leverage → Participation and Involvement Tactics

A metal fabrication plant in Kansas City hired a consultant to cure absenteeism. The consultant did not know the people, the personalities, or the town. Because she was an outsider, she had no power to demand cooperation for her investigation. She first had to gain the trust of the workers and begin to talk with them about the problems that prompted so many sick days. She needed their cooperation and involvement to define and solve a problem for the workers as well as for management.

Adjustment Problems → Support and Facilitation Tactics

As offices become computerized across the country, secretarial work has changed. There are no more typewriters. Secretaries are required to use word processor programs on computers. Instead of hiring new help, companies need to retrain their staffs. Companies must hire computer support staff to help with this adjustment.

Your Desired Changes Will Cause Losses and Opponents Have Power to Block You → Negotiation and Agreement Tactics

In the 1980s robotics were introduced in the American auto industry. Japanese imports were taking jobs overseas. GM, Ford, and Chrysler chose to negotiate new agreements with the powerful United Auto Workers union to allow work-rule changes required by the new technology. If the corporations had decided to play hardball and impose their will upon the UAW, the union could have struck, and both parties would end up losing. By cooperating both have a chance of surviving.

You Have No Alternatives and No Money for Facilitation → Manipulation (Give No Choices)

In distressed companies there are often no alternatives to layoffs and wage cuts. A manufacturer of electronic switches in Trenton, New Jersey, gave its employees the choice of lower wages or no jobs at all. They took the pay cut, but the company failed anyway.

Frank Lorenzo of Texas Airlines, in his leveraged buyout of Eastern Airlines, saddled the air carrier with a huge debt. As a result he obligated the company to make huge interest payments. To salvage the situation, Lorenzo demanded across-the-board pay cuts, but he underestimated the union's resolve to resist his demands. In 1990 Eastern ceased operations.

Speed Is Needed and You Have the Power → Explicit Orders and Coercion Tactics

This situation is most common in the consulting, law, and public accounting professions. The familiar scene begins with a client requesting a project due "yesterday." The partner calls in a lowly associate and demands that the assignment be completed "the day before yesterday." The partner says jump and the associate jumps. The partners hold the power. The rub is that employees burn out and leave. Fortunately for the firms, there are legions of eager college graduates to replace their ranks. If you choose coercion tactics, you have to be sure you have the power and are willing to deal with the consequences.

AN OVERVIEW OF ORGANIZATIONAL BEHAVIOR

Above all, MBAs should think before they act. When MBAs need to take action they should thoroughly analyze the situation, first from the perspective of the individual and then from an organizational vantage point, to create a coordinated and effective action plan. MBAs are not trained to be "organizational experts" by any means, but with a few theories and frameworks, they should have a better chance of acting effectively.

KEY OB TAKEAWAYS:

Want Got Gaps — Organizational problems
Causal Chains — The relationship of problems to one another
Action Planning — A specific series of activities to solve an organizational problem
APCFB Model — A human psychology model
Goal Congruence — People with similar goals work better together.
Expectancy Theory — Motivation is a function of how an employee's actions translate into a reward.
VCM Leadership Model — The vision, commitment, and management aspects of leadership.
Active Listening — Listening to gain insight
The 5 Forms of Power — Power is derived from more than a title.
The Basic Organizational Model — Strategy, policies, structure, systems, climate, and culture
Structure — The way a company organizes itself

Span of Control — The number of people a manager directly controls
Paradigm — A corporate mindset or pattern of doing things
Systems Theory — An organization functions much like a body.
The Evolution and Revolution Pattern — Organizations go through a se-
ries of growth and crisis periods during their lifetime.

DAY 5

QUANTITATIVE ANALYSIS

QUANTITATIVE ANALYSIS TOPICS

Decision Tree Analysis
Cash Flow Analysis
Net Present Value
Probability Theory
Regression Analysis and Forecasting

Quantitative analysis (QA) is probably the most challenging and most important course in the MBA curriculum. It provides the basic tools principally used in finance, accounting, marketing, and operations. Therefore, these pages are not to be skipped over simply because you are not accustomed to dealing with numbers and statistics. Give it a chance!

Quantitative techniques provide MBAs with a way to distinguish themselves from their non-MBA peers. MBAs can make a splash with their bosses by creating sophisticated charts and graphs and by using impressive language. Hopefully, the conclusions they have to deliver are a welcomed story.

Using QA theories to solve business problems is the MBA's main job. Quantitative analysis helps MBAs remain objective when solving complicated problems. The theories behind the techniques are inconsequential. Their application to solve real business problems is what is important. Yet it should be noted that no matter how

"It's my fervent hope, Fernbaugh, that these are meaningless statistics."

mathematically precise the tools of quantitative analysis may appear, they are no substitute for an MBA's own best judgment.

DECISION THEORY

Decision theory teaches how to break complex problems into manageable parts. Without a framework to attack difficult situations, such cases quickly become unmanageable. For example, QA can be used to help a wildcatter decide whether or not to drill for oil. The inherent risks of oil exploration, however, cannot be eliminated. A *decision tree diagram* can organize the problem's alternatives, risks, and uncertainty.

Decision tree analysis consists of the following 5 steps:

1. Determine all the possible *alternatives and risks* associated with the situation.
2. Calculate the *monetary consequences* of each of the alternatives.
3. Determine the *uncertainty* associated with each alternative.

4. Combine the first three steps into a tree diagram.
5. Determine the *best alternative* and consider the nonmonetary aspects of the problem.

Decision tree diagrams include *activity forks* and *event forks* at the juncture where different alternatives are possible. For example, the decision whether to drill for oil or not represents an activity fork in the tree for an oil wildcatter. It is symbolized on a decision tree by a *square*. If the different alternatives are *subject to uncertainty*, that is an *event* fork. The uncertain outcome of a well producing oil would be considered an *event*. It is symbolized on a decision tree by a *circle*.

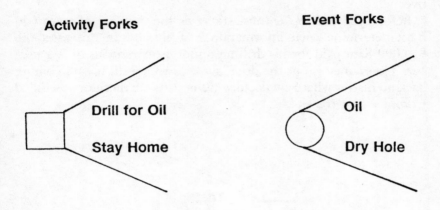

Activity Forks   **Event Forks**

Drill for Oil   Oil

Stay Home   Dry Hole

Decision Tree Example

As an illustration of a situation where the decision tree could be helpful, consider Mr. Sam Houston of Texas. Mr. Houston is about to exercise his option to drill for oil on a promising parcel. Should he drill? If he hits a gusher there is an estimated $1,000,000 to be gained. When he investigated all of the alternatives, Mr. Houston made the following list:

1. Sam paid $20,000 for the drilling option.
2. Sam could lower his risks if he hired a geologist to perform seismic testing ($50,000). That would give him a better indication of success and lower his risk of wasting drilling costs.

3. Should he roll the dice and incur $200,000 in drilling costs without a seismic evaluation to guide him?
4. Sam consulted with oil experts. They believe Sam's parcel has a 60 percent chance of having oil without the benefit of any tests.
5. It has also been the experts' experience that if seismic tests are positive for the oil, there is a 90 percent chance there is "some" oil. And conversely, there is a 10 percent chance of failure.
6. If the seismic tests are negative, Sam could still drill but with a 10 percent chance of success and a 90 percent chance of failure.
7. Sam could decide not to drill at all.

Each piece of information above is incorporated into a tree diagram. A tree diagram graphically organizes Mr. Houston's alternatives.

Before you get too enthusiastic over the drawing of trees you must determine what information is irrelevant. In this case, the $20,000 Sam paid for his drilling option is extraneous; it is a *sunk cost*. The money is out the door, sunk down a well. It isn't coming back no matter what Sam decides. Sunk costs are therefore excluded from decision trees.

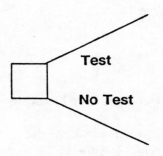

Drawing a Decision Tree

The first step to drawing the tree is to determine the first decision (or *fork of the tree*) that needs to be made. Should Sam choose to test first? If seismic testing is chosen, it would precede all of the other activities that follow. It is reflected in the tree as a *square* at the first fork.

If Sam tests, it could result in a positive *event* (60 percent chance) or negative event (40 percent). If there are no tests, he can still choose to drill or not (square). Regardless of the results of the seismic report, Sam can still "choose" to drill or not. But once the oil rig is drilling, the existence of oil is an *uncontrollable* event. Either there will be a lucrative oil event or not.

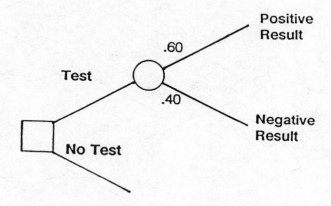

The next step is to add the monetary consequences — they are like the "leaves to a tree." If there is oil, there would be a $1,000,000 payday. Drilling costs are $200,000 per well. Testing costs are $50,000 per well.

To know the potential financial outcomes of each decision, multiply the possible dollar outcomes by their probabilities at forks where there is an "event circle." [($1,000,000 payday × .90 probability) + ($0 payday × .10 probability) = $900,000]. This gives you the *expected monetary value* (EMV) of the event. At any circle, the probabilities must add up to 100 percent (.90 + .10 = 1.00) to denote that all possibilities are accounted for. Each fork is *mutually exclusive* of other alternatives and within that alternative the probability is 100 percent or *collectively exhaustive*.

At *activity squares* the decision maker has the ability to choose the best outcome. To determine the best alternative, subtract the applicable cost from the payoff of the alternative. You calculate the monetary consequences by beginning at the far right and working your way to the left. This process is said to be "folding back" or "pruning" the tree to arrive at your best action plan

The Decision Tree
Oil Drilling

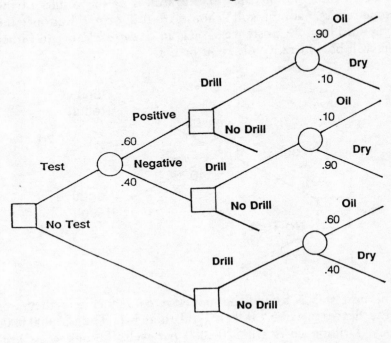

decision. At square forks you should choose the highest dollar alternative. At the circle multiply the possible payoffs by their probabilities.

The decision dictated by the tree is to throw caution to the wind and forego the seismic tests. The expected monetary value of going ahead with testing is $370,000 (420 − 50), while the EMV of going ahead without tests is $400,000. You choose the highest *expected monetary value* (EMV). This relatively simple conceptual framework can be applied to new product development, real estate development, and store inventory level decisions. Whatever the decision to be considered, a decision tree structure forces the decision maker to take a comprehensive view of all the alternatives, to make an evaluation of the uncertainty (you often have to make your best guess about probabilities), and to explicitly calculate the dollar out-

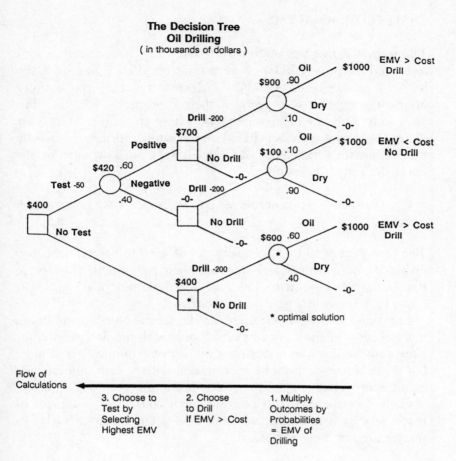

**The Decision Tree
Oil Drilling**
(in thousands of dollars)

Flow of Calculations ◄───────────────────

3. Choose to Test by Selecting Highest EMV

2. Choose to Drill If EMV > Cost

1. Multiply Outcomes by Probabilities = EMV of Drilling

comes possible. The tree forces decision makers to state their assumptions explicitly. Others looking at the same situation could see it otherwise. By comparing trees, analysts can debate specific assumptions in an organized way.

"Draw a tree and get a B" was the saying on exams involving decision trees. The complexity of seemingly simple problems can be seen using decision trees. Therefore, just creating an accurate tree framework was a challenge during a four-hour exam; it takes a lot of practice to become proficient.

CASH FLOW ANALYSIS

The term *cash flow* was often used in the 1980s in connection with leveraged buyouts (LBOs) of companies on Wall Street. It is the basis of financial analysis. Wall Street technicians may ponder briefly the qualitative aspects of their investment decisions, but ultimately, only the cash consequences have any real relevance for them. Cash flow analysis is based on the same information used by the accountant's Statement of Cash Flows. Cash flow analysis answers the simple question:

> What does the investment cost and how much cash will it generate each year?

The cash generated by a company can be used to pay off debt, pay dividends, invest in research, purchase new equipment, or invest in a real estate development. The goal is to determine when and how much cash flows in a given case scenario.

In making an investment there may be several objectives in mind, but cash flow analysis concerns itself only with the dollars. A company's advertising may create goodwill with the public, for example, but if the benefits cannot be measured in dollars, cash flow analysis is not appropriate.

Cash flow analysis is as relevant to the purchase of a piece of machinery as it is to the acquisition of a corporation. So let us restate the first question asked:

> What is the current investment and what are the future benefits?

The steps to answer the questions are:

1. Define the value of the investment
2. Calculate the magnitude of the benefits
3. Determine the timing of the benefits
4. Quantify the uncertainty of the benefits
5. Do the benefits justify the wait?

One important issue to consider is that cash flow analysis indicates cash flows, not profits. For example, a successful computer start-up company in Silicon Valley, Astro Computer, may be making an "accounting" profit of $3 million. But if the company requires a $20 million investment in research and a $30 million outlay to build a factory, the company is actually a net user of cash. In this case the company's profitability lies in the future.

Accounting profits, as reported in the income statement, are a short-term measurement of an investment in a time frame shorter than the life of the investment, whereas cash flow analysis is a technique used to evaluate individual projects over the life of the project.

The following specific information would be required to quantify the initial cash flows of a project:

Cash Uses

- **Construction Costs**
- **Initial Inventory Stock**
- **Equipment Purchases**
- **Increases in Accounts Receivable (allowing customers to borrow from you for goods sold to them)**

Cash Sources

- **Sales of Equipment (if disposed of)**
- **Increases in Accounts Payable (borrowing from suppliers on materials purchased)**

To determine the cash uses during the life of the project:

Cash Sources

- **Revenues or Sales**
- **Royalties**

Cash Uses

- **Costs of Goods Sold**
- **Selling Costs**
- **General and Administrative Costs**
- **Taxes**

Depreciation, which appears in income statements, is not relevant in cash flow analysis. Depreciation is an accounting allowance that says that if a piece of equipment has a useful life of five years, then one fifth of the cost in each year of use can be deducted from income. In a cash flow analysis, hard cash is used to buy the machine today, therefore it is shown as a use of cash at the time of purchase. Depreciation is only applicable inasmuch as it is used to reduce "accounting income," thereby reducing the "cash" out the door for taxes. In the Bob's Market example in the accounting chapter, the store expensed its cash registers and shopping carts over a ten-year period even though they were paid for at the store's opening.

A second important point is that financing costs are not included in cash flow analysis. The investment decision is separate from the financing decision. At General Electric there are thousands of projects and many classes of financing — debt (bonds, bank debt) and stock. To match debt with individual projects would be impossible. In reality, the finance department borrows to meet all of its current corporate needs and it is the capital budgeting department that decides which projects to adopt. If the two decisions were linked, all projects that were financed by debt would look much better than those for which cash is paid up front, even though in substance they are the same.

A Cash Flow Example

Quaker Oats is considering a $100,000 investment in a cereal filling machine for its plant in Kansas City. The fiber craze has spurred the demand for oatmeal to the point of exhausting plant capacity. If the machine is purchased, additional cereal sales of $80,000 could be made each year. The cost of goods sold is only $20,000 and the profits derived would be taxed at 30 percent. The increased sales will also require holding $10,000 in inventory. Quaker will partially offset that use of cash by increasing its payables by $8,000 to farmers for the oats and Stone Container for the boxes to net a $2,000 additional cash investment.

At the end of three years the machine will be worn out, but the equipment will still be useful to a milling company in Mexico. Quaker plans to sell it to Molino Grande at a price of $10,000.

The Timing of Cash Flows
Quaker Oats Filling Machine Project
(in thousands of dollars)

	Year 0	Year 1	Year 2	Year 3
Investment	− $100			
Revenue		+ $80	+ $80	+ $80
Cost of Goods Sold		− $20	− $20	− $20
Taxes*		− $ 9	− $ 9	− $ 9
Increase in Inventory	− $ 10			
Increase in Payables	+ $ 8			
Sale of Equipment				+ $10
Total Cash Flow	− $102	+ $51	+ $51	+ $61

* Tax Calculation

Revenue	$ 80	
Cost	− 20	
Margin	$ 60	
Depreciation	− 30	(100 − 10)/3
Earnings Pre-Tax	$ 30	
Tax Rate	× .30	
Tax	$ 9	

In this example the timing of cash flows is critical to determining the project's value. A commonly used representation of the timing of cash flows is a bar graph. Each period, cumulative cash flow is reflected either below the line for cash investments or above the line for returns. Our Quaker example is shown in the following bar graph:

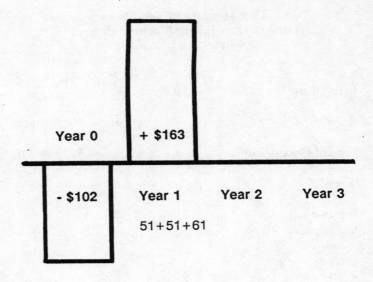

Suppose that the cash flows are the same but the timing of the cash is advanced as follows:

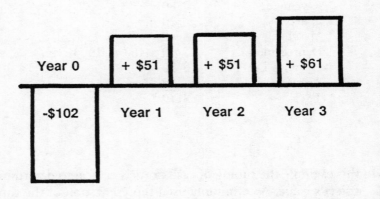

or prolonged as follows:

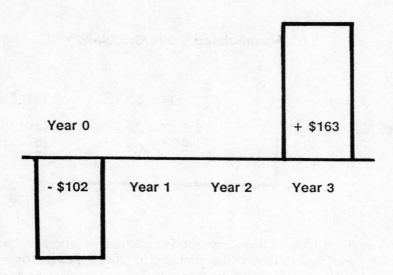

These diagrams raise the critical issue of the "value" of timing.

Accumulated Value

When the milling project produces cash, Quaker *reinvests* it rather than let it remain idle. Therefore if Quaker ˙receives $51,000, $51,000, and $61,000 as described earlier, the company earns income with the cash for two more years in Scenario A than in Scenario B.

If the company has investment opportunities that yield 10 percent, then Scenario A will produce $34,230 more than Scenario B.

The flows have an *accumulated value* at the end of three years of $163,000 plus earned interest of $34,230 that equals $197,000. Scenario A is clearly the better scenario.

A simpler calculation is to use the formula for the accumulated value or *future value* of a dollar:

Future Value of a $ in x periods = ($ today) × (1 + Reinvestment Rate)$^{\text{Number of Periods}}$

At 10% the factor for 1 year = $1 × (1 + .10)^1 = 1.10

Accumulated Value Calculation

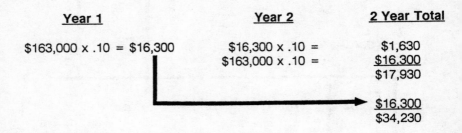

Year 1	Year 2	2 Year Total
$163,000 x .10 = $16,300	$16,300 x .10 = $163,000 x .10 =	$1,630 $16.300 $17,930
		$16.300 $34,230

You don't have to memorize the factors or calculate them each time — you can use the tables provided in the Appendix, or any basic business calculator. (The best calculator in my opinion is the Hewlett-Packard 17B or 19B. Owning an HP, an MBA icon, also sends a strong signal to others that you are serious about numbers.)

Per the tables at Appendix A, the *accumulated value* factors for varying rates and investment periods at 10 percent are:

Accumulation Factors

$1 today   = $1 today
$1 invested = $1.100 in 1 year
$1 invested = $1.210 in 2 years

Using our factors on Scenario B, on the $163,000 received at the end of Year 1 and invested for two years till the end of Year 3, the accumulated value is:

Year 1's $163,000 × 1.2100 = 197,000 in 2 years
or $197,000 − $163,000 = $34,000 of reinvestment income

When evaluating projects or investments that extend into the future, it is not only the magnitude of the cash flows that is important, but also the timing and the subsequent use to which those flows can be reinvested.

Net Present Value (NPV)

Accumulated value analysis is a good tool to determine how much a retiree needs to invest today to have an adequate pension in thirty years, but it doesn't solve the problem of evaluating investments and projects today. Investments need to be evaluated in today's dollars. How much is Quaker's milling project worth today? How does it compare to a similar piece of equipment that costs $150,000 but lasts four years?

Cash flow analysis determines the flows and the NPV technique values them in today's dollars. In that way different projects can be compared regardless of timing.

If Apple Computer, for example, knows that a new Tangerine computer will be a surefire $100 million hit, but that it will take ten years to develop, it may not make sense to invest in this project. Not only will that $100 million be worth less due to inflation, but Apple could also use the money to invest in robotics, which will save Apple production costs *today*. Even if an NPV analysis justifies the Tangerine, there may be strategic reasons that overshadow it. That's where the MBA must use management judgment.

Securities analysts see stocks and bonds as an equipment purchase. The stocks provide dividend payments and bonds provide interest payments in the future. The securities' values lie in the *present value* of their future cash flow. Just as Quaker Oats uses NPV analysis to evaluate the merits of buying a new piece of production equipment, corporations evaluate new factories, and the worth of increased advertising. Lawyers involved in wrongful death suits can use *net present value* techniques to value the total of a man's future earnings when considering a settlement. The basic idea to remember is: *A dollar today is worth more than a dollar received in the future*.

The Quaker Oats project yielded $163,000 over three years (51 + 51 + 61). As previously calculated, the $163,000 in cash flows would yield an additional $34,000 if the cash produced was reinvested at a rate of 10 percent in other company projects or an interest-bearing investment. Would you pay $163,000 for $163,000 to be received over three years? Of course not! You would be giving up the *time value of money*, or $34,000.

Using this simple logic, NPV analysis takes future cash flows and *discounts* them to their present-day value. This is the inverse of *accumulated value*. The formula is as follows:

NPV = ($ in Future) $\times$ (1 + Discount Rate)$^{-\text{Number of periods}}$

One dollar received one year from now, with a discount rate of 10 percent, would be worth:

$1 \times (1 + .10)^{-1} = .90909$

Using this formula, tables of *discount factors* tell the NPV of $1 at varying rates and for varying periods. Considering the 10 percent reinvestment opportunities available and the project's riskiness, $1 in the future is worth the following amounts today per the formula and tables:

Discount Factors

$1 today	=	$1 today
$1 in 1 year	=	$.90909 today
$1 in 2 years	=	$.82645 today
$1 in 3 years	=	$.75131 today

The cash flows of the Quaker project would be valued in the following way:

Future Cash $\times$ Discount Factor = NPV

Start Year 0	$-$102,000 $\times$ 1	=	$-$102,000 today
in year 1	$51,000 $\times$ .90909	=	$46,363.59 today
in year 2	$51,000 $\times$ .82645	=	$42,148.95 today
in year 3	$61,000 $\times$ .75131	=	$45,829.91 today
The Quaker project NPV		=	$32,342.45 today

The evaluation of any project depends on the *magnitude* of the cash flows, the *timing,* and the *discount rate,* 10 percent in our case.

The discount rate is highly subjective. The higher the rate or *hurdle rate* the less a dollar in the future would be worth today (see the Appendix). It is called a hurdle rate because a project with a higher discount rate must generate more cash in the future to be worth the same value of today. The project thus has a higher hurdle to jump to stay even. In cases where the future outcome of an investment is risky, as in our oil well example, a higher discount rate is appropriate. If the outcome of an investment is certain, as in the investment in a labor-saving device or in a United States Treasury Bond, a lower rate is warranted. Companies not guided by an MBA's expertise will use only one hurdle rate for all investment decisions and thereby ignore the relative riskiness of projects. They end up rejecting sure things, and chasing high-risk projects. Under no circumstances should the interest rate of a company's bank debt be the rate that is used, unless it is just coincidence. *The risk of the project should determine the discount rate.* Very stable companies can borrow at very low interest rates, but they can invest in risky projects.

Internal Rate of Return (IRR)

IRR is a derivative of NPV. Simply stated: The internal rate of return of an investment is the rate at which the discounted cash flows in the future equal the value of the investment today.

To find the IRR one must try different discount rates until the NPV equals zero. (Of course the HP calculator yields the IRR at a push of a button!) For the Quaker project the IRR is 26.709 percent. To confirm that number we can calculate the following:

Using "26.709% Discount Factors"

today	$1.00	×	−$102,000	=	−$102,000
1 year	$.78920	×	$51,000	=	$ 40,250
2 years	$.62285	×	$51,000	=	$ 31,765
3 years	$.49155	×	$61,000	=	$ 29,985
			NPV	=	− 0 −

Using IRR to rank projects is useful, but it does not consider the magnitude of the values. A small investment with proportionately large returns would be ranked higher than very large investments with adequate returns. If General Electric has a billion dollars allocated to research, it needs to deploy large sums of money to large projects which may have lower IRRs.

Ranking by IRR also neglects the hurdle rates or discount factors used in NPV analysis. Those hurdle rates, as I said, adjust for risk. All things being equal, the investment in equipment by Quaker may have a lower IRR than highly speculative research into a Swedish cancer cure by Merck, but the Quaker project could have a higher NPV. The equipment project's smaller cash flows would be discounted at a 10 percent rate because of the lower risk involved. This could result in higher NPV. The cancer research would be assessed using a very high discount rate of 50 percent. *Remember, the higher the discount rate, the less the cash is worth today and the more risk is implied.*

PROBABILITY THEORY

Probability theory is a nice word for statistics, the subject that creates fear in the hearts of even the brightest CPAs in business schools. Actually, probability theory is a more accurate term because it describes how statistics are used to solve problems. Given the *probabilities* of striking oil, what should Sam do? Out of eight hundred married MBA students in the Top Ten programs, how many spouses are likely to be ignored during the first year of the MBA program? It's all probability theory. Because most businesspeople shy away from statistics, here is an *opportunity* for MBAs to excel. I took a statistics course as an undergraduate and learned virtually nothing because I was taught theory, not problem solving. MBA programs concentrate on the practical aspects of statistics and tend to leave theory for mathematicians to sort out. If you are not familiar with statistics *do not* skip this section. I cannot make you statistically proficient in a few pages, but if you give it a chance with some patient reading, I promise you that you will have enough working knowledge of the discipline to ask for help whenever appropriate. Preparing students by giving them a working knowledge of different subjects is the main thrust of an MBA education. In only two years, professors do not expect their students to become technical experts, but they expect them to recognize where they should seek the help of an expert to solve a particular problem.

Probability Distributions

In situations where multiple outcomes are possible, the result is a *distribution* of outcomes. Each possibility is assigned a probability.

Through careful analysis, intuition, and judgment, all the possible outcomes of any *event* add up to 100 percent, like the event fork of a decision tree. The graph that shows a distribution of outcomes is called a *probability mass or density function*. If there are many possible outcomes, the curve is smooth and is called a *probability density function*. If there are only a few, an uneven curve is drawn, called a *probability mass function*.

A Rainfall Example. Rainfall in Seattle is an event resulting in a probability distribution. Seattle's rainfall, using hypothetical data, looked as follows in a table and in probability distribution charts on the next page.

Table of Seattle Daily Rain Measurements
April 1992

Daily Inches of Rain	Days with × Inches of Rain	Days as % of Month
0	5	16%
2	6	19
4	8	26
6	3	19
8	3	10
10	3	10
	28	100%

The Binomial Distribution

Flipping a coin results in two possibilities, heads or tails. Therefore the *distribution* of outcomes of two coin flippings could have several possible outcomes if you consider "heads" a success.

2 successes, Heads/Heads
1 success/1 failure, Heads/Tails, Tails/Heads
2 failures, Tails/Tails

Coin flipping gives rise to the most basic of distributions, called a *binomial distribution*. There are two outcomes in a binomial distribution, success and failure, each with an equal likelihood of occurring.

Probability Mass Function of Rain Measures
Daily Rainfall in Seattle
April 1992 (31 days)

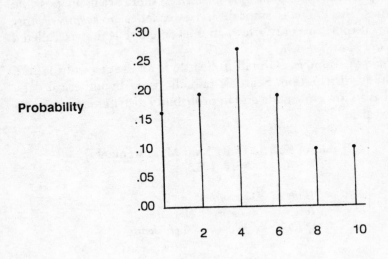

Inches of Rain

Seemingly arcane binomial distribution theories can be applied to such practical pursuits as stock market analysis. Success in a stock analysis would be a positive return on a stock in a month, and failure would be a loss or break even. In a study of AT&T share prices from 1957 to 1977, each month was examined to determine the rate of positive returns. It was found that 56.7 percent of the time there was a success.

The months studied were grouped into periods of three months each (quarters). Researchers noted that the frequency of actual successes was as follows:

# Successes	Frequency Occurred
0	.088
1	.325
2	.387
3	.200
	1.000

Probability Density Function of Rain Measurements
Daily Rainfall in Seattle
1962-1992 (1240 days)

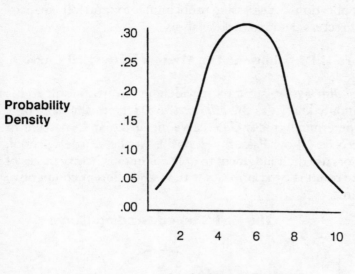

Probability Density

Inches of Rain

A coin-flipping mathematician created tables of numbers to solve all binomial distribution problems. In the AT&T case, the information needed to use a binomial table is:

r = number of successes possible = 0 to 3
n = number of trials = 3 (3 months in a quarter)
p = probability of success = 56.7%

Using this information, a binomial table predicts that the *expected* outcomes should be:

# Successes	Frequency Expected
0	.082
1	.318
2	.416
3	.184
	1.000

Surprisingly, the binomial distribution matches rather well the actual results of the AT&T case. Given a guess of *probability of success* (p), the probability of positive monthly returns in a given quarter could be read off the table. Binomial distribution therefore has practical applications for assessing probabilities for portfolio managers, sales directors, and research analysts.

The Normal Distribution: The Mystery of the Bell Curve

The *normal distribution* is the most widely used distribution and is most commonly known as the *bell curve*. At Harvard the bell curve is used to determine grades. The curve dictates that 15 percent of the class receive "Low Passes" ("loops"). At the Darden School, the professors use their judgment to dole out unsatisfactory marks of *C* or *F*. The result is two campuses with vastly different competitive environments.

The Bell-Shaped Grading Curve

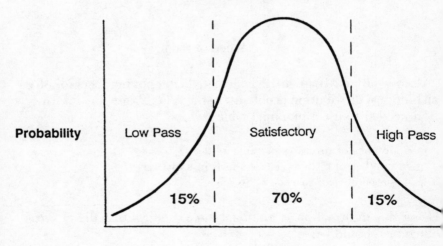

When a *probability mass function* is based on many trials, the curve tends to fill in and become bell shaped. We call this a *probability density function*. Such was the case with the two graphs describing rainfall in Seattle. The hump in the middle is caused by the *Central Limit Theorem*. It states that "the distribution of *averages* of repeated independent samples will take the form of the bell-shaped normal distribution." Why? Simply because a large number of independent samples tend to a central average.

The concept of "averages of samples" is a pretty vague one. In case applications the definition expands to include any large group of data. Why? Because the normal distribution is so easy to use and closely approximates reality anyway. Stock prices are the result of many market fluctuations which culminate in a return (profit or loss). The return can be considered an "average" of those market fluctuations. Just about anything can be rationalized as an average, hence the usefulness of normal distributions.

Measures of the Normal Curve. The bell-shaped curve is described by two terms, the *mean* and its *standard deviation* (SD). The mean (μ) is the center of the curve. The mean is commonly called the "average." It is the result of adding up the data and dividing by the number of data points. The standard deviation (σ) is how wide the curve appears. The SD can also be described as a measure of the "variability from the mean." These two terms are central to most probability concepts.

Other less-used measures of averages for a set of data are the *median*, the item in the middle of the list if sorted by size, and the *mode*, the item occurring most frequently in a data set.

Probability Density Functions with Curves of Different Standard Deviations

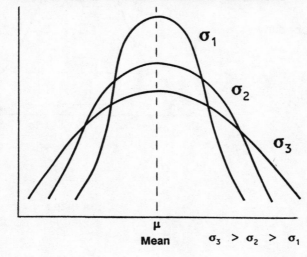

σ_1

σ_2

σ_3

Probability

μ

Mean $\sigma_3 > \sigma_2 > \sigma_1$

As with the binomial distribution, the sum of all the outcomes as represented by the region under the curve equals 100 percent. What makes the normal distribution's curve special is that for any given SD measure away from the mean or the center, the same probability exists for an event despite the normal distribution's shape.

Normal Distribution Retailing Example. Al Bundy, a shoe store owner, wants to make sure he has enough stock for all size requests. He purchased a study of ladies' shoe sizes from the Academy of Feet and received a stack of research data from survey responses.

He plotted the data on graph paper and it appeared as a normal distribution. He also entered the series of sizes in his calculator and hit the "Standard Deviation" key. The answer was 2. Al also took the average or mean of all the surveys' respondents' sizes and found it to be 7. Looking at the graph he created, he saw that it looked like our trusty normal distribution.

Normal Distribution of Shoe Sizes

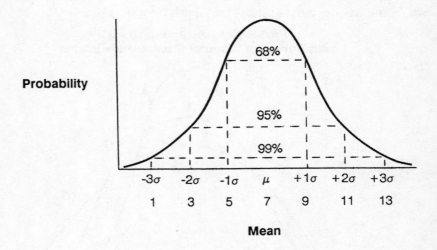

Just by recognizing the shape, Al could apply the laws of the normal distribution curve. The laws governing the area under all normal curves are the following:

$$
\begin{array}{lll}
1 \text{ SD} & = & .3413 \\
2 \text{ SD} & = & .4772 \\
3 \text{ SD} & = & .49865 \\
4 \text{ SD} & = & .4999683 \\
\end{array}
$$

Using these rules, if Mr. Bundy stocks sizes 5 to 9 he has covered .6826 (2 × .3413) of the population. Increasing the sizes to 3 to 11, he has covered .9544 of the feet out there. If Al stocked sizes 1 to 13, .9973 of customers at his store would be satisfied with his selection. He can always special-order for those feet beyond sizes 1 to 13.

Of course normal distribution tables have been developed to determine the probability for any specific point on the curve (noninteger SDs away from the mean). To use the tables, a *Z value* must be calculated.

$$
Z = \frac{[(\text{point of interest}) - \text{Mean}]}{\text{SD}}
$$

A Normal Curve Finance Example

Let's apply these new pieces of probability theory to finance. The monthly stock returns of a volatile stock, Pioneer Aviation, are assumed normally distributed as shown by a plotted graph. A summary of historical returns shows a mean (center) of 1 percent and an SD (dispersion) of 11 percent. Gerald Rasmussen wanted to know what was the probability that next month's return would be less than 13 percent.

Using our new Z value tool we can figure it out:

$$
Z = \frac{(13 - 1)}{11} = 1.09 \text{ SD away from the mean}
$$

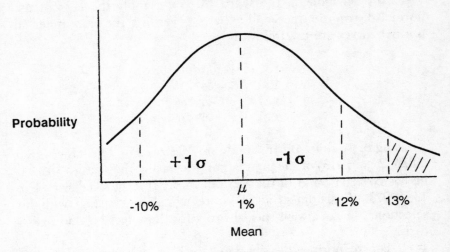

The Probability Density Function
Monthly Stock Returns of Pioneer Aviation

Probability

+1σ   -1σ

μ

-10%   1%   12%   13%

Mean

Monthly Stock Returns

The normal distribution table I have provided in the Appendix tells us that 1.09 SDs = .3621. The entire left side of the graph equals .5000, as any complete half of the distribution would. This holds true in all situations. There is a 50 percent chance of being above or below the center or mean in any normal distribution. Combining those pieces of information, I calculate there is an .8621 (.3621 + .50) probability that there will be a return of less than 13 percent and conversely a .1379 chance that it will be greater (1 − .8621). This is a real-world answer to a real-world business problem using statistics as our tools.

Statistics is not difficult if you do not dwell too long on theory. Other distributions exist, but are rarely used in business. The *Poisson Distribution* (pronounced "pwasaun") is similar to the normal distribution but has a flaring tail on the right side of the graph. But most distributions are assumed to be normal to take advantage of the normal distribution's laws of standard deviations.

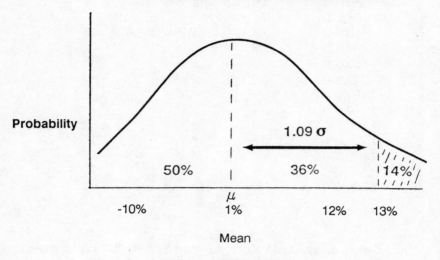

The Probability Density Function
Monthly Stock Returns of Pioneer Aviation

Cumulative Distribution Functions

A *cumulative distribution function* (CDF) is a cumulative view of a probability distribution. It takes a probability mass function, such as a bell curve, and asks, "What is the probability that the outcome is less than or equal to that value?" The normal curve tells you what the probability is for a given outcome, but the CDF tells you the probability for a given range of values. The CDF can also be used to marry our knowledge of uncertainty (probability theory) to our decision-making tool (decision trees). A CDF captures the range of possible outcomes of many-valued uncertain quantities.

To continue our oil well example, let's take the distribution of the possible values of oil that may be in the ground if oil is recovered:

Oil Value	Probability Mass Function	CDF Cumulative Probability "Equal to or <"
50,000	.005	.005
75,000	.01	.015 (.005 + .01)
150,000	.03	.045 (.03 + .01 + .005)
200,000	.08	.125
300,000	.12	.245
750,000	.15	.395
1,100,000	.21	.605
1,200,000	.15	.755
1,400,000	.12	.875
1,700,000	.08	.955
2,000,000	.03	.985
2,500,000	.01	.995
6,000,000	.005	1.00
	1.00	

In the tree constructed before, we used $1,000,000 as our payoff. That amount was the expected value (EMV) of the oil, because I conveniently chose it for the example. The distribution was actually a wide range of values. There was a .005 chance of a $6,000,000 payday and .005 chance of $50,000 as shown by the table of values. If you multiply each of the dollar values by their individual probabilities in the second column, the EMV equals $1,000,000, the EMV we used before.

Constructing a cumulative distribution function allows decision makers to arrive at the mean or EMV when they are not certain what it is to begin with. Drawing a CDF is a method of combining a series of your judgments about the probability of the upper, middle, and lower bounds of an unknown outcome to arrive at an EMV to use for decision making.

The CDF graph of ranges of outcomes resembles a big S. In the CDF, you see at a glance all the possible outcomes, not just static individual points. As shown by the following graph, Sam Houston believes that all his possible outcomes fall in the continuous "range" of $0 to $6,000,000.

The range of probabilities from 0 to 1.0 in the CDF is divided into *fractiles*, or slices, using the *bracket median technique*. The CDF

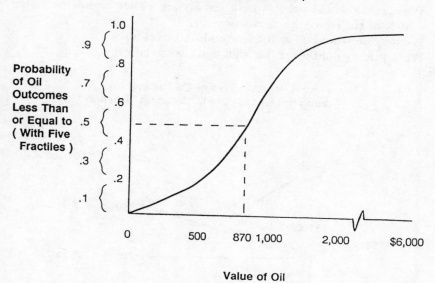

Cumulative Density Function
Values of Possible Oil Drilling Outcomes
(in thousands of $'s)

Probability of Oil Outcomes Less Than or Equal to (With Five Fractiles)

Value of Oil

above is divided in that way. To divide the CDF probability ranges into five fractiles, for example, one would take the .1, .3, .5, .7, and .9 fractiles. Each of those fractiles would represent the average of the "ranges of values," 0 to .2, .2 to .4, .4 to .6, .6 to .8, and .8 to 1.0, respectively.

The .5 fractile is the same as the median, because half of the values are on either side of it. The median is not necessarily the same as the mean we used as the center of the normal distribution. The median is merely the center of the value range. The mean is the result of multiplying all the probabilities by the values, as was done to arrive at the $1,000,000 EMV for an oil discovery.

To marry this CDF concept to the decision tree to make important management decisions, imagine how you would represent all the values an oil well may produce. It would be a *range* of values that would be represented by a *fan* of possibilities. One could not possibly draw the infinite possibilities of branches on the tree, so we use a CDF to help out.

Drawing a CDF. To draw a CDF as shown above, you use your own judgment and your research data. You need to ask yourself a series of questions:

What value would occur where results are either higher or lower 50% of the time (the median)?
What value would be at the low end (.10 fractile)?
What value would be at the high end (.90 fractiles)?

Decision Tree of Oil Drilling
Using the Cumulative Distribution Function

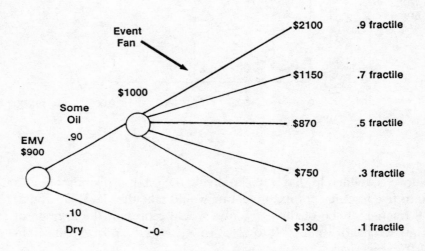

EMV = .9 [(.2 x $130) + (.2 x $750) + (.2 x $870) + (.2 x $1150) + (.2 x $2100)] = $900

With the answers to these questions, you can draw the CDF of what you believe the range of outcomes is. By picking five outcomes using the five fractiles from the CDF, you can draw the *event fan* of five possibilities and probabilities on a decision tree as five branches.

The expected monetary value is the same as in our first go-around, but that is only because I conveniently used the correct EMV to begin with.

A shortcut to using five fractiles is called the *Pearson Tukey Method.* Instead of five fractiles, the method uses only 3 — the .05, .5, and

.95 fractiles. Their respective probabilities are .185, .63, .185.

For large problems the decision tree has been computerized by *Monte Carlo* simulation programs. The tree and the parameters of the "event fan" CDFs are included in the computer model. The program runs many simulations to give you an idea of how things may really turn out. Some Fortune 500 companies use it.

CDF and fractile analysis can be used for situations where the EMV of a branch of a decision tree is uncertain. However, the judgment of the analyst is most important. The tree is simply a tool that the MBA must use in tandem with his/her knowledge and intuition.

REGRESSION ANALYSIS AND FORECASTING

Linear regression models are used in a variety of business situations to determine relationships between variables that analysts believe intuitively to be related. Once a relationship is established, it can be used to forecast the future. Commonly regression analysis is used to relate sales to price, promotions, and market factors; stock prices to earnings and interest rates; and production costs to production volumes. But of course one can use it as well to find answers to questions such as, "What is the effect of temperature on the sales of ice cream cones?" The *independent variable* (X) in this scenario is the temperature. It is the variable that is believed to cause other things to happen. The *dependent variable* (Y) is sales. Temperature affects sales, not vice versa.

Regression analysis involves gathering sufficient data to determine the relationship between the variables. With many data points, such as a year's worth of information on temperature and sales changes, a graph can be drawn with temperature along the X axis and sales along the Y axis. The goal of regression is to produce an equation of a line that "best" depicts this relationship. Regression tries to "fit" a line between the plotted data points so that the "squared differences between the points and the line are least." The *least squares method* requires a great deal of adding, subtracting, and multiplying. A business calculator or a Lotus 1-2-3 spreadsheet computer program will be necessary.

An Algebra Refresher Course

To set the stage for a *regression* example, let's review some basic algebra. You recall that a line is described by this algebraic formula:

$$Y = mX + b$$

Y = dependent variable (such as sales)
m = the slope of the line (the relationship between variables)
X = the independent variable (such as rain)
b = y axis intercept (where the line crosses the vertical axis)

The Lotus 1-2-3 spreadsheet will calculate the linear equation (Y = mX + b) that defines the relationship between the independent and dependent variables. The Lotus program will determine whether the line that it has calculated as the best "fit" can be used as an accurate tool for forecasting.

An Ice Cream Regression Example

The owner of a chain of twenty Ben & Jerry's ice cream shops noticed that as the temperature rose and fell, so did his sales. In an attempt to determine the precise mathematical relationship between sales and seasonal temperatures, he gathered the monthly sales data for the previous five years and the average temperatures for the months in question from the National Weather Service. His data looked as follows:

Month	Average Degrees F	Sales
January	33	$200,000
February	37	250,000
March	72	400,000
April	65	500,000
May	78	900,000
June	85	1,100,000
July	88	1,500,000
August	91	1,300,000
September	82	800,000
October	73	600,000
November	45	300,000
December	36	500,000

Using the "Data Regression" function of the Lotus spreadsheet, the owner generated the following output:

Regression Output
Constant	− 379,066
Std Err of Y Est	243,334
R Squared	.704

X coefficient(s)	16,431
Std Err of Coef.	3,367

What Does This Mean?

Wondrously enough that block of information contains the equation for the line that describes the relationship between temperature and sales at Ben & Jerry's. First let's interpret the data in the output to get the line equation.

"Constant" = b = − 379,066
"X coefficient" = m = 16,431

Placing that information into a standard linear equation as described in the algebra refresher, Y = 16,431 X − 379,066, plotting the data points, and drawing the regression line described by the equation, the Lotus graph looks like this:

Sales of Ben & Jerry's Ice Cream Regression Example

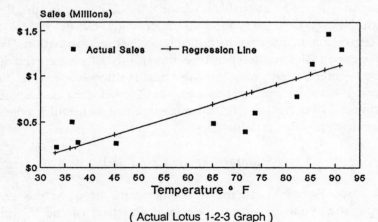

(Actual Lotus 1-2-3 Graph)

As shown by the graph, the regression line runs through the middle of the data points. By plugging temperature, X, into the equation, the *predicted* ice cream sales can be calculated. In Ben & Jerry's case, a temperature of 60 degrees would result in predicted monthly sales of $606,794.

$$Y = (16431 \times 60 \text{ degrees}) - 379{,}066 = \$606{,}794$$

But just how accurate is this equation in predicting the sales of ice cream? The answer to this question is given to us by another number in the Lotus "Regression Output."

R Squared Explained

The *R Squared* value tells us "what percent of the variation in the data is explained by the regression equation given." In our case 70.4 percent of the variation of sales is explained by the regression equation. This is considered very high. In broader economic analyses, an R Squared of 30 percent would be considered very high, since there are thousands of variables that could affect economies. In the ice cream business, one could imagine that in addition to temperature, store advertising, couponing, and store hours could also explain sales fluctuations.

But be careful! Do not read too much into the regression data results! Regression only says that changes in sales occur with changes in temperature in much the same way as described. It *does not* say that "temperature actually caused sales to move." But if a selected independent variable is reasonable and it is a good predictor of the desired dependent variable under study, use it.

Regression analysis points not only to positive correlations, such as ice cream sales and temperature, but also to negative correlations such as interest rates and housing sales. If interest rates are high, housing sales are low. In this case the X coefficient is a negative number. These negative relationships are just as useful predictors as positive/positive relationships.

Standard Error Explained

The "Std Err of Y and the X coefficients" shown in the Lotus output are synonyms for the *standard deviations* of the Y and X coefficients of the regression line. In the Ben & Jerry's example, the standard error of the Y estimate (sales) is plus or minus $243,334 68 percent of the time. In the same way the output shows that the standard error of the X coefficient (temperature) is 16,431. A variety of analyses about the ranges of possible data values can be performed using standard deviations to show the variability of those numbers and the reliability of the resulting regression equation.

The T Statistic Measure of Reliability

The *T statistic* can help determine if the regression equation calculated by Lotus is a good one to use for forecasting. The T statistic reveals if an X variable has a statistically significant effect on Y, such as temperature's effect on sales. You calculate the measure by dividing the X coefficient by the "Standard Error." The rule of thumb says if a T statistic is above 2 or below -2, the X variable has a statistically significant effect on Y. In our case 16,431/3,337 = 4.88, a very high T-stat. Therefore, an analyst would conclude that temperature is a very good predictor of sales.

When considering whether a model is a good forecaster, it is necessary to have both a high R Squared and a high T statistic. It is possible to create a model with more than one X variable. This is called *multivariable regression*. As the number of variables increases, so does the R Squared. However, adding more X variables with low T statistics creates an inaccurate model. It is necessary to play with the model, adding and dropping independent variables to achieve high R Squares *and* high T statistics.

Dummy Variable Regression Analysis

A trick employed in regression analysis is the use of *dummy variables* to represent conditions that are not measured in a numerical series. Ones and zeroes are used to represent these conditions. For example, at Toys "R" Us, having the "hot" toy of the season in stock, a nonnumerical condition, catapults sales. The in-stock condition could be indicated in a data set by a "1" and out-of-stock condition could be designated by a "0" using dummy variables.

Given a hypothetical set of data at a Toys "R" Us store, you can see how it works.

Date	"Hot" Toy Stock Status (1 = in, 0 = out)	Sales
12/1/92	0	$100,000
12/2/92	0	100,000
12/3/92	1	200,000
12/4/92	1	200,000
12/5/92	0	100,000
12/6/92	1	200,000
12/7/92	0	200,000

The following Lotus regression output of the relationship between "hot" toys and sales is the result.

Regression Output:

Constant	100,000
Std Err of Y Est	0.001
R Squared	1.00

X coefficient(s)	100,000
Std Err of Coef.	0.0009

This is a perfect model because the variation explained by the model's R Squared is 100 percent and the T statistic is excellent. The T statistic approaches infinity (100,000/.0009). The sales are $100,000 without the desired toys, and an extra $100,000 when they're in stock. The regression equation, using the Lotus output, is:

Sales = $100,000X + $100,000.

If the coveted toys are in stock, X = 1 and sales jump to $200,000. If not, X = 0, and sales total $100,000. Dummy variables are very useful and can be used to match nonscaled data, such as stock status or a holiday, with other regularly scaled data, such as temperature, interest rates, and product defects, to produce useful regression models.

OTHER FORECASTING TECHNIQUES

Time series techniques forecast outcomes based on changes in a relationship over time. In our ice cream example, the data points of temperature and sales were charted on the graph without regard to when they occurred. The regression relationship did not consider time. Obviously seasons affect Ben & Jerry's sales. Time series analysis considers time by plotting data as it occurs. The technique then attempts to "decompose" the fluctuations within the data into three parts:

- *The Underlying Trend* — up, down, flat (a long-term measure)
- *The Cycles* — hourly, daily, weekly, monthly (a short-term pattern)
- *Unexplained Movements* — unusual or irregular movements caused by unique events and quirks of nature

Regression and moving averages are used to determine the trend and cycles. As you can imagine, time series forecasting is a tedious process that does not lend itself to a short and simple example. However, it is helpful at least to know that time series techniques exist.

SUMMARY

This chapter has described the quantitative tools that perform the following functions:

Sort out complex problems with decision trees
Determine the value of cash received in the future — cash flow analysis and net present value analysis
Quantify uncertainty with probability theory
Determine relationships and forecast with regression analysis and other forecasting techniques

These are practical tools that MBAs use to meet business challenges. They give MBAs the power to make informed decisions and to distinguish themselves on the job.

KEY QA TAKEAWAYS

Decision Trees — A way to graphically show and quantify multiple outcomes of a business decision

Sunk Cost — Investments made in the past that have no bearing on future investment decisions

Expected Monetary Value (EMV) — The blended value of a decision based on the probabilities and values of all possible outcomes

Accumulated Value — The total future value of cash flows with all earnings reinvested

Net Present Value (NPV) — The total present value of all cash flows "discounted" to today's dollars

Internal Rate of Return (IRR) — The discount rate that makes the Net Present Value of the cash flows equal \$0 in today's dollars

Probability Distributions — The graph of all possible outcomes with their respective probabilities of occurring

Binomial Distributions — probability distribution with only two possible outcomes

Normal Distributions — The bell-shaped probability distribution of all possible outcomes

Standard Deviation (σ) — The measure of the dispersion (width) of the normal distribution

Mean (μ) — The arithmetic average of all outcomes

Z Value — A tool to measure probabilities of specific situations on the normal distribution curve

Cumulative Distribution Function (CDF) — A form of the normal distribution that shows the probability of being less than or equal to all possible outcomes

Regression — A mathematical method of forecasting using line equations to explain the relationships between multiple causes and effects

DAY 6

FINANCE

FINANCE TOPICS

Business Structures
Beta Risk
The Efficient Frontier
Capital Asset Pricing Model
The Efficient Market Hypothesis
Investment Valuations
Discounted Cash Flows
Dividend Growth Model
Capital Budgeting
Capital Structure
Dividend Policy
Mergers and Acquisitions

"I want to be an investment banker. If you had 10,000 shares I sell them for you. I make a lot of money. I will like my job very, very much. I will help people. I will be a millionaire. I will have a big house. It will be fun for me."

Seven-year-old schoolboy, "What I Want to Be When I Grow Up," March 1985. From Michael Lewis's *Liar's Poker*, 1989.

In the 1980s, finance was the place to be. Even kids dreamed of a life on Wall Street. Machiavellian young MBAs were beside themselves with glee as Wall Street hired them by the droves, offering them a shot at big bucks trading and deal making as investment bankers. Unfortunately, the bubble burst in 1987 with the stock market crash and MBAs were forced to seek less glamorous jobs by joining the financial staffs at banks and corporations. The heyday of the deal maker was over.

Even though finance is no longer the glamour job it once was, MBAs are still doing quite well in finance. MBAs from the top schools are put on the fast track and are paid significantly more than their non-MBA peers. On Wall Street MBAs make twenty to thirty thousand dollars more per year than non-MBAs in the same job. Moreover, job advancement is often limited to the MBA elite.

Do not read this chapter in isolation. If finance turns you on, a single-minded focus on this discipline could be hazardous to your business health. Finance is very quantitative, using numbers from the accounting and QA chapters. Finance also plays as much of a role in marketing as marketing does in finance. Marketers are responsible for their financial results. Financiers work hard to market themselves to new clients and to sell new stocks to old ones.

THE NATURE OF THE FIRM

Why do businesses exist? In a financier's eyes, the sole purpose of a firm is to maximize the wealth of its owners. In their pursuit of riches, there are several ways people can organize their businesses. There are three basic legal *business structures* that entities take on in the United States. Each is chosen depending on the complexity of the business, liability preference, and tax considerations of the owners.

Proprietorships

A *proprietorship*, commonly called a *sole proprietorship*, is a business owned by an individual or husband and wife. The owner reaps all the profits and has unlimited liability for all losses. If things go poorly, the owner's personal assets can be seized. It's a simple structure. As with a child's lemonade stand, no special government registration is required. Earnings are added to the individual's other income and taxes are paid on the total income. Because it is not a separate legal entity that can be divided and sold in pieces, it is more difficult for a proprietorship to raise money in the financial markets.

Partnerships

When several individuals form a business, they often enter into a *partnership*. As in a proprietorship, each owner's share of the earnings is included on his or her personal tax returns. Depending on the nature of the business, there are two types of partnerships. In a *general* partnership, active owners, called *general partners*, have unlimited liability for all business debts. When the accounting firm of Laventhol & Horwath went into bankruptcy in 1990 because of auditing malpractices, creditors went after the personal assets of the partners to pay off the partnership's debts.

In a *limited* partnership structure, *limited partners* are shielded to the extent of their investment. The "limited" form is often used in real estate and oil explorations ventures to protect the investing partners that do not participate in management. In the commercial real estate busts of the late 1980s and early 1990s, the limited partners in vacant office building projects were able to walk away from their investments with no further liability. On the other hand, the general partners of the same projects were personally on the hook. As in the proprietorship instance, the ability to raise money or to sell partial interests in partnership structures is rather difficult.

Corporations

Corporations, registered with a state, are legal entities that are separate from the individuals who own them. In the eyes of the law, a corporation is treated as an individual who conducts his own business independently. The assets and liabilities of the entity are owned by the corporation, not by the owners of the corporation. As with limited partnerships, owners of corporations have limited liability for the obligations of the business. In the case of a bankruptcy, the owners' personal assets are shielded from creditors.

A corporation's ownership is split into *shares of stock* that investors can purchase and trade in the financial markets such as the New York Stock Exchange. Shares can be traded among investors without disrupting the business. When management and the board of

directors who represent the owners decide that more money is needed, additional shares can be issued. An investor, whether he takes an active role or chooses to remain passive, is personally shielded from the liabilities of the company.

A major drawback of ownership in a corporation is *double taxation*. The corporation, like an individual, must pay taxes. When the corporation pays its owners a dividend, that dividend is taxable again as income to the individual.

There are variations to the *corporate* form. The *C Corp.*, as it is called by accountants and lawyers, works as described above, but there is also a *Subchapter S Corp*. These corporations have thirty-five or fewer owners. They agree to include the corporation's earnings in their personal tax returns as in the case of a partnership. In that way, the double-taxation hammer does not fall on the owners, while at the same time the corporation's limited liability advantage is maintained.

* * *

If you are interested in finance, you can take two different yet interconnected routes. There is the investments area, which is more glamorous, the thing that fortunes, headlines, and stock quotes are made of; and there is financial management, which is the "in the trenches" work that helps companies finance their growth, pay the bills, and make acquisitions. The two areas are interconnected because the performance of a business, for which the finance department is to a large extent responsible, affects its investors' share of the firm's profits. Let's start with the glamour.

INVESTMENTS

Risk and Return

How can I profit by owning a large or small share of a corporation or other business? This investment decision is really a two-pronged question: What is the potential income, and how risky is the venture? The basic concepts of discounted cash flows and probability explained earlier in the QA chapter can be used to answer these valuation questions. Refer to them as you would look up old class notes.

A basic tenet of finance dictates that the return should be commensurate with the risk. If you know that an investment is a sure thing, then you should expect a lower rate of return in compensation for the lower risk. Accordingly, certificates of deposit insured by the Federal Deposit Insurance Corporation (FDIC) pay low rates of return. Wildcatting for oil involves a great deal of risk, but it also promises a huge jackpot if a well turns out to be a gusher.

Types of Risk. If risk applies to a whole class of assets, such as the markets for stocks, bonds, and real estate, it is called *systematic risk*. For instance, when the public believes that the stock market is a good bet (a so-called *bull market*), the market as a whole will climb. When the public leaves, the market "lays an egg" or "melts down," as the headlines read in the crashes of 1929 and 1987. Movements in the economy, interest rates, and inflation are systematic factors that affect the entire market. In making any investment, you are exposed to the systematic risk of the market.

If the risk applies to a particular asset or to a small group of assets, it is called *unique* or *unsystematic*. An individual investment performance may be volatile because of specific risks inherent to the investment. If you own shares in Disney, for instance, and Mickey catches a cold, the stock could tumble. That type of risk can be largely compensated for by owning a number of investments. This is called *diversification*. By holding a broad portfolio of investments, investors can offset losses on some investments with gains on others. Diversification moderates the overall fluctuations of a portfolio.

Beta: Risk Within a Portfolio of Investments

The market prices of stocks, IBM for example, fluctuate daily on the stock exchanges of the world. That *volatility* is equated with risk. A distribution of historical outcomes would show the risk graphically, as was shown for Seattle's rainfall and for shoe sizes in the QA chapter. To refresh your memory of probability distributions, the mean long-term historic return on common stocks was 12.1 percent with a standard deviation of 21.2 percent. Within one standard deviation, 68 percent of the time, the stock market will return between + 33 percent and − 9.1 percent per year.

In addition to showing on a graph an individual investment's absolute volatility, financial analysts measure the risk of individual stocks or small groups of stocks by comparing their price movements with the entire market's movement. That measurement, *beta*, quantifies the risk of holding that particular investment versus owning a very large portfolio that represents "the market." An example of such "market" portfolios are the collection of 500 stocks called the *Standard & Poor's 500* (S & P 500) or the 5,000 stocks that are included in the *Wilshire 5000*. The *Nikkei* index of 225 stocks represents the Japanese market.

The famous *Dow Jones Industrial Average* ("The Big Board") is a diverse collection of 30 of the most stable industrial companies in America (e.g., AT&T, IBM, 3M, GM, P&G, Coca-Cola, Boeing, and Exxon). The Dow's thirty "blue chip" stocks are traded on the NYSE and are not representative of the broader market, even though the press might have you believe that they are.

If a stock or portfolio moves in tandem with the market, it is said

A Probability Distribution
of Historic Stock Returns

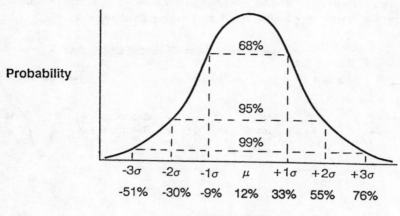

Probability

68%

95%

99%

| -3σ | -2σ | -1σ | μ | +1σ | +2σ | +3σ |
| -51% | -30% | -9% | 12% | 33% | 55% | 76% |

Rate of Return

to be perfectly correlated with a beta of 1. Heinz Foods is such a stable company that it moves with the market with a beta of 1. If a stock moves in perfect opposition to the market, it is said to be negatively correlated, or to have a beta of − 1.

There are no such perfectly negatively correlated stocks, but there are some stocks with very low betas. Pegasus Gold has a .45 beta. When the market fluctuates down wildly, the price of gold, the safe haven, stays relatively steady. However, in a big market rally Pegasus is less likely to rise dramatically. Electric utilities also have low betas. Theoretically, a beta of 0 would mean an absence of risk. In that case the investments' betas would perfectly cancel each other so that there would be no risk regardless of the movement of the market.

A risky stock, like Biogen, a biotech company, has a beta of 1.75. A 1 percent fluctuation in the market would be magnified in a 1.75 percent movement in Biogen's price. Moderately risky stocks such as MCI Communications and Wal-Mart have 1.2 betas.

The behavior of the market is so important because most large investment decisions are made in the context of a large *portfolio*, or collection of investments. Although the risks of individual investments may be high, the overall risk will be lowered by investing in the right mix of investments in order to lower the portfolio's beta. Large mutual funds that own hundreds of investments, such as Fidelity's Magellan Fund's $15 billion portfolio, provide this kind of *diversification*.

How Investments with Different Betas Act

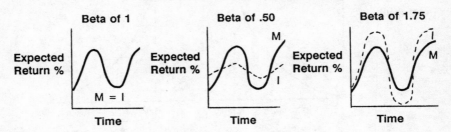

M = Market Movement   I = Individual Stock or Portfolio Movement

Of course the beta number does not appear from nowhere. Beta is a statistical calculation of a correlation coefficient, the covariance of a stock with the market divided by the variance of the market. Betas can be calculated, but financial analysts will admit that investment information services, such as the Value Line Survey, provide the beta coefficients. Calculating beta is tedious, and in true MBA fashion, this book will skip it.

The Efficient Frontier

Given all the possible portfolios of assets, theoretically there is a perfect mix of investments at each level of beta risk. The graphical representation of these theoretical "best" portfolios lies on a line called the *efficient frontier*. The area below the efficient frontier line encompasses the attainable or feasible portfolio combinations. Theoretically above the frontier are the unattainable returns.

The Capital Asset Pricing Model for Stocks

The *capital asset pricing model* (CAPM) determines the required rate of return of an investment by adding the unsystematic risk and the

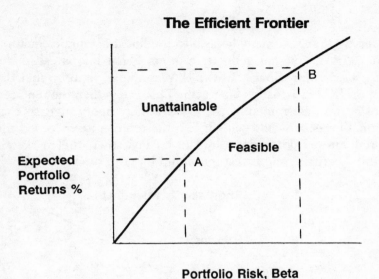

The Efficient Frontier

Expected
Portfolio
Returns %

Unattainable

Feasible

A

B

Portfolio Risk, Beta

systematic risk of owning this asset. A simple formula, the CAPM says that the required rate of return is the risk-free rate plus a premium for unsystematic risk. That risk is the beta that you are already familiar with.

$$Ke = R_f + (K_m - R_f) \; Beta$$

Required Return on an Equity Investment = Risk-Free Rate + (The Avg. Market Return Rate − Risk-Free Rate) × Beta

Suppose you want to know what IBM should yield to be a worthwhile investment. The Value Line Survey tells you that IBM has a conservative beta of 1.2. *The Wall Street Journal* tells you that the long-term risk-free United States Treasury Bond pays a return of 8 percent. The final CAPM input requires some more homework. A study conducted since 1926 shows that the average return on the Standard & Poor's 500 has exceeded the risk-free rate of investing in risk-free U.S. Treasury Bonds by 7.4 percent. With those three CAPM inputs, an investment in IBM should return on average 16.8 percent.

$$8\% + (7.4\%)\ 1.2 = 16.8\%$$

Plugging in many, many betas into the linear algebraic equation of the CAPM, you can generate a graph. That line is called the *security market line* (SML). In the IBM example, suppose that the return on IBM is actually 12 percent. That is less than the required rate of return determined by the CAPM. The theory suggests that a rational investor would sell IBM. If the return rate exceeded the required rate as determined by the CAPM, then the market is offering a bargain, and investors should buy the stock.

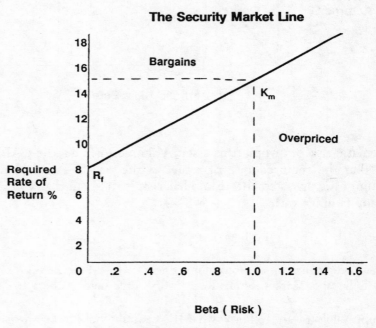

The Security Market Line

R_f = Risk-free rate, K_m = market rate

It sounds great, but the CAPM tells the required rate of return, not what an investment will actually return. For that you need tea leaves and a crystal ball.

Moreover, the whole CAPM is theoretically under attack. In an article entitled "Bye-bye Beta" in *Forbes*, March 1992, David Dreman, a noted investment advisor, reported on new and startling research, and pronounced CAPM and beta dead. A study by University of Chicago professors Fama and French saw no link between risk, as defined by the CAPM, and long-term performance. Because betas are based on historical volatility, betas may have no relevance for future predictions. Betas may have fallen into disrepute, but since there is nothing better, business schools still teach this theory.

The Efficient Market Hypothesis

The SML graph suggests that there are bargains in the market. But that begs the question, "If the market is efficient, then how can there be bargains?" The *efficient market hypothesis* (EMH) alleges that to varying degrees the market reflects all current information. Therefore, no one can take advantage of market aberrations to "beat the market." Investors competing for profits are so numerous that quoted stock prices are exact indicators of value.

There are three degrees of belief in the efficiency of the market: *weak, semistrong,* and *strong.*

Weak Form of Efficiency. All information that caused past price movements is reflected in the current market price. Believing in the weak form means that no benefit is gained by charting stock price movements using *technical analysis* as a predictor of the future. However, by doing in-depth *fundamental analysis* about companies' operations and profitability, analysts can gain insights that will provide opportunities for big profits.

Semistrong Form of Efficiency. This camp believes that market prices reflect all *publicly* known information. Therefore, without insider information, no "abnormal" returns can be gained by poring over financial statements. The *Securities and Exchange Commission* (SEC) acts as a policeman to try to ensure that investors do not trade based on insider information. Believing in the semistrong form of efficiency means that fundamental analysis, conducted by reading financial statements and all public information, will not result in big gains.

Strong Form of Efficiency. The true believers in market efficiency have faith that stock prices reflect all public and *private* information. That intense faith has been proven unfounded in many instances. The criminal convictions of Ivan Boesky, Dennis Levine, and Michael Milken were well-publicized cases in which insider information was used to reap hundreds of millions in profits that the public had no chance of making.

Research indicates that the *weak form* of market efficiency has held true over time. Naïve beliefs in complete efficiency are not warranted. Stocks are generally fairly valued, yet some people deny even the weak form of the efficient market hypothesis. As mentioned, *chartists* or *technical* analysts graph price movements seeking patterns that will indicate price movement in the future. Dan Sullivan's *The Chartist* investment newsletter has more accurately predicted the market's movements since 1980 than all other advisory newsletter services.

Investment Types and Valuation Methods

In the QA chapter the concepts of discounted cash flows and net present value were covered in detail. A dollar held today is worth more than a dollar received in the future. That simple concept, applied to the cash thrown off by an investment, is in most cases the method used to value investments.

The Bond Market

A bond's value comes from the present value of its future cash flows. Bonds are issued by companies or governmental agencies to raise money at fixed rates of interest. Most pay interest, a *coupon*, semiannually on the principal amount, called the *face* or *par value*. At the stated *maturity* date, the principal is repaid.

In most cases the longer the maturity, the higher the interest rate that a company has to pay investors. Higher rates compensate investors for tying their money up for lengthy periods. Investors could miss out on higher returns if the market rates go higher; therefore, they must be compensated for that risk. The basic concept that higher rates accompany longer maturities is graphically depicted in what the investment world calls the *yield curve*.

A Bond Valuation Example. In 1976 Caterpillar Inc., the maker of heavy construction equipment, issued $200 million worth of 8 percent coupon bonds maturing in 2001. In June 1992, the price for

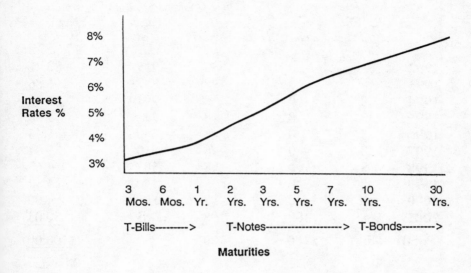

The Yield Curve for U.S. Treasury Securities
June 1992

Interest Rates %

8%
7%
6%
5%
4%
3%

| 3 Mos. | 6 Mos. | 1 Yr. | 2 Yrs. | 3 Yrs. | 5 Yrs. | 7 Yrs. | 10 Yrs. | 30 Yrs. |

T-Bills---------> T-Notes--------------------> T-Bonds--------->

Maturities

the bond was quoted in *The Wall Street Journal* as $100 for every $100 of face value. The value was determined not only by the rate of interest paid, but by three other factors:

The Stated Interest Rate (the *coupon* rate)
The Length of Time Until Maturity
The Risk of Default of the Issuer (investment researchers publish ratings)

The fact is that the market quote was $100. That indicated that the market valued the $100 payable in 2001, paying an 8 percent semiannual coupon, from a stable company at $100. The Moody's bond rating service confirmed a low default risk assessment by their "A" rating. Using the *net present value* concept, the cash thrown off by the bond, discounted at an 8 percent market discount rate, equaled the bond's market value. Because the market rate equaled the coupon rate, investors paid neither a *premium* nor a *discount* on the face value of the Caterpillar bonds. The bonds had an 8 percent *yield to maturity* (YTM) on the $100 market value of the bonds.

Caterpillar Bond Valuation
of Discounted Cash Flows

	Interest @ 8% Coupon	Principal Repayment	Payment Total ×	Discount Factors @ 8% Market =	Net Present Value
1992	$8	$0	$8	.9259	$7.41
1993	8	0	8	.8573	6.86
1994	8	0	8	.7939	6.35
1995	8	0	8	.7350	5.88
1996	8	0	8	.6806	5.44
1997	8	0	8	.6302	5.04
1998	8	0	8	.5835	4.67
1999	8	0	8	.5403	4.32
2000	8	0	8	.5002	4.00
2001	8	100	108	.4632	50.03
Total	$80	$100	$180		$100.00
		Face Value			Market Value

Here is the calculation in detail; normally, however, you should use a calculator to do the math. Seeing it in this form helps you visualize the time value of money. If the market thought Caterpillar was on the verge of bankruptcy, or if the market interest rates on all investments skyrocketed in a period of high inflation, then investors might have required a 20 percent rate of return on their money. If that were the case, the $100 bond would have been worth only $49.69 and quoted at "49¹¹⁄₁₆" in the paper. The increased riskiness of the cash flows would reduce the bond's value. Conversely, a discount rate of 5 percent would have yielded a market price of $123.16. In that case an 8 percent coupon would be higher than the market rate and investors would pay a premium for the higher cash flows.

Graphically, cash discounted at higher rates is worth less. The further out the cash is received the less it is worth to an investor today.

Duration. Another way of evaluating a bond is by calculating a bond's "average weighted maturity," called its *duration.* Duration is the time a bond takes to return half of its market price to the investor. It also measures the sensitivity of a bond to changes in market interest rates. The further in the future a bond is paid out the more volatile its value. If a bond matures in one year, it would be considered a short-term bond; all the proceeds would be paid quickly and the bond's volatility would be low. Long-term bonds offer a fixed interest payout over many years. If market rates climb, an investor is locked into lower rates for a long time. As a consequence, the bond will be devalued dramatically.

Time and Discount Rate Effects on Present Value

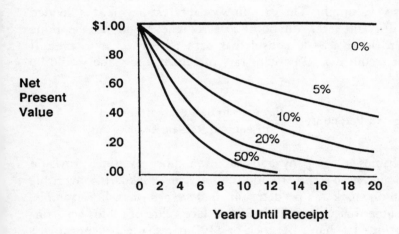

In the case of the Caterpillar bond, it paid back $50 of the investors' $100 investment in nine years. That's the bond's duration. This is a long time for a bond; as a consequence, its value responded dramatically to swings in interest rates, from $49.65 with a 20 percent rate to $123.16 with a 5 percent rate.

Don't worry about the math — computers will do the calculations for you. As a *Ten-Day MBA*, you can now ask your broker not only for the bond's yield, but also for its duration, and he will know that you are more than a retiree looking for a safe investment.

Other Types of Bonds

There are five more types of bonds of note: zero coupon bonds, consuls, convertible bonds, callable bonds, and junk bonds.

A *zero coupon bond* bears no interest, but pays a lump sum at maturity. Investors value the bond the same way as one that pays interest, but there are no interest payments to discount. For example, a Disney zero coupon bond maturing in 2005 at $100 was valued at $46.875 in 1992. Using a calculator to do the math, a 6 percent rate discounts $100 to be paid in 2005 to a value of $46.875 in 1992. The low rate denotes that Disney is a strong company.

A *consul* or *perpetuity* is a bond that never pays back the principal, but continues to pay interest forever. These bonds are unusual but they still are issued in the United Kingdom. The valuation technique is very simple. The cash flow or interest payment is divided by the discount rate. A hypothetical example: London Telephone agreed to issue a $100 consul that pays $8 each year forever. If investors require a 10 percent rate of return, the value would be $80 ($8/.10)

$$\text{Value of a Perpetuity} = \frac{\text{Payment to be Received Forever}}{\text{Required Rate of Return}}$$

Sometimes a company adds an even more exciting provision called a *conversion feature* to bonds. *Convertible bonds* are convertible to common stock at a predetermined *conversion ratio*. For example, let's assume that Caterpillar's $1,000 face value of bonds was convertible into 10 shares of stock or $100 per share. If Caterpillar's stock price rose above $100 per share, bondholders might consider converting their bonds into common shares of stock. Convertible bonds usually pay a lower interest rate than nonconvertible bonds, because they provide investors with an additional option.

The fourth type of bond is a *callable bond*. In some instances issuers want the option to buy back their bonds from the public if interest rates fall significantly after the issue date. In 1981, large corporations sold bonds paying 15 to 20 percent interest per year, the prevailing market rates. As interest rates fell later, in the 1980s and 1990s, the corporations that had included a *call provision* bought back their bonds at predetermined prices and issued new ones in

1992 paying 7 to 8 percent to save on interest expense. Because call provisions limit unusually high rates of return, corporations have to pay a higher interest rate for the privilege of calling back the bonds.

The last classification, a *junk bond*, is a bond that has a high risk of default. Often their risk lies in the fact that they may be *subordinated* to the claims of other bonds issued by a company. These bonds pay higher rates to investors and most still pay their interest and principal on time. If the company does not have enough money to make payments on its borrowing, the subordinated debt holders get paid last.

Although recent notoriety in the press might give the impression that they are new, junk bonds have been around as long as there have been bonds. During the Civil War the Confederacy issued risky bonds that could be termed "junk" bonds. Billions of junk bonds were issued for takeovers in the late 1960s and during the leveraged buyout binge in the 1980s, by such well-known firms such as RJR Nabisco, MCI, Macy's, Metromedia, and Chrysler. Junk bonds are not "junk"; they simply have a higher risk of default.

Bond Valuation Summary

Higher Risk of Default→Higher Disc. Rate→Lower Bond Value
Higher Market Rates

Lower Risk of Default →Lower Disc. Rate →Higher Bond Value
Lower Market Rates

Higher Coupon Rate →Shorter Duration →Value Less Volatile
Shorter Maturity   to Mkt. Rate Chgs.

Lower Coupon Rate →Longer Duration →Value More Volatile
Longer Maturity   to Mkt. Rate Chgs.

The Stock Market

Stocks have no contractual terms of payment and no maturity. If earnings are adequate, most companies regularly pay dividends to stockholders. But there are no guarantees. Building on the teachings of accounting, equity ownership of a company entitles the owner to the *residual* claim on earnings and assets after all the other obligations, such as bonds, have been met. If there are no earnings, there's little value to the stock. With adequate profits, bonds are paid on time and hopefully there is a portion left for stockholders.

Stocks are called by many names, depending on the company's characteristics.

Classes of Stocks

Class	Description	Examples
Growth Stocks	Rapidly Growing Companies	Wal-Mart
Blue Chip Stocks	Very Large Companies	Kodak, Coca-Cola
Cyclical Stocks	Fluctuate Greatly with Economy	Ford, GM
Penny Stocks	Risky, Small Companies with Low Share Prices	Jet Electro

The Dividend Growth Model. One way that investment analysts try to value stocks is by valuing the dividend cash flow. This value model heavily weights dividend growth in its formula. However, it does not always yield a reasonable answer.

$$\text{Value per Share} = \frac{D}{(K - g)}$$

D = Annual Dividends per Share
K = Discount Rate or Required Rate of Return
g = Annual Dividend Growth Rate

The stock of Caterpillar Inc. is a good example. In 1992 the company paid a $1.20 yearly dividend per share. Using the CAPM equation, the required rate for Caterpillar's beta of 1.2 was 16.8 percent, the same as IBM's. Caterpillar's board of directors raised their dividend an average 12 percent for the last few years. With those inputs in the dividend growth model, the stock should have been worth $25.

$$\frac{\$1.20}{(.168 - .12)} = \$25 \text{ per share value}$$

But Caterpillar actually traded at $56 per share in May 1992. Either there must have been more than just dividends to the company, or the market had gone nuts. But probably not. Investors must have also valued the company's assets and future earnings as well.

What is an analyst to do with Wal-Mart stores, the discounter that paid very small dividends? How do analysts value biotechnology firms that have no earnings and no dividends? There are no easy formulas, but the following are a few additional methods used by securities analysts to calculate value.

Price Earnings Ratio. Analysts compare the ratio of the current stock price to the current or projected earnings per share (EPS). This *price earnings ratio* (PE ratio) is probably the most widely used valuation method. It is simple. Everyone can divide price by earnings per share. Best yet, the EPS of most companies are widely published. If that ratio is in line with the industry of the business and with the market, then it may indicate the propriety of its current stock price. To illustrate the wide use of the PE ratio, the following is a stock picker's recommendation:

Corestates Financial at $44, the old Philadelphia National Bank, has a low price earnings multiple relative to other banks, and its dividend yield is higher than other banks mentioned. Strong buying interest exists.

Multiple of Book Value per share. This calculation using balance sheet information divides the share price by the book value of assets per share. In 1992 ImClone Systems, a biopharmaceuticals company, sold at 331 times its book value. *Forbes* highlighted it as possibly overvalued, but the ratios of small, new companies are often unusual. Investors often value the potential success of start-up companies, not their current size.

Multiple of Sales per Share. Sales divided by stock price is the formula. Cryomedical Sciences, another company on *Forbes*'s questionable list in 1992, had a sales-to-price ratio of 1,699. With very few sales, the multiple was very large. Investors were buying the future.

Asset Value per Share. When a company's assets value divided by the outstanding shares is more valuable than the price of the stock indicates, then analysts might overlook other ratios. The buyout binge in oil stocks was due to the fact that the share prices were below the value of their oil and gas reserves. As a result, Getty, Gulf, Mesa, and Phillips engaged in a bidding war that made their shares soar in the 1980s.

Multiple of Cash Flow per Share. Some analysts value companies because of their ability to generate cash as measured by the company's cash flow statement. In Caterpillar's case, it produced $5.90 for each share outstanding in 1992. At $56 per share, the stock was priced at 9.5 times cash flow. Looking forward, analysts projected $11.10 in 1993 and $17.80 in later years, or three times the projected cash flow. That is where some investors saw the value of Caterpillar. If a group of analysts valued the $17.80 cash flow per year in perpetuity at a 16.8 percent discount rate, the stock would have a net present value of $100 (17.80/.168). To them, at $56 Caterpillar was still cheap.

In a stock market there are always buyers and sellers. Imbalances cause price movements. Many yardsticks of value exist, but the only one that truly matters is the current quote, no matter how crazy it may appear. If the market is willing to buy Caterpillar at $200, then *that* is its value. Of course, if there is more supply than demand, prices fall. But that's for our economics chapter.

Preferred Stock is the privileged cousin of common stock. Preferred shares, a hybrid of a bond and a common stock, are issued by many utilities, banks, and steel companies. Preferreds have the characteristics of a bond inasmuch as they pay a fixed dividend rate and have no voting rights. As in the case of common stocks, their dividends can only be paid if debt payments are made first, and there is no maturity. However, most issuers make provisions to purchase and retire their preferred stock over time. A preferred stock's claims on the assets of the firm are superior to common stock but are subordinated to debt.

Companies issue preferred stock when they want to borrow money but don't want to be contractually obligated to pay interest on time. Most preferred issues are *cumulative*, meaning that the total of all unpaid dividends must be paid before dividends on common stocks can be paid. Investors who like a more secure dividend, but like to have the benefits of partial equity ownership, choose preferred stocks.

The Options Market

Options are contractual rights to buy or sell any asset at a fixed price on or before a stated date. Options can be traded on real estate, bonds, gold, oil, and currencies. An option is a way to gain control of a great deal of assets with very little money. The opportunity for profits is high, and, accordingly, so are the risks.

For example, imagine G. R. Quick, a house buyer, who believes that prices are about to skyrocket in Beverly Hills. However, he needs six months to raise the down payment and get financing. A willing owner agrees to sell him his bungalow at $500,000, but wants $5,000 for the *option* to hold it off the market for six months. For six months Mr. Quick, the option holder, has the right, *but not the obligation*, to purchase the house for $500,000. If the real estate market falls, Mr. Quick can let his $5,000 option expire at a 100 percent loss.

But options can also be *very* profitable. If the bungalow increases in value to say $550,000, the return on the $5,000 option would be 1,000 percent. If he buys the house outright for $500,000, his return would be only 10 percent. The essence of options is to control the destiny of an asset with an investment of a fraction of that asset's value. The payoff is a leveraged payoff or a possible total loss if the underlying asset's value fluctuates.

Stock options work in the same way as in the real estate deal discussed. An *option* is "the right" to buy or sell a stock:

at a stated price — the *strike price*
by a certain date — the *expiration date*
at a cost for the privilege — the *option premium*

Options to purchase stocks are called *calls*. ("Call" in the stock to buy.) Rights to sell a stock to somebody else are called *puts*. ("Put" it to somebody else for sale.) The values of call and put options move in opposite directions. If a stock price rises, then the value of a call option to buy it, at a fixed price, increases. If a stock's price falls, its call value decreases. Conversely, the value of a put option increases when the underlying stock price falls and decreases when the stock price increases.

The Way Option Values Fluctuate

Underlying Stock Price Movement

	UP	DOWN
CALL	Gain	Loss
PUT	Loss	Gain

On the Chicago Board Options Exchange (CBOE), the oldest and largest exchange, traders buy and sell options on blocks of one hundred shares of stocks in the same way as Mr. Quick bought an option on real estate. Buyers of stock options buy the right to the appreciation (calls) or depreciation (puts) of a stock for a period of time. Sellers, called option *writers*, of *covered* options sell to buyers the rights on the stocks that they own. If an option writer sells an option on a stock not owned, the options are called *naked* options. They are not covered.

There are two types of option valuations, *theoretical* and *market value*. The theoretical value is the difference between the underlying stock's market price and the option's strike price. For example, a call option to buy Coca-Cola at $40 when the market price of the stock trades at $45 would have a theoretical price of $5. However, options are written for extended periods of time. Therefore, the market value is the sum of the theoretical value plus a premium for the chance of profitable price movements until the expiration date.

As the date of expiration approaches, there is less time for profits, so the premium erodes. On the expiration date, the option is settled for cash based on the optioned security's market value. The market value equals the theoretical value because there is no longer a premium for future gains.

Option Valuations. In 1973 Fisher Black and Myron Scholes published a model that became the industry standard for option valuations throughout the world. In the *Black-Scholes Option Pricing Model,* an option's calculated value is determined by five factors:

Time until expiration — The longer the optioned time, the more chance of a desired price movement. That's the time premium.

The difference between the current stock price and the strike price — The closer the strike price is to the current price the more probable it is that current price movements can meet or exceed it by expiration date.

The price volatility of the stock — The more volatile the price movement of a stock, the more likely that a price movement could jump near the strike price.

The market rate of interest on short-term government securities — If the cost of financing the transaction is high, then the option price has to be higher to cover the handling costs of the transaction.

Dividend payments on the stock — Option owners do not collect the dividends on the underlying stock, but the stock price that influences the option price is affected.

One can calculate the approximate prices of calls and puts by placing these five inputs into a simple Lotus 1-2-3 computer spreadsheet. Because everybody uses some form of the Black-Scholes model, the prices produced by these models are very close to the market price. That is in sharp contrast to common stock valuations, in which investment analysts use thousands of methods to determine their own "correct" value.

A Call Option Example. Optimistic stock options traders buy calls to purchase stock if they believe the underlying stock will increase. For example, let's call our options trader Billy Peligro. On June 15, 1992, Billy saw Wal-Mart stores common stock quoted at $54 per share in *The Wall Street Journal.* The call right to purchase one share of Wal-Mart by September at $55 traded at $2.69. Billy bet that Wal-Mart would trade significantly above $55 by September (SEP), and he paid $2.69 for the chance. If the option expired on the day of purchase in June, the optioned purchase price of $55 would have been "out of the money," by one dollar, and the option would be worthless. The value of a $55 call option of Wal-Mart graphically looks like a hockey stick. It varies with the stock price.

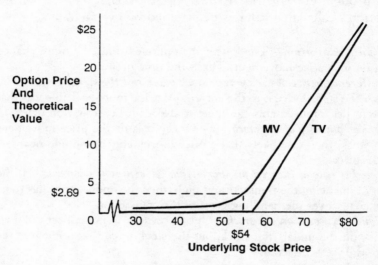

The Value of a Wal-Mart SEP $55 Call Option

MV = option market value   TV = option theoretical value

But is $2.69 the correct price? Plugging the five factors of Wal-Mart's common stock and the particulars about the option into the Black-Scholes black-box Lotus spreadsheet, the outcome for your author was a $2.66 price. Pretty close!

Put Option Example. Let's look at the opposite situation, a pessimistic Billy Peligro. He bought a put option to sell Wal-Mart at $55 for settlement in September when the market price was $54 in June. That was one dollar "in the money" because he had the right to sell at $55 when the market was at $54. The market price for the option was $2.75 on June 15, 1992. One dollar of the value was "in the money" and the other $1.75 was the premium for three months to make more money. If the stock fell further, Mr. Peligro had the right to sell a share of Wal-Mart stock at $55, no matter how low it might have gone. Checking Black-Scholes for reasonableness, the $2.75 market value was close to the modeled value of the put. The put's graph of possible values is the call's hockey stick in reverse.

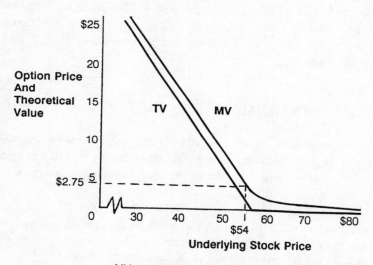

The Value of a Wal-Mart SEP $55 Put Option

MV = option market value   TV = option theoretical value

Options Strategies and Hedging. Options are highly risky investments, but their risk can be reduced by *hedging*. Hedging is buying an option to offset a possible decline in value in an owned investment. Like other options, it can be taken on many types of assets. Suppose that a risk-adverse investor, Mr. Scared E. Cat, owned the same share of Wal-Mart stock trading at $54, but because of the downside risk, he wanted to protect himself from a steep decline. The investor could have bought a three-month put option at a $50 strike price for $1 in June 1992. The put would have ensured that he could have sold his Wal-Mart share for at least $50 in the next three months. The person who wrote the option believed that there was little risk of that happening and was happy to take the $1 premium, hoping it would have no value to Mr. Cat.

If Wal-Mart fell to $40, the put option that cost only one dollar would be worth $10 at expiration. The put writer would be obligated to pay up. For Mr. Cat, the option's $10 gain would partially offset the $14 loss in the value of the stock from $54 to $40. That is why many people view the options market as a way to shift risk from one investor to another.

There are many options strategies that option traders and portfolio managers use in addition to simple hedges. Sophisticated investors combine options and stocks in many ways. There are many option strategies that traders use, including *spreads, butterflies, condors, straddles,* and *boxes*.

FINANCIAL MANAGEMENT

How a company funds itself and maximizes the return on money raised from its shareholders or debt holders is the essence of *financial management*. MBAs who choose to go into financial management perform two major functions:

Business Investment Decisions — What assets should the firm own? In what projects should the business invest?
Financing Decisions — How should those investments be paid for?

Business Investment Decisions

There are many investments that a company can make. It is a financial manager's job to help the management team to evaluate investments, rank them, and suggest choices. The MBA term for such activity is *capital budgeting*.

In the Quantitative Analysis chapter, the Quaker Oats example described the techniques used to decide whether or not to invest in new cereal filling equipment. Quaker managers used discounted cash flows to calculate the net present value (NPV) of the project. In the marketing chapter, the decision to launch a new coffee brand was evaluated by a simpler measure, the payback period. Some investments, however, defy financial analysis. Charitable donations, for example, provide intangible benefits that financial managers alone cannot evaluate.

Investment decisions fall into one of three basic decision categories:

Accept or Reject a Single Investment Proposal
Choose One Competing Investment over Another
Capital Rationing — With a limited investment pool, capital rationing tells which projects among many should be chosen.

Each corporation uses its own criteria to ration its limited resources. The major tools that MBAs use are:

Payback Period
Net Present Value

Payback Period Method. Many companies believe that the best way to judge investments is to calculate the amount of time it takes to recover their investments:

Payback = Number of Years to Recover Initial Investment

Analysts can easily calculate paybacks and make simple accept or reject decisions based on a required payback period. Those projects that come close to the mark are accepted, and those falling short are rejected. For example, the managers of a small company may believe that all energy- and labor-saving devices should have a maximum three-year payback, and that all new equipment should "pay back" in eight years, whereas research projects should pay back in ten years. Those requirements are based on management's judgment, experience, and level of risk aversion.

By accepting projects with longer paybacks, management accepts more risk. The further out an investment's payback, the more uncertain and risky it is. The concept is similar to the measure bond investors use, *duration.* The longer it takes an investor to recover half of his bond investment, the riskier it is.

Payback period criteria are desirable because they are easy to calculate, use, and understand. However, they ignore the timing of cash flows, and accordingly, the time value of money. Projects with vastly different cash flows can have the same payback period. For example, a research project that repays a $100,000 investment evenly in $33,333 installments over three years has the same three-year payback as the single $100,000 return received at the end of three years.

Another shortcoming of using payback is that it ignores the cash flows received after the payback. What if the $100,000 research project with a three-year payback continued to churn out a stream of royalties forever as a result of a new invention? Clearly it would be worth much more than a project that had a one-time payout of $100,000 in the third year of the invention's life.

Net Present Value Methods. The same method used for valuing the cash flows of bonds and stocks is also used to value projects. It is the most accurate and most theoretically correct method.

The further in the future a dollar is received, the greater the uncertainty that it will be received (risk) and the greater the loss of opportunity to use those funds (opportunity costs). Accordingly, cash flows received in the future will be discounted more steeply depending on the riskiness of the project.

$$\text{NPV} = \text{Cash to Be Received} \times (1 + \text{Discount Rate})^{-\text{Number of Periods}}$$

(as calculated in tables in Appendix or by using business calculators and computers)

The ways in which a corporation wishes to fund itself are "financing" decisions independent of "investment" decisions. A *glaring* non-MBA mistake in evaluating projects is to use a discount factor equal to the cost of borrowing for the corporation as a whole. In 1992 stable corporations could borrow money at the prime interest rate of 6 to 7 percent. The individual projects that businesses may want to invest in are not as stable. Accordingly, financial managers *must* use a discount rate commensurate with the risk of the particular project.

In the Quaker Oats factory example from the QA chapter the cash flows looked as follows:

10% Discount

	Cash Flow	Factor	NPV
Today	− $102,000	1.0000	− $102,000
Year 1	$51,000	.90909	$46,364
Year 2	$51,000	.82645	$42,149
Year 3	$61,000	.75131	$45,830
Total	$61,000		$32,343

The NPV method says that the project returned $32,343 in excess of the required rate of return for a project with that level of risk. Projects that have NPVs of $0 are also acceptable because they return the required rate. Those below zero are flatly rejected.

NPV has many advantages. It is flexible in making calculations that are useful in comparing different projects.

Riskiness of Projects. In calculating the NPV an analyst can use different discount rates. For example, if he considered the profits from Quaker Oats' new oatmeal filling equipment more risky, a 15 percent or 20 percent discount rate would value the project at $21,019 or $11,217 respectively.

Unequal Lives of Projects. An analyst does have the ability to value cash over many years by using different discount factors based on the risk-adjusted discount rate. The Quaker project could be compared with many other projects with cash flows of one year, ten years, or unlimited. The discount factor can be used to discount all cash flows to their present value for comparison.

Scale Differences in the Size of Projects' Cash Flows. The ability of the NPV method to discount cash at different amounts yields a "net" present value that is comparable among different size projects. The discount factor also values the cash flow at any time in the future.

Since capital needs to be rationed, what is an MBA to do if he or she needs to choose? NPV tells you the best projects, but not the best *group* of projects. The *profitability index* (PI) can be of help. The PI divides the NPV of the *future* cash flows by the initial investment. For example, the Quaker project has an index of 1.317.

NPV of Future Cash Flows
    Initial Investment

$$\frac{\$46,364 + \$42,149 + \$45,830}{\$102,000} = 1.317$$

In situations where money is unlimited, all PIs above 1.00 would be accepted. All projects with a return over the risk-adjusted rate are attractive. With constrained resources, only the investment opportunities with the highest PI are chosen so that the group of investments may yield the highest NPV for the shareholders.

In those cases, it is up to the MBA analyst to try different combinations of the best projects using NPVs and PIs as guides to get the highest possible NPV for the entire group.

Business Financing Decisions

A large number of MBAs devote their lives to finding the financing for the capital needs of businesses. The goal of corporate finance is to raise sufficient capital at the least cost for the level of risk that management is willing to live with. The risk is that a business will not be able to service its debt and will be forced into bankruptcy.

There are five basic ways of financing a company's needs:

Receive Credit from Suppliers
Obtain Lease Financing
Obtain Bank Loans
Issue Bonds
Issue Stock

Supplier Credit. Supplier credit is the easiest way that companies obtain financing. Companies buy goods and services and have anywhere from seven days to a year to pay their bills. When companies need more credit from suppliers, financial managers negotiate longer credit terms or larger credit lines. Cash managers can also *stretch their payables* to vendors by paying them late. In the case of Federated and Allied department stores in 1990, vendors refused to extend them additional credit. The combination of creditors and debt holders forced the company into bankruptcy.

Lease Financing. Instead of buying equipment, many companies choose to lease equipment. This is a form of financing. Automobiles, computers, and heavy machinery can be financed for short periods or for longer periods. If the lease is for a shorter period, it is called an *operating lease*. At the end of the lease the property is still useful and is returned to the finance company. This is the case with two-year car leases.

Long-term leases are, in substance, ways of financing a purchase, rather than buying the temporary services of a piece of equipment. Such long-term leases are called *capital leases*. The *useful life* of the leased equipment is used up by the lessee, and at the end of the lease the equipment usually stays with the lessee for a *bargain purchase* price like $1. The accountants have specific rules that deal with the different kinds of leasing arrangements. For capital leases, the leased assets and the financing liability are recorded on the leasing company's books as though the company had bought the equipment outright.

Bank Financing. The next level of financing involves banks. Banks can loan money for long-term or short periods of time. If a company has a credit line or *revolver* with a bank, it draws down and pays back up to set limits of credit as cash is needed and generated by the business. The credit is often secured by the assets of the firm. If a business runs into trouble, it may not be able to pay the bank and goes into bankruptcy. The once mighty Olympia & York real estate investment firm declared bankruptcy in 1992 when bankers refused to extend its owners, the Reichmann brothers, any more credit for floundering real estate projects.

Bond Issuance. Bonds have fixed interest rate contractual payments and a principal maturity. The risk to the firm's owners comes if they cannot be serviced. In 1990 the Southland Corporation (7-Eleven stores) defaulted on its bond payment and Ito-Yokado Corporation, the majority bondholder, exchanged its bonds for the ownership of the company and ousted the Thompson family from the company they had founded.

The After-Tax Cost of Borrowing. Interest payments for borrowing from vendors, bankers, or bondholders are tax-deductible, while dividends to shareholders are not. The after-tax cost of borrowing is the interest cost less the tax benefit.

After-Tax Cost of Borrowing = Borrowing Rate × (1 − Tax Rate)

In 1993, the Caterpillar bond used in the earlier example paid 8 percent interest on the issue maturing in 2001. In 1993 Caterpillar's corporate tax rate was projected at 34 percent. By deducting the interest expense on the tax returns, the company received, in effect, a 34 percent discount on its borrowing. The after-tax rate was 5.28 percent (8% × (1 − .34)).

As you learned in the Accounting chapter, dividends are not tax-deductible, but interest payments are. That difference is an incentive for businesses to borrow rather than issue stock and pay dividends. This phenomenon is called a *tax shield* for borrowing. In the leveraged buyout binge of the 1980s, the tax shield was a spur to borrow huge amounts, such as the $26.4 billion Kohlberg Kravis Roberts borrowed to buy RJR Nabisco in 1989. That year the government subsidized this venture to the tune of approximately $800 million (26.4 × 10% × 30%). Not surprisingly, many taxpayers favor eliminating or restricting the tax subsidy for interest expenses.

Stock Issues. Stock issues have noncontractual, non–tax deductible dividend payments. Stock represents an ownership interest in the business and in all of its assets. If additional shares of stock are issued to raise cash, this is done at the expense of the current shareholders' ownership interest. New shareholders share their ownership interest equally on a per-share basis with the current shareholders. That is why analysts say that the new shares *dilute* the interest of existing shareholders.

There are several markets available to sell new stock issues: the New York Stock Exchange (NYSE), the less important American Stock Exchange (AMEX), and the emerging National Association of Securities Dealers Automated Quotations System (NASDAQ). When a stock is not listed on an exchange, but is *publicly* traded, it is traded *Over the Counter* (OTC). If a company's shares are not publicly traded, the company is said to be *privately* held.

Financial advisors called *investment bankers* assist in the sale of new shares in companies. Noted investment bankers such as Salomon Brothers; Goldman, Sachs; Alex Brown; Bear Stearns; and Merrill Lynch, employing many MBAs, work on these *initial public offerings* (IPOs) for large fees. These *I-bankers* assist in the preparation of the selling document, called the *prospectus*. The prospectus outlines the issuer's history and business plans. The Securities Act of 1933 governs the disclosures required in this document.

The Financing Mix's Risk and Reward. The financing decisions in a corporation revolve around what is the best mix of debt and equity. That mix is called a company's *capital structure* policy. When managers make large changes in the debt-to-equity mix, they call it *restructuring*.

Theoretically, there is an optimal mix of debt and stock; however, there are no magic MBA formulas to establish that perfect ratio. MBAs can look to what worked in the past and to the mix of successful competitors. If the industry is cyclical, lighter debt loads are preferable in order to survive downturns. Good financial managers don't decide on a financing plan and forget it. Capital structures are *dynamic*. Decisions to shift the balance from equity to debt and back again should be continually reviewed to make sure the capital structure is appropriate at any given point in time.

Although there are no handy MBA formulas to solve once and for all the debt versus equity conundrum, there is a useful MBA acronym, FRICTO, whose initials stand for a useful checklist in sorting out capital structure issues.

Flexibility. How much financial flexibility does management need to meet *unforeseen* events, such as new competitors or lawsuits? For example, Nutri/System, Inc., the diet center chain, never planned for the gall bladder litigation that crippled the company in 1990.

Risk. How much risk can management live with to meet *foreseen* events, such as downturns in the business cycle, strikes, and material shortages? Toy companies are known to produce hot toys that turn cold. Savvy managers should plan for the eventual sales dropoff by providing enough financial flexibility to survive the downturn. Accordingly, most toy companies have low debt-to-equity ratios.

Income. What level of interest or dividend payments can earnings support? Financial managers are required to forecast the results of operations to determine cash flows. Using those forecasts, and the degree of confidence a manager has in his or her projections, he or she can determine what level of payments the company can make.

Control. How much stock ownership does management want to share with outside investors? Many family business owners are leery of letting an outsider even know their income, let alone have a vote.

Timing. Does the debt market offer very attractive rates? Has the market overvalued the firm's shares in the opinion of management? If so, then it makes sense to sell shares to the public. Conversely, if the stock is too cheap then it is better to buy back shares from the public. After the crash of 1987, many firms took the opportunity to buy back their own shares. By reducing the number of shares outstanding, their share of debt financing grew as a portion of their capital structures.

In 1991 investors could not buy enough biotechnology stock. They paid very high prices for even questionable start-ups. Smart managers tapped that market, and sold shares to the eager public at high prices. In 1992, the days of easy money ended when biotech fell out of favor with investors. A company's capital structure should be dynamic to take advantage of market conditions.

Other. Many other factors affect the paths managers take. At times, a company just can't find a bank to lend money, forcing an equity choice. In other circumstances interest rates are just unaffordable, forcing an equity choice. The reasons for capital structure decisions are many.

Key to financial structure is the discussion of ratios. In the Accounting chapter, I explained the concept of *financial leverage*. Companies that maintain high levels of debt and little equity *leverage* their earnings for shareholders if there are profits. There are simply fewer shares to divide income by, yielding higher earnings per share. Conversely, highly leveraged firms wipe out the entire value of their equity when earnings falter and interest payments eat up all the profits.

Managers of highly leveraged firms must decide whether it is worthwhile to risk bankruptcy if their cash flow projections don't pan out in order to offer high returns to their shareholders. The Thompson family guessed wrong with Southland, while the happy and rich management of ARA Services, the food service company, calculated correctly in their leveraged buyout in 1984. Who knows? Maybe if the Thompsons had used FRICTO, they might have avoided their losses!

The market value of shares already issued is also related to the risk of a firm's capital structure. If investors believe that debt levels are excessive, then they will pay less for the company's shares, since the debt payments could put earnings in jeopardy. Investors will also discount the market value of a company's debt for risk. That was the case in the early 1990s with leveraged companies such as Black & Decker, RJR Nabisco, and Owens-Corning Fiberglass. Many investors felt uncomfortable with the riskiness of their capital structures and avoided both the debt and equity of these highly leveraged companies.

Modigliani and Miller, a famous duo from MBA academia, created a series of "propositions" that discussed how debt affects the values of firms. In 1958, Franco Modigliani and Merton Miller did their pioneering work on the effect of debt financing with and without a tax advantage. In a perfect world, the more debt the better. The value of the firm increases with higher debt levels. However, in the real world, as seen in the previous paragraph, investors do consider the risk of insolvency in their valuations of both debt and equity.

To summarize, the higher the percentage of debt to total capital, the higher a company's value, to a point. At the point where the risk of bankruptcy becomes significant, values fall. The cost of financing decreases as a company adds lower-cost tax-shielded debt to displace the higher returns required by equity investors. But like stockholders, debt holders become nervous at a certain point and require higher rates of return to compensate them for their risk. Study the two graphs on page 230 that illustrate the workings of capital structure.

A Detailed Capital Structure Decision Example. Although choosing the optimal capital structure is difficult, financial managers try to put together some numbers to make choices. If you are curious about the details and want to graduate from the *Ten-Day MBA* "cum laude," read on. If not, just skip to the next section. Making capital structure decisions involves a two-step process:

1. Calculate the WACC.
2. Value the *Free Cash Flows* of the company, the value of the firm.

The first step is to calculate the *weighted average cost of capital* (WACC) of the entire firm by using the following formula and calculating a number of variables. The cost of equity (Ke) is the most difficult.

$$\text{WACC} = K_d (1 - t) \frac{\text{(Market Value of Debt)}}{\text{Total Debt and Equity}}$$

$$+ K_e \frac{\text{(Market Value of Equity)}}{\text{Total Debt and Equity}}$$

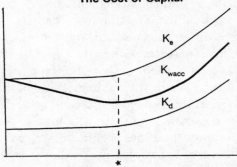

Optimal Capital Structure
The Cost of Capital

Cost of Capital

Debt to Capital Ratio %

Capital = Debt + Equity
K_e = Cost of Equity
K_d = Cost of Debt
K_{wacc} = the Weighted Average Cost of Capital

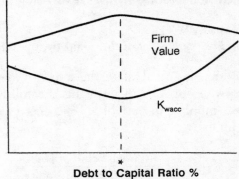

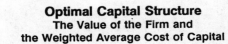

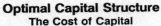

Optimal Capital Structure
The Value of the Firm and
the Weighted Average Cost of Capital

Value of the Firm
Cost of Capital

Debt to Capital Ratio %

Capital = Debt + Equity

t = tax rate
K_d = cost of debt
K_e = cost of equity

Review the formula. Notice that the WACC uses the market values of debt and equity. The market is the true measure of how current bondholders and shareholders value their investments. The cost of debt can be obtained from the company's treasury department or can be found in the footnotes of the financial statements. It takes large boosts in debt financing to change the cost of debt. However, the cost of equity is a bit more complex to figure out.

The cost of equity heavily depends on the leverage of the firm. Because leverage means risk, we can use beta from the *capital asset pricing model* (CAPM). The CAPM helps calculate the required return on equity under different leverage scenarios.

$$K_e = R_f + (K_m - R_f) \times Beta$$

$$(K_m - R_f) = \text{Risk Premium}$$

The risk measure, Beta, changes according to the risk of leverage. Financial MBAs take the current levered beta and unlever it to a no-debt, *unlevered* state (Step A), then lever it back up to any hypothetical capital structure (Step B).

Step A

$$Beta_u = \frac{Beta_l}{\left(1 + (1 - \text{tax rate}) \times \dfrac{Debt}{Equity}\right)}$$

Step B

$$Beta_l = Beta_u \times \left(1 + (1 - \text{tax rate}) \times \frac{Debt}{Equity}\right)$$

l = levered structure with debt
u = unlevered structure without debt

To illustrate: The treasurer of Leverco, Inc. wants to decide whether to choose a 0 percent, 25 percent, or 50 percent debt capital structure. In order to do so he has laid out the facts and calculations in the following columns of numbers. The conclusion is that Leverco should have a 50 percent debt/50 percent equity capital structure. That's the structure that maximizes the value of the firm while minimizing the WACC.

The same calculations demonstrated in Leverco's case were used to derive the two theoretical graphs of the "Optimal Capital Structure." The first is the calculation of the weighted average cost of capital. The second graph, using the lowest WACC shown, describes the maximum value of the firm. If you wish, you can try to recompute the calculations that are noted with an asterisk (*). These are the same computations that MBAs throughout the world use for capital structure decisions.

Dividend Policy. Financial managers must decide how much of a firm's profits should be paid out as dividends and must determine the size of dividends per share. This is called *dividend policy*.

To guide them in their policies financial managers use at least two measures — *dividend yields* and *dividend payout ratios*. The market plays a big role in determining the *dividend yield* since it is derived by dividing the annual dividend payment by the current share price. Dividends may also be paid out as a certain percentage of earnings, called the *dividend payout ratio*.

$$\text{Dividend Yield} = \frac{\text{Annual Dividend}}{\text{Market Price per Share}}$$

$$\text{Dividend Payout Ratio} = \frac{\text{Annual Dividend}}{\text{Net Income}}$$

Dividends are extremely important because they show clearly the cash-generating ability of the firm. Many analysts value companies based on the dividend cash flows. You saw that valuation method with the Dividend Growth Model earlier in this chapter.

Investors love stable, steadily growing dividends, and hate any cuts. Therefore, managers try to avoid swings in dividend payouts at all costs. If an MBA miscalculates the ability of the company to maintain a dividend, his or her job will be in real jeopardy.

Capital Structure Decision Calculation
Leverco, Inc.

Scenarios

Book Value of Debt Ratio	0% Debt	25% Debt	50% Debt
Book Value of Debt	$0	$2,500	$5,000
Book Value of Equity	10,000	7,500	5,000
Market Value of Debt	$0	$2,500	$5,000
Market Value of Equity	10,000	8,350	6,700
Market Value Debt Ratio*	**0%**	**23%**	**43%**
Pretax Cost of Debt	.07	.07	.07
Tax Rate	.34	.34	.34
After-Tax Cost of Debt*	**.0462**	**.0462**	**.0462**
Pretax Cost $\times$ (1 − t)			
Unlevered Beta	.8	.8	.8
Levered Beta*	**.8**	**.958**	**1.194**
Using the Step B formula			riskiest
Cost of Equity*	**.139**	**.151**	**.168**
Using the CAPM formula:			riskiest

$K_e = R_f +$ Levered Beta $\times$ (Risk Premium)
$K_e = .08 +$ Levered Beta $\times$ (.074)

WACC*	**.139**	**.127**	**.108**
Using WACC formula given			least cost
Annual Cash Flow	$2,000	$2,000	$2,000
Before Interest and Taxes			
"Free Cash Flow"			
Value of Company*	**$14,388**	**$15,748**	**$18,518**
(Value Cash Flow as a perpetuity)			highest value
Free Cash Flow / WACC			

*denotes a calculation using a formula provided

Adapted from "An Introduction to Debt Policy and Value," Case UVA-F-811, Copyright © 1989 by the Darden Graduate Business School Foundation, Charlottesville, Virginia.

There are five questions that astute MBAs ought to mull over as they formulate a policy that may directly affect their careers.

Can the company do a better job by investing its earnings back into the firm than investors could by investing elsewhere? If a company is growing and has many exciting investment opportunities, dividends should be small and earnings should be used internally. In 1991 Wal-Mart paid a puny 16-cent dividend per share against $1.40 in earnings, but investors were happy because Sam Walton was busy investing in many new and profitable stores.

Who is your stockholder? Do widows and orphans depend on your dividends for their incomes? This is the case with utility stocks, but not with start-up computer companies.

What will stockholders' reaction be to any changes in dividend payments? Changes in dividend payments are a very powerful signal to investors. Investors react violently to any cuts in dividends, since they signal that the company is in trouble. Increases are not such a big deal. More often than not, dividend increases are expected and greeted with little fanfare. Increases in dividends show management's confidence that the business's earnings are strong enough over the long-term to sustain an increased payout.

What is the degree of financial leverage of the company? To ensure that dividends will not be interrupted, companies should see to it that they can comfortably pay the dividends investors expect and demand.

What is the growth strategy of the company? Growth companies usually pay little to no dividends. They need cash to finance their own growth. Biotechnology companies, for example, retain all their cash to support long-term research needs.

If a company is strapped for cash and yet still wants to make investors happy, it can pay a *stock dividend*. This is a dividend that the company pays in shares of the company, not cash. Such dividends usually range from 2 to 5 percent of shares owned. For example, if you were to own one hundred shares you would receive two to five new shares. Investors end up with a greater number of shares, but since all shareholders receive the same percentage share dividend, their percentage ownership of the firm remains the same.

MERGERS AND ACQUISITIONS

Mergers and acquisitions (M&A) is one of the most exciting areas of finance. The same investment bankers who help companies raise money also help companies spend it. Many highly paid MBAs work in this field. "Strategic" reasons and methods for M&A are covered in the strategy chapter. This chapter will cover the legitimate financial reasons for mergers and acquisitions.

Diversify the Company

Many companies attempt to lower risk by owning other businesses. Philip Morris bought Kraft, General Foods, and Miller Brewing because it wanted to diversify. Tobacco usage was declining, lawsuits loomed, and new regulation limiting advertising was pending.

Improve Sales and Earnings

Procter & Gamble, the leader in soaps, detergents, and paper products, decided to expand sales and earnings by buying Norwich Easton (Pepto-Bismol), Richardson-Vicks, Noxell, and Hawaiian Punch. Their brand management expertise served them well in enhancing the values of these acquisitions.

Purchase an Undervalued Company

Based on market conditions, corporations can sometimes buy companies at a bargain. Companies may also be a bargain if investors do not recognize the potential of valuable assets on the books. Turner Broadcasting bought MGM/United Artists in 1986, because MGM had an extensive movie library of classics that Turner felt was undervalued and not fully exploited.

Lower Operating Costs

When companies merge many cost savings are possible. With the absorption of a company, some of the acquired company's corporate overhead expenses can be cut. In manufacturing mergers, factories can produce larger quantities more efficiently. When Chemical

Bank and Manufacturers Hanover merged in 1991, their larger transaction volumes caused the costs of processing to go down. They were also able to lay off 6,200 employees.

Types of Acquisitions

If two companies decide to join forces to become one company, this is called a *merger*. When Sperry and Burroughs merged in 1986, the merged entity was named Unisys.

If one company buys another company it is called an *acquisition*. If both parties agree to the purchase, it is called a *friendly acquisition*; if not, it is called a *hostile takeover*.

Smaller companies that are attractive takeover candidates often agree to be purchased in friendly takeovers. In 1989 Procter & Gamble made a friendly purchase of Noxell, the maker of Cover Girl and Clarion cosmetics. Both saw the advantages of the two marketing companies joining forces.

In other cases, the purchase can be nasty. In 1984, T. Boone Pickens tried to buy Phillips Petroleum in an unsuccessful hostile takeover. The management of Phillips was so opposed to the idea that in 1985 it borrowed $4.5 billion to buy back 47 percent of its common stock. This thwarted Pickens's efforts because it borrowed against the same assets that he was planning to mortgage.

The fourth type of acquisition that I have mentioned several times already in this chapter is the *leveraged buyout* (LBO). In the 1980s, there were many lenders who were willing to loan money to takeover artists. In the same way that a mortgage company makes a loan to a home buyer for a down payment of only 5 percent, banks, insurance companies, and bond investors lent money to these financiers to buy companies. The company that emerges from a leveraged buyout carries a high level of debt on which it must pay interest and principal.

The Valuation Process

To engage in M&A, you must assess the value of the targets. Cash flow is the main consideration. A business's cash flows are the result of operations, investing, and financing activities (the same activities that the accountant's Statement of Cash Flows describes). In the

Accounting chapter, I used the example of tiny Bob's Market. By adding a few zeroes to the numbers, it could be Safeway, Kroger, or A&P. Because you are already familiar with Bob's Market, this section will continue with this example.

There are five steps involved in calculating and evaluating a business's cash flows:

1. **Analyze operating activities.**
   Forecast the Income Statement; sales, cost of goods sold, selling, general and administration expenses
2. **Analyze the investments necessary to replace and to buy new property, plant, and equipment.**
3. **Analyze the capital requirements of the firm.**
   Determine the corporate working capital requirements.
4. **Project the annual operating cash flows and terminal value of the firm.**
5. **Calculate the NPV of those cash flows to calculate the firm's value.**

There are many techniques or approaches that MBAs use to value firms. With all the flair a marketer displays in putting together a marketing strategy, finance jocks show their stuff in M&A valuations. The following is one popular method used by many in the financial community.

Bob's Market
Income Statement
for the Year Ending December 31, 1992
(in thousands)

		% of Sales
Sales	$5,200	100%
Cost of Goods Sold	3,900	75
Gross Margin	$1,300	25%
Selling, General and Administrative (SG&A)	1,256	24%
Operating Income	$44	
Add Back: Depreciation (not a cash use)	3	
"Free Cash Flow" Earnings Before Interest and Taxes (EBIT)	$47	

1. Analyze operating activities and the firm's capital spending requirements.

The first thing is to forecast sales and calculate the gross margins on sales and other operating expenses. But financial analysts must do more than just look at numbers. They must also review the industry, the competition, the markets for raw materials, and management's plans to run and grow the business. All these factors will affect the cash flow of business.

Discussions with Bob, his accountant, and his assistant manager revealed that the business is healthy and they expect sales to grow by 10 percent a year over a four-year period and then stabilize. They are confident that they will maintain a gross margin of 25 percent or a variable 75 percent cost of sales. They also believe that their SG&A expenses will remain a steady variable 24 percent of sales. The depreciation for equipment, which does not cost cash, can be added back, but Bob believes that he will be upgrading the store each year by reinvesting the $3,000 in new store fixtures. With that information, the cash flow forecast would look as follows:

Cash Flow Projections
(in thousands)

	Prior Year	Year 1	Year 2	Year 3	Year 4
Sales	$5,200	$5,720	$6,292	$6,921	$7,613
COGS @ 75%	3,900	4,290	4,719	5,190	5,709
Gross Margin @ 25%	$1,300	$1,430	$1,573	$1,731	$1,904
SG&A @ 24%	1,256	1,373	1,510	1,661	1,827
Operating Income	$44	$57	$63	$70	$77
Add Back Depreciation	3	3	3	3	3
Less Equipment Purchased	3	3	3	3	3
Free Cash Flow (EBIT)	$44	$57	$63	$70	$77

2. Analyze the investments necessary to replace and to buy new property, plant, and equipment.

Don't be shy. Consult with the engineers, purchasing department, and the accountants to get a good estimate of costs and useful lives.

3. Determine the working capital needs of the business.

Businesses need cash to operate. The level of working capital is most often a function of the volume of sales. The more sales that are generated the greater the cash needs for making change at the cash registers and purchasing inventory. This need is balanced somewhat by the credit that vendors increasingly extend as the market's purchases from them grow in volume. This is a very important part of the process; failing to consider the working capital needs could result in a cash squeeze.

When we look back at the balance sheet of Bob's Market, we see that Bob had $115,000 in current assets and $87,000 in current liabilities. That is a net working capital position of $28,000 (115 − 87).

Bob says that every week he needs 28 cents for every dollar of sales ($28,000/[$5,200,000 annual sales/52 weeks per year]). That covers his cash needs for inventory and register money offset by the additional financing extended by his grocery vendors. Added to the valuation calculation, the cash flow projection would look as follows:

Cash Flow Projection
(in thousands)

	Year 1	Year 2	Year 3	Year 4
Free Cash Flow (EBIT)	$57	$63	$70	$77
Less Additional				
Cash Flow Needs*	3	3	4	4
Net *Free Cash Flow*	$54	$60	$66	$73

*(Sales / 52) × 28% − Prior Year's Working Capital Level

4. Determine the terminal value of the firm.

A business is presumed to be a *going concern* that will continue to operate indefinitely into the future. By valuing the cash flow to a certain point in time, you are ignoring ongoing value. That is why at the end of the financial projection, a *terminal value* must be calculated and added to the cash flow valuation.

At Bob's Market the fourth year's cash flow was $73,000. If that cash is forecasted to be the same year after year, you could use the same valuation method that is used to value a perpetuity.

$$\text{Terminal Value} = \frac{\text{Terminal Cash Flow}}{(\text{Discount Factor} - \text{Growth})}$$

The proper discount factor to use in this case is the weighted average cost of capital (WACC). We use WACC because the *free cash flow* of the company is available to pay interest on debt *and* to pay dividends to equity holders. Therefore the proper discount factor takes into account the firm's entire capital structure, its debt *and* equity.

Bob's Market's capital structure is very conservative. Its balance sheet lists only $10,000 of debt and $45,000 of equity. Its debt carries an interest rate of 10 percent. The cost of equity can be calculated using the Capital Asset Pricing Model. Using the long-term risk-free treasury rate of 8 percent, the risk premium of 7.4 percent, and a .85 beta representing the lower risk of a low-debt grocery store, the cost of equity is 14.3 percent.

$$K_e = R_f + (K_m - R_f)\text{Beta}$$

$$14.3\% = 8\% + (7.4\%)\ .85$$

Plugging the cost of equity into the WACC equation, the firm's weighted average cost of capital is 13 percent.

$$\text{WACC} = K_d(1 - t)\left(\frac{\text{Market Value of Debt}}{\text{Total Debt and Equity}}\right)$$

$$+ K_e\left(\frac{\text{Market Value of Equity}}{\text{Total Debt and Equity}}\right)$$

$$13\% = 10\%(1 - .30)\left(\frac{\$10,000}{\$55,000}\right) + 14.3\%\left(\frac{\$45,000}{\$55,000}\right)$$

Putting it all together in a valuation, the terminal value cash flow calculation would be:

$$\text{Terminal Value} = \frac{\text{Year 4 Free Cash Flow}}{\text{WACC} - \text{growth}}$$

$$\$510{,}000 = \frac{\$73{,}000}{14.3\% - 0\%}$$

5. Calculate the NPV of those cash flows to calculate the firm's value.

Add the terminal value to the present value of the first three years' projected cash flows, and the entire value of the firm can be calculated as follows:

Net Present Valuation of Free Cash Flows
(in thousands)

	Year 1	Year 2	Year 3	Year 4
Free Cash Flow	$54	$60	$66	$510
Discount Factor @ 14.3%	.8780	.7593	.6666	.5861
Net Present Value	47	46	44	299
Total NPV	$436			

That's it! The grocery store is worth $436,000. After subtracting the $10,000 in debts, the net equity that Bob owns is worth $426,000. That's how the MBAs value companies large and small. Yes, it's a bit tedious, but mathematically not difficult to calculate. By keeping M&A a mysterious process, MBAs can charge more for their M&A services. Now you have the inside story.

Additional Things MBAs Include in Their Valuations

The valuation of Bob's Market assumes that the grocery store will be operated as Bob said it would. MBAs sometimes have different ideas. Companies being analyzed for potential acquisition are just like meat in a butcher shop — cut, sliced, and ground up as necessary. Analysts investigate the company from all angles. MBAs look at any opportunity to improve operations, lower expenses, and increase cash flow. They consider the sale of assets. The process is colored by the type of acquisition it is: merger, friendly, hostile, or leveraged. If the company is being taken over by a new management, then many changes are possible and likely. If the purchase is made with a great deal of debt, the new owners will want to increase cash flow and sell assets as soon as possible to pay off the debt incurred in purchasing the company. A sampling of things new owners will look for in these situations are:

- **Wage Concessions, Break Labor Unions**
- **Layoffs**
- **Lower Production Costs**
- **Reduce Working Capital Needs**
  Lower Inventory
  Lower Receivables
  Increase Payables
- **Gain Access to Employees' Pension Money**
- **Sell Real Estate**
- **Sell Patents and Rights**
- **Sell Divisions, Subsidiaries, Product Lines**
- **Sell Unnecessary Luxuries for Executives** (jets, company apartments)

The MBA Touch: Asking "What If?" All the steps outlined can be investigated and plugged into mathematical formulas and spreadsheets. Analysts have to make many informed guesses. The real contribution an MBA can make to the process is not only an accurate evaluation of specific company information, but an experienced evaluation of the external factors that may affect the cash flows forecasted. How would a change in product costs affect the forecasted cash flows? How could the competitive environment in the industry affect sales? What if?

A proper MBA forecast of cash flows includes variations or "sensitivities" of key assumptions, so that decision makers can assess the risk inherent in the cash flows they are forecasting. The use of Lotus 1-2-3 is imperative and its "Data-Table" function is the MBA tool to perform variation analysis. If you're not familiar with it, consider yourself Lotus-illiterate.

In the airline industry, for instance, fuel prices, fares, and passenger load factors can produce swings in cash flows. Variations in key assumptions such as these three items dramatically change valua-

" GOOD NEWS!
ITS NOT A TAKEOVER, MERELY SOMEONE TAKING THE COMPANY FOR A JOYRIDE. "

tions and cash flows. In a leveraged buyout, owners are counting on projected cash flows to pay interest on the debt they carry. If they are caught short of cash, companies go into bankruptcy. Carl Icahn was caught short, and his TWA was forced to operate under the protection of bankruptcy in January 1992.

Making a Bid

MBA calculations and forecasts are fine and dandy, but often they are ignored. Sometimes the thrill of the hunt overcomes buyers, and they act like bidders in the heat of an art auction. Instead of a net present value cash flow valuation, bidders use simpler rule-of-thumb methods, a multiple of earnings or a multiple of sales. In leveraged buyouts, the bid often simply represents the maximum amount of financing the acquisitor can obtain, or the maximum debt the targeted company's cash flow can carry. People differ, and accordingly, they have different motivations and methods in their M&A quests.

FINANCIAL OVERVIEW

Simply stated, there are two main functions in the financial world, buying and selling. Businesses require funding, therefore they either sell equity shares in their companies (stocks), or fixed interest payments securities (bonds). The investment community values these securities and buys and sells them.

The theoretical basis for financial analysis is the risk/reward equation, in which higher risks are associated with higher returns. Returns are calculated by determining the amount and the timing of cash flows.

The guiding principle of financial management is to maximize the firm's value by financing cash needs at the least cost possible, at a level of risk that management can live with.

KEY FINANCE TAKEAWAYS

Present Value — The value of a dollar received in the future is less than a dollar on hand today. There is a time value of money.

Beta — A measure of risk inherent in a security or a portfolio of securities as it reacts to general market movements

The Efficient Frontier — The graph depicting the highest portfolio returns for a given risk level

The Capital Asset Pricing Model — $K_e = R_f + (K_m - R_f)$ Beta

Duration — The time it takes for a bond to pay back half of an investor's investment

Bond Value Fluctuations — If market interest rates go up, bond values go down, and vice versa.

The Dividend Growth Model — Value = $D/(k - g)$

Call Option — The right to purchase an asset at a fixed price for a limited amount of time

Put Option — The right to sell an asset at a fixed price for a limited amount of time

The After-Tax Cost of Borrowing — After-Tax Rate = Borrowing Rate $\times (1 - $ tax rate)

Capital Structure — The mix of debt and equity of a company

FRICTO — Flexibility, Risk, Income, Control, Timing, and Other matters, the checklist to be considered in making capital structure decisions

The Optimal Capital Structure — One that minimizes the weighted average cost of capital and maximizes the value of the firm

DAY 7

OPERATIONS

OPERATIONS TOPICS

The History of Operations Research
The Problem Solving Framework
Flow Diagrams
Linear Programming
Gantt Charts
Critical Path Method
Queuing Theory
Inventories
Economic Order Quantities
Material Requirements Planning
Quality
Information Technology

Operations is the only MBA subject that concerns itself with actually making products and providing services — the ultimate purpose of business. That is the line Production and Operations Management (POM) professors deliver each year to incoming MBAs. It must fall on deaf ears, since most MBAs go into finance, marketing, and consulting. Only one student from the 1990 Dartmouth MBA graduating class took an operations job, while only 2 percent of Stanford's and Michigan's graduating classes went into operations. It may be that recruiters feel MBAs are not sufficiently trained to be worth the high salaries paid in their plants and factories. They may also believe that MBAs are best kept at headquarters with their computers and Waterman pens. From my interviews with recruiters and students, lack of interest on both sides is responsible for the lack of operational-bound MBAs.

Operational subjects are not all engineering and numbers. POM classes also have a humanistic side. The technical or quantitative approach presents students with a variety of mathematical tools with which to attack operational problems in a clinical fashion. The humanistic approach teaches students to look at operational problems from a worker's perspective as well. Clearly many business solutions lie in employee motivation.

THE OPERATIONS HISTORY LESSON

Studies on methods to improve the production of goods and services have been conducted since the beginning of the century. Academics believed that if they had only researched closely enough how businesses worked, they would have stumbled on that magic formula that would result in total efficiency. Much of that pioneering research was done on the factory floor. Because their names and theories are frequently mentioned in articles and MBA conversation, you had better add them to your business vocabulary.

Frederick Taylor

Frederick W. Taylor, considered the "father of scientific management," developed his scientific management theories in the late 1800s and the early 1900s. He studied, measured, and documented the behavior of steel workers. He showed that by breaking down a complex task into smaller component tasks, through a process that he called *job fractionalization*, each smaller task could be studied to find the most efficient way of accomplishing it. By successfully combining the most efficient elements, the best production methods could be adopted. Taylor performed countless *time and motion studies* using a stopwatch to find the "one right way" of doing things. In Taylor's opinion, it was in a worker's nature to "soldier," meaning to slack off. Therefore, it was management's responsibility to control the workplace and to force lazy workers to be efficient in spite of themselves.

Frank and Lillian Gilbreth

The Gilbreths also studied ways to achieve peak factory efficiency. Their investigations led them to the development of a spectrum of seventeen types of body movements that covered the range of a factory worker's motion. Each motion was called a *therblig*. Like Taylor, the Gilbreths broke a complex task into its component parts. By understanding each element, one could simplify a job through the elimination of wasteful motion. Streamlining the task to its essential therbligs was key. Lillian wrote about her attempts to streamline the chores of parenting a family of twelve children in a humorous book entitled *Cheaper by the Dozen*. In 1984 the U.S. Postal Service commemorated her contribution to business and literature with a forty-cent stamp.

Elton Mayo

Elton Mayo is considered the father of the *human relations* movement of production management. In his search for efficiency, Mayo believed that the emotional state of workers is just as important as finding the right combination of movements.

Mayo's claim to fame came as a result of a series of experiments he conducted in 1927 at the Hawthorne Works of the Western Electric Company. In those studies, he varied the intensity of light on the shop floor in an effort to discover the degree of lighting that would result in the greatest productivity. He found that regardless of changes in lighting, worker productivity increased. Knowing that they were the subject of a study made the workers act differently. That phenomenon came to be known as the *Hawthorne Effect*. Puzzled by the results, Mayo interviewed the workers and found that they had performed better because during the experiment they were being treated better by their supervisors. The assembly line workers were further motivated because their menial tasks acquired greater meaning as part of an experiment.

World War II and the Management Science Approach

As the technology and the scale of industrialization became more complex, operational problems became more difficult to solve. During World War II production bottlenecks forced the government to turn to scientists and engineers to help achieve maximum military production. In seeking solutions, these pioneers created mathematical models to apply to production problems. Today this branch of operational study is called *operational research* (OR). Some of those models are presented later in this chapter.

Theory X, Theory Y, and Theory Z

In 1960, Douglas McGregor of MIT renamed Taylor's scientific approach to management *Theory X*, and dubbed Mayo's behavioral approach *Theory Y*. By repackaging these theories, he made a place for himself in the operational history books.

Theory X adherents, like Taylor, take a more "pessimistic" view of human behavior. They believe that people are inherently lazy and need to be pushed to produce with rewards and punishments. Workers lack creativity and ambition and have little to offer management other than their labor.

Theory Y adherents, like Mayo, believe that workers are self-motivated given a supportive work environment. Workers are inventive and should be consulted for ideas to improve productivity. They are also capable of assuming more responsibility for their work.

In the 1980s Theory Y was taken a step further. William Ouchi called the benevolent Theory Y used by Japanese management *Theory Z*. In the mid-1980s some "experts" thought Theory Z was the secret of the Japanese competitive advantage. Using Z, the Japanese bring together management and workers in cohesive work groups. Everyone is part of a consensual decision-making process. To improve quality, workers and management work together in *quality circles*. Every employee is involved in *kaizen* — the continuous struggle necessary to improve all aspects of the self and of the company. When workers feel like partners in the business, they become more productive and committed to their jobs.

The Contingency Approach

Because neither the scientific methods nor human relations approaches can be used successfully at all times, the proponents of the *contingency approach* believe that managers should alter and combine the two theories to fit the situation. If the classical methods of Taylor can be combined with a bit of Japanese Theory Z, so much the better if the result is good.

THE PROBLEM SOLVING FRAMEWORK FOR OPERATIONS

Now that you have acquired a little historical perspective, you are ready to experience the core MBA operations education. There are five issues that arise when trying to produce a product or service:

Capacity — How much can I produce?
Scheduling — How am I going to do it?
Inventory — How much inventory is there and how can I reduce it?
Standards — What do I consider efficient production and quality output?
Control — Is the production process working?

An MBA's operations education is very rudimentary. The object is to turn out not engineers, but managers who understand the manufacturing and service-rendering process. Each of the five issues raised above can and should be studied in great detail to achieve the most efficient production methods; however, in the spirit of this book, I will present only the highlights of some popular theories to offer you the basics.

The Six M's of Capacity

To answer the question of how much you can produce, MBAs use six M's to guide them in manufacturing analysis. The M's focus on the areas that determine the limits of any production facility. Some schools teach only four M's, while others stretch the six into seven. In any case, M's are taught at all the Top Ten schools.

Methods — Have you chosen the best method of accomplishing the operational task? Are the machines placed in the most efficient factory floor configuration?

Materials — Are the materials you need available and of good quality? Do you have the capability to purchase efficiently, store, and distribute the materials when needed by the production process?

Manpower — Do you have well-trained and productive workers and managers to accomplish your production goals? Are your workers sufficiently trained to operate any new technology that you may acquire?

Machinery — Do you have the right tools for the job? Do your machines meet your needs: capabilities, speed, reliability, technology?

Money — Is the cash to fund production available as needed? Is the investment in factories, equipment, and inventories justified in light of the entire organization's priorities, capabilities, and other opportunities? Does the projected cash flow justify the investment? (a finance question)

Messages — Do you have a system for sharing accurate and timely information among all members of the production team — people and machines? A machine needs to electronically share information about output and quality on an assembly line with its operator, as well as with other machines.

Production methods are of three basic types:

Continuous Process
Assembly Line
Job Shop

The more *standardized* the product, the more likely that a repetitive, high-volume production method is best. Oil refineries, for instance, use a *continuous* production process. Refining equipment works twenty-four hours a day. The operational focus at the refinery is to keep the equipment functioning smoothly. The downside of this kind of operation is that it is not flexible. Changes in the system usually require costly shutdowns.

The old Henry Ford *assembly line* is a somewhat less continuous process. Auto production is broken down into separate tasks; each is performed repetitively in a series of work stations. The challenge is to coordinate the outputs of each task to maximize efficiency, and to minimize the need to hold a great deal of costly inventory. The assembly line method allows for some flexibility. Minor changes can be made to the process without a shutdown. Auto assembly lines can accommodate different combinations of optional equipment without interrupting the process.

The assembly line system can also be used to perform services. An enterprising surgeon in the former Soviet Union who specialized in the removal of cataracts, broke the operation into its component tasks and created a surgical assembly line.

To produce customized products, the *job shop* system is often best. In a job shop, the factory is set up to do many different tasks. Machinery is organized in work centers to tackle unique production jobs. Metal machine shops, print shops, hospital operating rooms, and furniture makers are commonly organized in this way. Each order is somewhat different, but the same basic equipment or instruments may be used for each job.

Diagnosing Capacity Problems with Flow Diagrams. Most MBAs are sent to factories as consultants rather than as plant managers. Instead of a wrench, they usually carry a flat plastic *flow diagram* template. These templates are plastic stencils with rectangles, triangles, and diamonds cut out. They are used to represent the manufacturing process. By mapping out the process, MBAs hope to find bottlenecks, inefficiency, and information-sharing problems. A clear sign that you are in the presence of an MBA is when he or she refers to production flows as *throughputs*.

In my experience, changing my car's oil at the gas station takes approximately twenty minutes; at Jiffy Lube, it takes only ten minutes. A simple process flow diagram analysis tells why.

Jiffy Lube specializes in oil changes using an assembly line technique. The facility, the tools, and the workers are set up for only this task. Teams are used to complete the job as quickly as possible. Armed with your own template, you can act like a consultant too by diagramming any production process.

Linear Programming: Dealing with Capacity Constraints. Production is always faced with constraints. Materials may be scarce. Machines have production limits. Skilled labor is tough to find. The goal is to choose the best course of action within the prevailing constraints. What is considered best is the decision that will yield the largest

Corner Gas Station – I must leave my car, appointment necessary

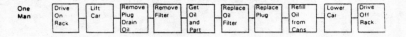

Jiffy Lube – I wait for my car, no appointment necessary

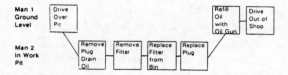

output, the most revenue, and greatest profits at the least cost. Because often there are dozens of production constraints, to try to find an optimal solution by trial and error can be nearly impossible. Mercifully, a computer technique exists to do the work. It's called *linear programming* (LP).

Consider the Tangerine Computer factory, which produces two types of computers: a Deluxe and a Standard. The Deluxe model requires a special chassis and two disk drives, whereas the Standard model requires one standard chassis and one disk drive. However, the parts supply is limited to 30 Deluxe chassis, 60 Standard chassis, and 120 disk drives. If the profit on the Deluxe model is $500 and the profit on the Standard model is $300, how many of each unit should the factory produce? How do you sort it out?

The first step is to define the linear equation that will either maximize or minimize the desired results. In this case, Tangerine wants to maximize profits.

(X Deluxe Models × $500) + (Y Standard Models × $300)
= Total Profits

The constraints on production are the parts supplies:

Deluxe Chassis Use: (X units × 1) + (Y units × 0) < 60 units
Standard Chassis Use: (X units × 0) + (Y units × 1) < 50 units
Disk Drive Use: (X units × 2) = (Y units × 1) < 120 units

The computer program tries many combinations until it has determined the production level that maximizes profits. In this case the solution is:

(30 Deluxe Models × $500) + (60 Standard Models × $300)
= $33,000 Max. Profit

In most production settings there are many models that a company can choose to produce. There are also many production constraints. LP can determine the best plan.

Linear programming techniques can also be used to solve transportation and distribution problems. For example, McDonald's vendors have many warehouses, many franchisees, and a limited truck fleet. The goal is to find the cheapest way to ship the merchandise from a thousand or more possible warehouse/restaurant route combinations. Linear programming can do the job.

Scheduling

Henry Gantt and Gantt Chart Scheduling. In the late 1800s Henry Gantt postulated that standards should be set not only for the performance of tasks, but also for their scheduling sequence. "Mr. Scheduling" felt that optimal timing should be determined so that the sequence of production tasks could be efficiently planned, coordinated, and performed. If scheduling ran amok, bottlenecks would occur and inefficiency would poison the system.

The *Gantt chart*, Henry Gantt's contribution to efficiency, is a grid in which tasks required in a production cycle are listed along one axis and their time sequence along the other. With a Gantt chart the entire production process can be scheduled and critical tasks or bottlenecks can be identified readily. Gantt charts can be used in a variety of settings; they are not restricted to a factory. In fact, a project such as buying a house can be depicted in a Gantt chart.

Critical Path Method of Scheduling (CPM). The 1950s brought us a more sophisticated way of determining optimal scheduling: the *critical path method* (CPM). CPM is used for complicated production projects that require the coordination of many tasks. An even more

Gannt Chart for Buying a House

Week	1	2	3	4	5	6	7	8	9	10
Select Realtor	X									
Qualify for Mortgage		X								
House Hunt	X	X	X	X						
Win Bid				X	X					
Obtain Appraisal & Inspections					X	X	X			
Obtain Mortgage					X	X	X	X		
Close on House									X	
Move In										X

complex form of CPM exists called *PERT*, Program Evaluation and Review Technique. However, today most businesspeople use PERT and CPM interchangeably.

Using CPM, production managers arrange each task or *activity* in sequential order and estimate the time needed to complete each one. Each time a task begins or is completed it is called an *event*. The CPM chart displays graphically all the events of a project. This enables a production engineer to estimate and manage the time to complete the job. Because all tasks are shown, the *critical* activities can be identified. The tasks that could potentially hold up a project are considered critical. The chart organizes and highlights the critical tasks, and it forecasts the time necessary to complete the entire project.

To illustrate, Kip Mustang, production engineer at General Dynamics, would like to produce a new switch for a fighter plane. The switch in question controls the ejection seat which pilots reported as sticking during Operation Desert Storm in 1991. Kip determined the five main activities involved in the project:

A: Design production machinery and prepare manufacturing drawings = 2 weeks

B: Prepare production facilities to receive new machines and parts = 4 weeks

C: Buy tooling and parts for production = 3 weeks

D: Stock parts and install production machinery = 1 week

E: Test new production line = 1 week

The CPM chart would look like this:

Ejection Seat Switch Project
Critical Path Chart

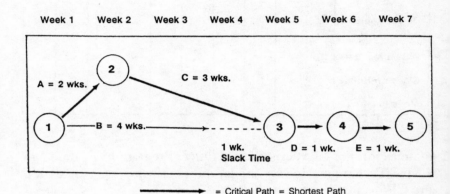

= Critical Path = Shortest Path

Each task at General Dynamics is represented by an arrow for the activity and a circle for each event. As shown in the diagram, the shortest path to set up the production line for the switch is seven weeks. These activities along the shortest path, called the *critical path*, determine and control the length of the project. When critical tasks can be accomplished faster, this is called *crashing the project*, because the project can be finished sooner. If designing the tooling could be sped up, that would crash the switch project. If any of the critical activities, such as designing the production tooling, is delayed, the project is delayed. Noncritical activities, such as preparing the facility, do not hold up the project. They have built-in *slack time*.

With large engineering, construction, and manufacturing projects, there are myriad tasks to keep track of. For these projects, computer software is available to help create the chart and do the timing calculations. The drawback to this wonder tool is the time needed to set up and manage the tedious CPM charts. "We all did them [CPM charts in the 1950s]," recalls Donald N. Frey, chief executive of Bell & Howell Co., "but it took so much effort to get the charts done, you might as well have spent the time getting the job done."

Queuing Theory to Schedule. Ever been stuck in line at a bank? Trapped on hold while trying to order something by phone? Then queuing theory is a topic that you might find interesting. A *queue* is any line that either people or products wait in before they are serviced. Each person servicing a person in a queue is called a *channel*. MBAs use queuing theory to schedule workers and to design waiting lines to save money and improve service. The question of efficiency lies in the optimal number of channels needed per queue. For instance, a bank manager would like to have few tellers and short lines.

To answer queuing questions, you must determine several things:

A = Average number of random arrivals per unit of time
S = Average number of services provided per channel per unit of time
M = Number of available channels

With those items of information and a series of tables, you can make several calculations:

Utilization factor of the system = A/MS
Average Number Waiting = Total Number in Line − (A/S)
Expected Waiting Time in Line = $\dfrac{\text{Average \# Waiting}}{A}$

Let's continue the banking example: consider a Citibank in lower Manhattan with one express teller that can process deposits at a rate of 50 per hour with an average customer arrival rate of 45 people per hour.

One Teller:
S = 50 customer per hour capacity per teller
A = 45 customers arriving per hour

$$A/MS = \frac{45}{1 \times 50}$$

$= 90\%$ utilization of one teller expected (very busy)

With that information and the abbreviated table below, the average number of people waiting in line should be 8.1.

A/MS	M = 1	M = 2
.45	.37	**.23**
.50	.5	.33
.60	.9	.67
.70	1.6	1.3
.8	3.2	2.9
.9	**8.1**	7.7

It would seem logical that by adding a second express teller, the average line would be cut from 8 to 4, wouldn't it?

Two Tellers:

$$A/MS = \frac{45}{2 \times 50} = .45$$

Expected Average Waiting Line
$= .23$ customers (from the table above)
No wait!

The waiting line would be reduced by over 97 percent by adding an extra teller. When the line is very busy, the second teller makes a *big* difference. Only queuing theory could tell you that. This teller problem is the simplest of examples. A whole "science" has been born around queuing. Academics have created books of tables and charts to answer many queuing dilemmas. Although you may not be an expert, you now know of the existence of queuing theory. That's how most MBA courses work. They teach you the fundamentals, but they expect that as an MBA, you'll seek out an expert to implement the program.

Inventory

The Balancing Act. The optimal inventory level is a delicate balancing act. Inventory decisions are tough because different departments of the same company have different goals. When it comes to automobiles, marketers prefer to have too much rather than too little inventory. Salespeople want product for their customers. They hate to lose a sale because they are out of the hot minivan or sports car. Finance people want to carry the least amount of inventory possible. A smaller inventory investment leaves them with more cash on hand for other investments or to pay higher dividends. Production departments like to run as efficiently as possible. Long runs reduce the waste of multiple starts and stops, but, of course, can also be responsible for significant inventory buildups.

Inventory Vocabulary. Inventory exists in one of three forms, be it in a factory or in a bakery:

Raw Materials — flour, sugar, shortening, ready-made icing, etc.
Work in Process — dough, pastry in the oven, pastry on cooling trays.
Finished Goods — cakes, cookies, and donuts ready for sale.

Inventory includes not only the investment in materials, but also the investment in labor. As long as inventory remains in a company's possession, money is being tied up. A simple and illustrative way of analyzing inventory levels is the *inventory flow diagram* on page 260. It shows the type and value of a factory's inventory. As a product is made, raw materials are combined with labor to create finished goods of higher value.

Reasons for Holding Inventory. There are five major and legitimate justifications for holding inventory:

Pipeline — Inventory on hand to minimize production delays and maximize efficiency.
Cycle — Suppliers have minimum order amounts that are greater than immediate need.
Safety — Stocks held to avoid a shortage because of uncertain production demands. Stockouts cost money when production is halted.

Inventory Flow Diagram

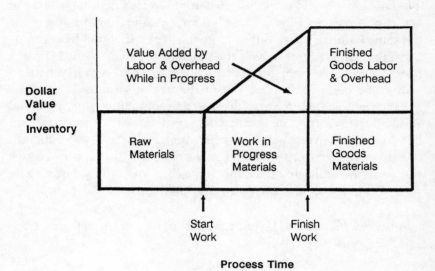

Anticipatory — Inventory held in anticipation of known demand.
Speculative — Items purchased to beat supplier price increases.

In efficient companies, materials arrive just in time for production. This is called *just-in-time* inventory (JIT). The Japanese are famous for this. Factory line workers request parts as needed with inventory order cards called *kanban*. However, JIT does not necessarily mean that parts suppliers produce at the exact rate of the automaker's assembly line needs. In reality the parts inventory sits in the warehouse of less powerful suppliers until it is called in by the auto manufacturers. True JIT has all manufacturing participants working in concert to meet production demands.

Economic Order Quantity (EOQ). Special EOQ formulas help MBAs to find just the right quantity of inventory to order to keep parts, raw materials, or shelf items to a minimum.

The Economic Order Quantity formula is based on the trade-off of two costs associated with inventory.

Carrying Costs — the costs associated with storage, insurance, and financing of inventory. The opportunity cost of using the company's funds elsewhere should be considered.

Ordering Costs — the costs of ordering that include all the accounting and clerical labor and materials associated with placing an order.

There are two extremes. A factory manager may choose to order huge quantities of parts infrequently, which reduces order costs, but maximizes carrying costs. Or he may order frequently to reduce carrying costs, maximizing ordering costs. The graph below shows that the least total cost is the inventory level when both ordering and carrying costs are minimized.

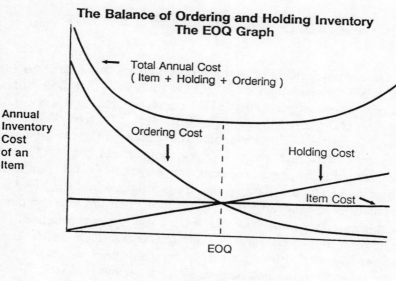

**The Balance of Ordering and Holding Inventory
The EOQ Graph**

Annual
Inventory
Cost
of an
Item

Total Annual Cost
(Item + Holding + Ordering)

Ordering Cost

Holding Cost

Item Cost

EOQ

Order Size (Q)

The EOQ formula tries to find that optimal point at which the total cost of both ordering and carrying is minimized.

The EOQ formula is:

$$\text{Economic Order Quantity } (Q^*) = \sqrt{\frac{(2 \times R \times O)}{C}}$$

Where:
Q* = Optimal inventory order quantity
R = Annual unit requirements (Demand)
O = Cost of placing an order
C = Cost of carrying a unit of inventory per period

Consider an auto parts distributor that supplies Kansas City with replacement lamp bulbs for car dome lights. Its sales history indicates that a level demand of 2,000 bulbs throughout the year is most likely. Each time the distributor orders a shipment from General Electric it costs $14 to process the order. A detailed study of costs reveals that it costs $.50 to carry each bulb in inventory for a year.

$$\text{Economic Order Quantity} = \sqrt{\frac{(2 \times 2000 \times \$14)}{\$.50}} = 335 \text{ units}$$

The formula calculates the most economic inventory order as 335 bulbs. Since the demand is 2,000 bulbs, this means that there will be about 6 orders per year (2000/335). Sounds simple. But it is not. The simple EOQ formula only works if the demand is *level*. When demand fluctuates wildly throughout the year, as in the case of a grocery store's demand for bagged ice, egg nog, or beer, the EOQ model has little value. Sophisticated computer programs exist that perform a modified EOQ calculation more frequently to adjust the EOQ for fluctuating demand projections. In those situations the computer calculates varying optimal order sizes many times throughout the year. Even though the formula's application is limited, an MBA can talk intelligently with inventory experts if a problem arises. Because when inventory piles up unexpectedly, it is serious business.

Material Requirements Planning (MRP): Inventory and Capacity Management. The knowledge of production scheduling and inventory control makes state-of-the-art manufacturing possible. MRP is a method for planning and controlling inventories required in a factory. Some say that MRP means "manufacturing resource planning," but under any name, MRP is a sophisticated system to improve manufacturing efficiency. MRP schedules production and

"WE'RE STUCK WITH 700,000 BUSHELS OF CORN AND SOMEONE IS GOING TO HAVE TO EAT IT."

calculates the optimal amount of inventory needed for efficient production. With products that have many parts such as automobiles, appliances, and electronics, such a calculation can only be arrived at by using a computer.

To set up the system the computer programmer must be familiar with the production process and material requirements. Then the computer can translate customer product demand into detailed orders to guide factory production and material requisitions from vendors.

The MRP process begins when production engineers determine the most efficient production method. For autos like a Honda Civic, for example, the assembly line is the most efficient production method. The process investigation must include every step of assembly, from sanding the raw steel body to driving the Honda out of the factory. Time and motion studies, such as those Taylor conducted nearly a century ago, might be necessary. The capabilities of both machine and worker must be known to determine the capacity of the factory. For instance, production engineers know exactly how many front quarter panels can be stamped out per hour and how many man-hours are required to operate the press.

Process engineers also have to detail *all* the part and material requirements of a product. The requirements list is called a Bill of Materials (BOM). It is recorded in the computer so that production demands can be "exploded" into exact material needs. For each Honda Civic, the MRP system would know that it needed two headlamps, 46 two-inch screws, 4.2 quarts of paint, and hundreds of other parts. The inventories of the materials are also tracked by MRP. In that way MRP can direct the factory manager to keep adequate part inventories to feed the production line needs. At the same time, MRP minimizes inventory levels by telling inventory clerks to order economic order quantities.

A "complete" MRP system coordinates the manufacturing process from forecasting customer demand to the shipment of the finished product. The Master Production Schedule (MPS) within the computer sorts and stores all the information about demand, production, and materials and sends out orders to direct and coordinate the manufacturing process.

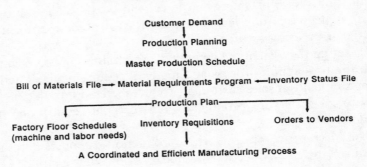

Material Requirement Planning System

Customer Demand
↓
Production Planning
↓
Master Production Schedule
↓
Bill of Materials File → Material Requirements Program ← Inventory Status File
↓
Production Plan
↓
Factory Floor Schedules   Inventory Requisitions   Orders to Vendors
(machine and labor needs)   ↓

A Coordinated and Efficient Manufacturing Process

STANDARDS AND CONTROL

All the information about the production process necessary to create an MRP system or to use the other MBA efficiency tools provides the basis for the standards that managers use to measure and control performance. An MBA buzzword for using standards is the term *benchmarking*. This is where accountants jump in to help the operational side of the business. The *managerial accounting* section of the Accounting chapter explained how accountants track and report production efficiency through the use of variances. The factory can vary by paying more than planned for materials (price variances) or using more materials or labor per unit produced (material and labor usage variance). By setting standards and seeing if they are met, production managers control the process.

Quality

Operations classes take the concept of standards a bit further and deal with the issue of "quality," an issue that is vital to America's competitiveness. What is quality, anyway? Quality only means that the product or service "meets the standards" set by either the manufacturer or the consumer. Quality does not necessarily mean a flawless product or service. Nor does it mean the most expensive product in its class like a Rolls-Royce. Quality products perform "as expected." Mundane things such as paper clips could be considered of high quality if they are not rusted and hold paper together well.

There are three important "quality gurus" whose prescriptions are touted as the cure for America's troubled manufacturing: Joseph Juran, W. Edwards Deming, and Philip Crosby. Each has made a fortune writing, lecturing, and consulting about quality.

Juran and Fitness for Use. Joseph Juran uses the phrase "fitness for use" when speaking about quality. "Consumers should be able to count on the product for what they need or want to do with it." Manufacturers should produce quality products while "achieving high yields and minimal downtime."

Fitness for use has five "dimensions": quality of design, conformance to manufacturing standards, lack of breakdowns, satisfactory performance, and the ease of maintenance of product after purchase.

Deming and Statistical Process Control. W. Edwards Deming is famous for having taught the Japanese about quality in the 1950s, when American industry showed little interest in the subject. Deming quite simply proposed that quality could be achieved by identifying the causes of production problems and by carefully monitoring production to stop errors before too many products were produced.

He divided problems into two categories, "common causes" and "special causes." Common causes are systemic problems, shared by many workers, machines, or product types. Special causes are those problems that relate to individual workers, machines, or material shipments.

Deming, with the help of Juran and W. A. Shewhart, developed a tool for identifying problems called *statistical process control* (SPC). "It is unlikely that two parts, even when produced by the same operator on the same machine, would ever be identical. The issue, therefore, was distinguishing acceptable variations from variations that could indicate problems." Statistical probability provides a method of making that distinction.

Production engineers make that distinction by studying the expected tolerance of each production task. For example, the filling machine at a Coca-Cola bottling plant does not pour exactly two liters into the two-liter jugs. The range of error is a few milliliters above or below two liters. Production engineers need to perform detailed studies to determine the usual amount of liquid squirted into each bottle. This exercise will result in a determination of the bell curve or statistical frequency distribution of filling quantities. If you remember the *Normal or Bell Curve* discussion in the QA chapter, the range of variation that occurs 68 percent of the time was called "one standard deviation" or "one sigma" from the expected quantity. Any production measure outside a "one sigma" tolerance quality standard would signal a production problem. If a production manager desires, he can choose two- or three-sigma tolerances. Three-sigma is very common in the United States.

In my Coca-Cola example, the production engineer selected a one-sigma tolerance and found that 68 percent of the time, the bottles measured in his sampling were filled within a range of ten milliliters above or below the desired two-liter level.

Using Deming's SPC, a filling machine operator could take hourly batches of ten 2-liter jugs off the assembly line. Using one-sigma tolerance, samples above 2 liters and 10 milliliters would be above the *upper control limit* (UCL). For those measuring below 2 liters, 990 milliliters would be below the *lower control limit* (LCL). Measurements outside the limits would signal a "special problem,"

Bell Curve of Cola Fill Quantities

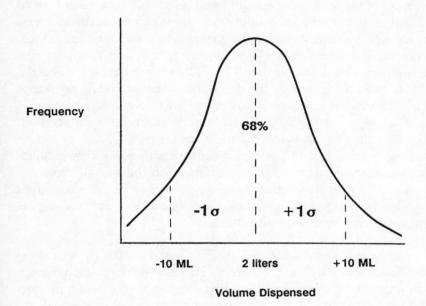

meaning a feeding line is crimped or clogged. The process would be considered "out of control," and the operator would be instructed to take corrective action. If after the correction the next samples are within the 10-milliliter tolerance, the process is "in control" and the machines are allowed to operate. (My Coca-Cola example of selecting the UCL and LCL was greatly simplified merely to expose you to the subject. The frequency and number taken in each sample by the operator greatly affects the statistical calculation of limits.)

Using SPC, the filling machine operator records his sample Coca-Cola measurements on SPC charts. On *X Bar Control Charts* the operator records the average (X Bar) of the sample measurement he takes every hour. The X Bar chart shows any tendency of the machine to drift or jump over time. If the chart is approaching a limit, the operator can investigate before the filling machine gets out of statistical control.

The *R (Range) Control Chart* reveals any tendency of the process to behave more or less randomly over time. It measures the range between the largest and smallest measurement in the same sampling used to create the X Bar charts. Within each group sample, the average of the sample measurements might mask unacceptable deviations. For example, a sample of a one-liter measurement and a three-liter measurement would average to two liters and appear acceptable on an X Bar chart. However, it is safe to expect that customers would be upset with half-filled bottles as well as bottles sticky from being grossly overfilled. In the case of being outside of an R chart's limit, the operator must also take corrective action.

The hypothetical SPC X Bar and R charts of a twelve-hour bottling shift on page 269 highlight problems.

The sudden change in X suggests that there is a mechanical problem or a new employee unfamiliar with the specifications.

The rise in R may signal that a machine may be deteriorating, a machine control may be vibrating and slipping out of specification, or a worker could be getting tired.

Crosby and "Quality Is Free." Philip Crosby's claim to fame is the proclamation that "quality is free." He believed that if manufacturers improved quality, "conforming to requirements," total production costs would fall. Crosby proposed that the ultimate goal of a quality program is zero defects. Management must make a concerted effort to alter both the design and the production method to improve quality. In his opinion, any costs incurred in improving quality would be paid for by the saving of materials and labor that were once expended in correcting defects.

HOT TOPICS

With the basics of capacity, scheduling, standards, and control behind you, this chapter would not be complete without mentioning some of the trendy stuff that keeps popping up in the business press.

Cycle Time

The time it takes for a company to convert a product idea into a new product or to improve an already existing product is called the

Statistical Process Control Charts
Coca Cola Bottling Plant
X Bar and R Charts

Sample Average Chart
X Bar

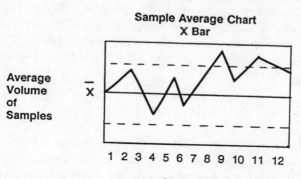

Average
Volume
of
Samples

$\overline{X}$

1 2 3 4 5 6 7 8 9 10 11 12

Shift Hours

The sudden change in X suggests that there is a mechanical problem or a new employee unfamiliar with the specifications.

Range of Sample Chart ·
R Chart

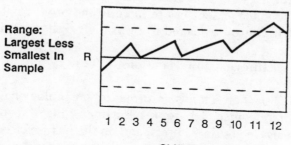

Range:
Largest Less
Smallest In
Sample

R

1 2 3 4 5 6 7 8 9 10 11 12

Shift Hours

The rise in R may signal that a machine may be deteriorating, a machine control may be vibrating and slipping out of specification, or a worker could be getting tired.

cycle time of introduction. In Detroit the design and retooling for a new automobile may take two or more years. The turnaround for a new fashion item is often six months from design to store delivery. The faster a company can turn out a new product to meet consumer demand, the better the corporation will compete in the marketplace. Accordingly, rapid cycle times are a competitive advantage and a hot MBA topic. Some trendy MBAs call the battle to act faster *time-based competition*.

New Technology and Integration

New technology in and of itself is not necessarily a good thing unless it can be used effectively. General Motors spent billions of dollars in the 1980s for robotics in order to automate its assembly lines. According to ABC's *Business World*, with this lavish spending, GM hoped to achieve both higher quality and lower costs. However, GM lacked the technical expertise to integrate the new technology effectively into its operations.

Using traditional low-tech tooling and American workers, Japanese auto companies have met high productivity and quality standards in their U.S. assembly plants, to the chagrin of Detroit. In Honda's case, the use of flexible work rules, production work teams, and participative management has resulted in the productivity and quality gains that Detroit expected from its high-tech investments.

Information Technology (IT)

At many of the Top Ten schools, information technology has been added as a separate course. The topic has gained a life of its own in academic journals, the business press, and on the lecture circuit. As computers have become more powerful, they have become a very valuable tool in the gathering and integration of useful information for competitive advantages.

Those companies that know the most about their customers' preferences have an advantage over their competitors. Sales registers linked to large computers can yield daily information on consumer demand and preferences. Department stores, such as Macy's and Wal-Mart, can track daily rack movement of their apparel to try to spot a hit dress, or to cut back on orders for a fashion dud. The supermarket checkout scanners serve the same purpose. With limited shelf space, grocers can cull slow-moving items and replace them with more promising ones to maximize every foot of the aisle. Using the information in computer data bases, direct mail pitches can be targeted to the most likely prospects.

MBA students are taught a lot of computer jargon so that they can be conversant in technospeak. MBAs hate to be out-jargoned. Here's a small lexicon sampling:

EDI — electronic data interchange, computers that talk
CAD/CAM — Computer-Aided Design/Computer-Aided Manufacturing
On-line/Real Time — computer system with continuous updating (airline reservation systems)
POS — Point of Sale systems, checkout registers
Hardware — computer equipment (IBM, Apple, Compaq)
Software — computer programs (Lotus, WordPerfect, Super Mario Bros.)
Applications — synonym for software
Mainframe — a big computer
Microcomputer — a desktop or portable computer
CPU — Central Processing Unit, a computer's brain
LAN — Local Area Network of many computers
AI — Artificial Intelligence, computers that think like people

Besides the vocabulary, it is important that MBAs become knowledgeable computer buyers. The same equipment that can create a competitive advantage can also become a disadvantage if the equipment or the programming cannot be changed to suit the company's needs. Therefore computers and other technology purchases should be made after considering the company's long-range strategy.

OPERATIONS WRAP-UP

In all operational situations a five-issue framework applies: capacity, scheduling, inventory, standards, and controls. With that framework, a little history, some vocabulary, 6 M's, and a few formulas, the top MBA schools thrust their students into the business world. Imagine yourself as a consultant reviewing the operations of Onoff, Inc., a switch supplier to IBM. Onoff has been running short of cash. Product defects have plagued the factory and costs have been rising. Based on the MBA knowledge culled from this chapter, you would start your investigation by asking a few questions:

What is the management style used in the plant? Theory X, Y, or Z?
Are the workers properly trained?
Is the production equipment adequate? efficient?
Are there material supplier problems? quality, delivery problems?
Is the production process efficiently configured? Consider a flow diagram.
Can linear programming help develop a more profitable product mix?
Could an MRP system be used to coordinate the entire production process?
Are Economic Order Quantities used for inventory ordering to minimize inventories and to free up cash?
Are there quality improvement programs in place? SPC, quality circles?
Are adequate standards being set, monitored, and followed up on a timely basis?

Those are the types of questions that run through an MBA's head. With this chapter in mind, you too are able to ask the right questions.

KEY OPERATIONS TAKEAWAYS

Frederick Taylor — Father of "scientific" production management (Theory X)

Elton Mayo — Father of the "human relations movement" of production management (Theory Y)

Operational Problem Solving — Capacity, Scheduling, Inventory, Standards, Control

6 M's of Capacity — Manpower, Machinery, Materials, Money, Methods, Messages

Flow Diagramming — Mapping out work flows to spot efficiency opportunities

Linear Programming — Computer method of determining the optimal solutions in situations with constrained capacity

Gantt Chart — A simple project scheduling tool

Critical Path Method (CPM) — Sophisticated scheduling method for projects

Queuing Theory — Mathematical tool to make waiting lines more efficient

Inventory Types by Stage of Production — Raw materials, work in process, finished goods

Inventory Types by Reason for Holding — Pipeline, Cycle, Safety, Anticipatory, Speculative

Economic Order Quantity (EOQ) — Mathematical formula to minimize inventory costs

Material Requirements Planning (MRP) — Sophisticated operational inventory and capacity management tool

Quality Gurus — Joseph Juran, W. Edwards Deming, and Philip Crosby

Statistical Process Control (SPC) — Statistical quality control technique

DAY 8

ECONOMICS

ECONOMICS TOPICS

Supply and Demand
Microeconomics
Opportunity Costs
Marginal Utility
Elasticity
Market Structures
Macroeconomics
Keynesian and Monetarist Theory
Gross National Product Accounting
International Economics

"Like kings of old dispensing with their astrologers, big business is sacking its economic soothsayers. Their stargazing proved entertaining and interesting – but not very useful."

"Dreary Days in the Dismal Science," *Forbes*, January 21, 1991

That may sound like a good excuse to play hooky on the day for economics, yet there is value in studying the subject. Economics cannot provide a clear picture, but it can supply some insights into the "invisible forces" that underlie the movement of business around the world. As in the case of all other MBA subjects, a

"I HAVE NO IDEA WHAT IT MEANS BUT I LOVE THE ACTION."

certain amount of familiarity with this subject provides the chance to impress people at the office with how smart we are!

Schools like Chicago and MIT place a great deal of emphasis on learning classical textbook economics, but most others treat economics a bit more on an applied basis. Harvard and Darden have integrated economics into their international studies courses.

Economics can boast about only a few basic concepts. So how does one explain the endless volumes of complex academic literature that try to explain the booms and busts of business cycles? Like the holy grail, the perfect economic model is an elusive target that seduces many zealous professors and thousands of Ph.D.s in private industry. In their wake over the past hundred years they have left thousands of magic formulas, graphs, and charts. An MBA should aim at understanding the fundamentals and the vocabulary of economics, and then move on and leave the windmill theories for theoretical Don Quixotes to chase after. With that in mind, this chapter sticks to the basics. It does not dwell on complicated formulas and difficult concepts that you would probably skip over, have no real use for, and forget in short order anyway.

Economics studies how society allocates the limited resources of the earth to the insatiable appetites of humans. Supply and demand are the forces at work. At what is referred to as *equilibrium* (E), the market price allows the quantity supplied to equal the quantity demanded. Suppliers are willing to sell, and consumers are willing to buy. Supply equals demand for a price. That, in a nutshell, is the basis of all economic theory.

For example, let's take a look at the local pub, Porth Tavern, which brews its own beer, Spud beer. Imagine you are a Heineken drinker and the bar is running a twenty-five-cent special on mugs of Spud. The owner has ten kegs on hand, but feels if he were to charge the usual dollar per mug, he might only be able to sell one or two kegs. You like Heineken, but at twenty-five cents, you decide to try the cheaper brew. Here, in this bar, the "invisible hand" of economics is at work. At the "right" price, there is a demand for the ten kegs. The graph shows that as the price per mug increases, the brewery would be willing to produce more, but people would be less willing to buy.

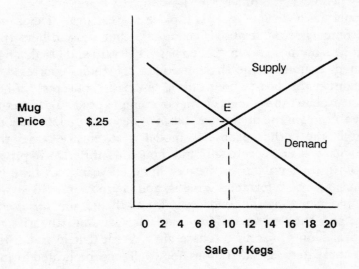

Supply and Demand For Beer

Generalizing from this simple relationship to an entire economy, aggregate supply (AS) equals aggregate demand (AD) at an equilibrium price and level of economic output. The graph is similar to the beer graph, the same relationship holds, but the elements measured constitute a much more serious MBA subject.

Supply and Demand For An Economy

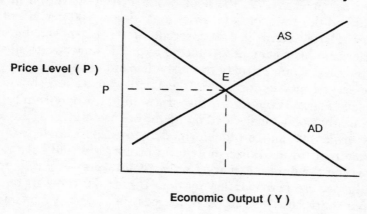

LEVEL OF ECONOMICS: MICRO OR MACRO?

Students can study either *microeconomics* or *macroeconomics*. Microeconomics deals with the supply and demand equation of individuals, families, companies, or industries. The Heineken versus Spud competition was an example of a microeconomic battle. Macroeconomics, on the other hand, concerns itself with the economies of cities, countries, or the world as shown in the second graph. Simply put, "micro" economics deals with "small," specific situations; "macro" economics looks at the "big" picture of entire economies.

MICROECONOMICS

Microeconomics is less glamorous than macroeconomics, but is a little more practical. Since most of us are not likely to have a macro-effect on a whole economy, it is better if we concentrate on the few basic concepts that make up microeconomic knowledge.

Opportunity Costs

Because our appetites for goods and services are insatiable, decisions have to be made to determine how to allocate limited resources. Most often, the increase in production of a good or service requires that a cost or sacrifice be incurred. Economists call these costs *opportunity costs*.

For example, in 1992 the demand for Harley-Davidson motorcycles had the company's factories operating at 100 percent of capacity. Harley controlled 60 percent of the big-ticket, big-bike market, and management was forced to decide how best to allocate limited production capacity to satisfy demand. They chose to produce several models for sale in the United States and abroad. As a result, Harley-Davidson incurred a significant opportunity cost because the company decided not to devote its entire capacity to its most expensive and profitable models for export to Japan. Had Harley tried to maximize short-term profits, it would have risked alienating the domestic market of devoted bikers — the very group that helped create the Harley mystique that the Japanese are buying. Opportunity cost, therefore, is the cost of choice, when output, time, and money are limited.

Marginal Revenue and Cost

A concept closely associated with opportunity cost is *marginal revenue and marginal cost*. Companies are motivated to maximize total profits by maximizing revenues and minimizing costs. If a business has the *opportunity* to sell even a single additional unit at a profit, it should produce it. The *marginal revenue (MR)* from the sale should exceed the *marginal cost (MC)* to produce.

Enterprises should continue to produce until their MR = MC. At that point of equilibrium the marginal profit on the next unit sold will equal zero. No profits are left on the table. Past that level, the marginal revenue of each additional unit sold decreases and the marginal cost increases. Experience tells us that the more units businesses try to push on the market, the less the market is willing to pay for these goods. The cost of producing one additional unit is minimal. But if there is no excess capacity and a company wants to produce more units, new workers will need to be hired, new

equipment purchased, and a larger factory leased or built. Therefore, once a factory reaches capacity, the marginal cost of producing
one additional unit increases beyond the cost of the last unit produced.

In the case of a cattle rancher, Bud Montana, the marginal cost
of adding a steer to the herd is minimal. Fences still have to be
mended and the pasture maintained. Since he is a *rational* decision
maker, Bud will add cattle to the point that the marginal revenue
from the sale of an additional steer will cover these marginal costs
of raising this steer (MR = MC). If the cost of raising one additional
unit becomes higher than the current market price, then Bud Montana will stop adding steers to his herd.

Marginal Revenue and Cost Equilibrium

Competitive Environment

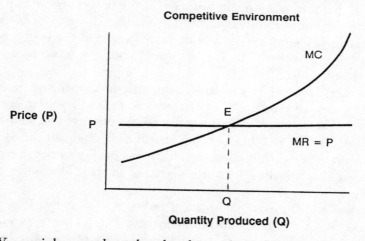

Quantity Produced (Q)

You might wonder why the demand curve is flat rather than
downward sloping, as in the case of other demand curves. It is
because the price of beef is determined in a competitive auction.
The few additional head of cattle that Bud might bring to the
market will not affect the price that is determined by the output of
thousands of ranchers and meat processors. If Bud had a corner on
the beef market, or a monopoly, then presumably he would always
produce and sell at the point where MR = MC. In that case, his
marginal revenue curve would slope downward to the right as in
the instance of the standard demand curve shown in the beer and
macroeconomic illustrations.

The marginal cost and revenue concepts would also hold true for a cookie factory manager faced with a large special order. Imagine yourself in his apron. The customer wants to pay $1.00 per dozen for 100 dozens to be sold at a church fair. You have some excess capacity and so you go to your accountant and ask what your cost is to satisfy this order. She asserts that it would cost $1.45 per dozen. She gives you this breakdown as proof:

Cookie Batter	$.80
Labor	.25
Factory Utilities	.20
Factory Upkeep	.20
Total Cost	$1.45

From that information you can see that the only *marginal* cost of running the automated cookie production line is the extra batter. The machine operator would be there anyway, and the large oven would be on anyhow. The factory would continue to require the usual maintenance.

The factory manager should welcome the order because he can make a marginal profit. The only reason to reject the order would be if word were to get out to regular customers that you sold the $2.00 cookies for $1.00. The rub is that if everyone paid the $1.00 special price per dozen, there would be no profits to pay for the fixed costs, such as the operator's salary and the cost of running the factory.

As shown in the example of steers and cookies, "marginal" costs and revenues are critical in making "marginal" pricing and production decisions. However, to evaluate profitability of an entire business, rather than one transaction, *total* revenue must exceed *total* costs to make a bottom-line company profit.

Marginal Utility

Utility is a term used to describe the value of a product to a consumer. *Marginal utility* (MU) means the usefulness or utility of having an additional unit of a product. At some point a buyer is fully satisfied, and an additional unit is of no value. Going back to the beer example, suppose you are looking to forget whatever troubles you have and you order one beer at Porth Tavern. A second beer would be welcome and in fact would be of great marginal utility. Five hours later you've had twelve beers, played pool, danced, and in the process forgotten your troubles. At this point, an extra beer would be of little value. The marginal utility of the thirteenth beer is negligible.

Price Elasticity of Demand

In the first illustration of supply and demand, Heineken drinkers were willing to buy Spud beer at a price. When the price was lowered, demand increased. Conversely, if the price had been higher, demand would have fallen. Buyers' responsiveness or *sensitivity* to changes in price is called *elasticity*.

Elasticity of demand happens to be one of the few economic theories that my MBA alumni friends have reportedly used. Brand managers at Procter & Gamble, for example, want to know how a price change will affect demand for their brand of soap. Production foremen at Ford Motor Company want to know how price changes will affect their production requirements.

If consumers are very sensitive to price changes, their demand is termed *elastic*. Consider the fast food junkies' buying habits at Taco Bell. In 1988, Taco Bell lowered its prices by introducing "value meals." Consumers responded strongly by increasing their purchases. With tacos priced at fifty-nine cents, only fifty-nine cents stood in the way of having a third or fourth helping. Competitors followed. Package deals at McDonald's gave permission to fence sitters to order the large fries, large Coke, and apple pie with their Big Macs at savings of twenty to fifty cents over ordering each item separately.

When consumers are not sensitive to prices, economists call their demand *inelastic*. Their purchasing behavior does not change with price changes. Necessities such as medical services or cigarettes fall into the inelastic category. When patients are in pain because of an appendicitis attack, they pay whatever the surgeon wants. Hard-core nicotine addicts accept cigarette price increases in the same way.

As you can see by now, the *price elasticity* of consumer demand for product is very important to consider when pricing a product. To quantify elasticity, a descriptive *elasticity coefficient* is used:

$$\text{Elasticity of Quantity Demanded} = \frac{\% \text{ Change in Quantity Demanded}}{\% \text{ Change in Price}}$$

OR

$$\text{Elasticity of Total Revenue} = \frac{\% \text{ Change in Total Revenue}}{\% \text{ Change in Price}}$$

The higher the elasticity coefficient, the higher the price elasticity. A coefficient equal to or greater than 1 is considered elastic. For example, researchers have calculated elasticities for restaurant meals at 2 and medical services at .31. Usually a great deal of research is necessary to determine elasticity, but of course the process may be simplified at the expense of accuracy. Managers must analyze historical data and also try to sort out the nonprice influences that may have caused a demand change, such as weather and competition.

Another important aspect of elasticity is that it is not constant at all price levels. At different price levels elasticity may vary. This phenomenon is illustrated in a hypothetical table showing how people responded to price changes of hamburger meat sold by a particular butcher.

Elasticity of Demand for Hamburger
(hypothetical)

Price per Pound	Total Pounds Demanded	Total Revenue		Elasticity of Quantity Demanded	Elasticity of Total Revenue
$5	1,000	$5,000			
+ 25%	− 50%		− 38%	2.00 E	.67 I
$4	2,000	$8,000			
+ 33%	− 50%		− 33%	1.50 E	1.00 E
$3	4,000	$12,000			
+ 50%	− 56%		− 33%	1.10 E	.67 I
$2	9,000	$18,000			
+100%	− 56%		+13%	.43 I	.13 I
$1	16,000	$16,000			

E = Elastic   I = Inelastic

If you were a butcher, this information would confirm what you might expect. At lower price levels, affordable to most families, changes in prices do not prompt the cook of the house to switch to other meats. However, when prices are higher in the $2 to $5 range per pound, hamburger loses its broad appeal. Shoppers demonstrate elastic demand by selecting hot dogs or even pasta instead of beef. Those with unlimited cash tend to be more price inelastic and buy regardless of the price. That is why the elasticity of "quantity demanded" differs from the elasticity of "total revenue." The die-hard beef eaters who are willing to buy at higher prices make up for the lost revenue of higher sales volumes.

The same concept of elasticity of demand can be applied to the supply side of the economy, but in the opposite direction. Higher prices encourage more production while simultaneously discouraging more consumption. Lower prices discourage production but encourage more consumption. At the point that the quantity supplied and the quantity demanded meet at a market price, the market reaches equilibrium.

Competitive Market Structures

In addition to elasticity of demand, the competitive environment drives supply, demand, and prices. The greater the competition in a given market, the more sensitive the market price is to changes in supply and demand. In the diamond trade, DeBeers of South Africa controls the supply of diamonds, thus prices remain high and relatively stable with predictable annual price increases. In the gold market, there are many suppliers worldwide and the price fluctuates daily on commodity exchanges. The same holds true in the beef market in which Bud Montana operates. Now that you understand the principle involved, let's look at the four basic *market structures*.

Pure Monopoly. If there is only one seller with a unique product, then the seller is said to have a *pure monopoly*. The National Basketball Association controls professional basketball. Electric utilities are another monopoly. They are "price makers" because they can set the price of stadium tickets and of your utilities. And when a pharmaceutical company holds an exclusive patent, as Burroughs Wellcome does for its AIDS drug AZT, it can charge thousands of dollars for treatments that cost very little to produce. Government regulation is usually the only restraint on greed. For a monopoly to exist there shouldn't be any close substitutes to which consumers can switch.

Oligopoly. When there are only a few suppliers for a product for which there are few substitutes, then what prevails is an *oligopoly*. With only a few competitors, prices can be maintained at high levels if the producers choose not to compete on price. If not, the market players can engage in price wars that can push prices down. Airlines are a good example of both of these conditions. Occasionally on busy routes price wars break out, but once it becomes clear that nobody can win, oligopolists return prices to higher levels.

Monopolistic Competition. In a market where there are many producers with products that can be differentiated, *monopolistic competition* can occur. Copy stores are known for this. The copies may be the same, but the service varies. Kinko's copy centers, for example, sell copies for seven cents each, while some economy shops charge only five cents a copy. Kinko's justifies the higher price by being open twenty-four hours, and offering competent and friendly service in clean stores. The lower-priced shops provide bare-bones service. But the existence of discounters places a lid on copy prices for the whole market. Kinko's would most likely experience a downturn if its prices were two or three times those of economy shops.

Pure Competition. In *pure competition* there are many competitors selling a similar, substitutable product. Marketing does not affect the price producers can get. Gold, silver, wheat, and corn are products that fit into this category. Many suppliers and buyers compete on commodity exchanges and the prices are determined by the market forces of supply and demand. The producers are "price takers" from the market that arrives at prices by competitive bidding.

In summary, when you are thinking about the specific market conditions of an industry, a company, or the buying behavior of individuals, microeconomic theory governs. Industries produce the quantity that meets demand at an equilibrium price based on the competitive market structure. Companies produce the quantity at which the marginal revenue of the last unit produced equals the marginal cost. Individuals purchase based on their elasticity of demand.

MACROECONOMICS

The reason MBAs study macroeconomics is to understand the forces that shape the larger economy in which their companies operate. Is a recession coming? Are interest rates heading up? Is inflation a threat? Those are legitimate questions that business owners need to ask and consider. Even though theories may not offer you the answers, knowing the fundamental principles of macroeconomics may provide the framework within which to make intelligent guesses about the future.

The Battle over How the Economy Works: Keynes vs. Friedman

Economists rarely agree on what *drives* the economy. Just as there are Democrats and Republicans in politics, there are Keynesians and Monetarists in economics. Keynesians hold that government intervention can significantly improve the operation of the economy. On the other hand, Monetarists believe that markets work best if left alone with minimal government interference.

The fathers of these opposing economic camps were profoundly influenced by the times in which they lived. John Maynard Keynes of Cambridge wrote *The General Theory of Employment, Interest and Money* (1936), the cornerstone of modern Keynesian macroeconomics, in the midst of the chaos of the worldwide Great Depression of the 1930s. Keynes saw the hands-off policies of world leaders as a failure and felt that judicious and timely government intervention could have a stabilizing and beneficial effect on the economy.

In the boom years following World War II, Milton Friedman of the University of Chicago became a forceful advocate of the Monetarist view of economics. He is the same person who asserts that a business's sole function is to make profits (see the Ethics chapter). Having witnessed the prosperity of the Eisenhower and Kennedy years, he believed in the power of the market to heal itself. Friedman was convinced that government ought to keep its hands off the economy. In areas as varied as income tax policy, agricultural subsidies, public housing, and others, he thought governmental regulation had done more harm than good.

The macroeconomic debate of good versus evil government occupies an inordinate amount of time at MBA schools. The mostly conservative Republican MBA majority frequently clashes with a small but vocal Democratic minority. Using the following chart as a guide, I feel confident you can argue both sides if you wish to, in true MBA form!

Keynesian Thought	Monetarist Thought
Free enterprise without government intervention does not cause full employment.	Free market economics are best in the long run even at the cost of unemployment.
Unemployment is the big problem that needs a solution.	Inflation is the big evil; it is a tax on everyone.
With government spending and monetary policy, government should smooth out the business cycles.	Government tinkering makes the economy worse off in the long run.
Adequate information is available to take government action.	Available economic data are usually inaccurate and too late for useful government intervention.
Government spending can help spur efficient economic growth.	Government spending crowds out efficient private activity.

This rather simplistic table covers the major theoretical macroeconomic arguments. When Sam Donaldson and George Will clash about the economy on Sunday morning TV, theirs may appear to be a liberal/conservative argument, but one must realize that their battle is rooted in Keynesian and Monetarist theories.

Gross National Product, Inflation, and the Keynesian View

The centerpiece of macroeconomics is understanding a nation's *gross national product* (GNP). GNP is the total market value of all *final* goods and services produced by an economy in a year. Changes in GNP are used as a measure of the health of an economy. The qualifier "final" is important. There is no double counting. An automobile, for example, is the sum of many components. Steel is counted in production only once, when the car is finished.

Because prices change from year to year, economists must adjust GNP for year-to-year comparisons. The cost of a pound of steel usually increases from year to year. If price levels rise it is called *inflation*. GNP adjusted for inflation is called *real GNP*. If left unadjusted, the so-called *nominal GNP* could show dollar growth, even if the economy produced the same amount of goods and services.

To convert the unadjusted nominal GNP to real GNP, economists use a *GNP deflator* index. Using 1982 as a base year, the GNP deflator index equaled 100 in 1982. In 1950 it equaled 24. To translate, in 1950 the price of goods and services was 24 percent of what it was in 1982. During recessions and depressions real GNP falls, and during booms, it grows.

For example, imagine that in 1992 you produced one pound of saltwater taffy worth $1 in your kitchen. Then the following year, you made an identical pound of candy, now worth $1.04 due to inflation. "Nominally," in "current" dollar terms in 1993, you produced 4 percent more value. But did you really? No. Your output was the same. Therefore, economists adjust nominal GNP numbers with a deflator to yield real GNP. With "real" figures analysts can measure and compare "real" growth in the economy.

In addition to a GNP deflator, there are two more measures of inflation that economists use to gauge inflation's impact on the economy. The *Consumer Price Index* (CPI) measures the price changes of a specifically defined basket of consumer goods and services that people buy most often. This shopping basket or collection of goods is kept constant from year to year. The *Producer Price Index* (PPI) measures price changes of a collection of raw materials used most often by producers. These indexes use 1967 as their base year (1967 = 100). In 1985 the CPI was 322 and the PPI 309. That means that prices in 1985 were more than three times what they were in 1967 for identical goods.

There are also two additional variations of GNP measures called *net national product* (NNP) and *gross domestic product* (GDP). NNP considers the cost of using up machinery, factories, and equipment in the process of production. In accounting, as I know you remember, they call that wasting of assets *depreciation*. NNP is GNP less the depreciation on the fixed assets used in the economy.

Gross domestic product is the part of GNP that is produced within a country's borders. It is an important statistic for economies heavily involved in trade. For example, Japan's GNP includes profits from Honda's assembly plants in the United States, but these profits would be excluded from its GDP.

The GNP Equation. The gross national product, in the Keynesian view, is composed of four types of spending that result in income for others. Each component can and should be influenced by the government's desire to maintain steady economic growth and low unemployment. When MBAs refer to the components of GNP they call them the *drivers* of GNP.

GNP = C + I + G + X where:
C is Personal Consumption
I is Private Investment
G is Government Purchases
X is Net of Exports over Imports

As illustrated by the equation, any increase in consumption, investment, or government spending will result in growth for the economy. Countries such as Japan and Taiwan use exports as their engines for growth. The United States, by contrast, drags its economy with a yearly trade deficit.

As mentioned previously, the Keynesians' main goal is full employment. A lowering in GNP is distressing since it means fewer jobs. If the economy is operating at a level below full employment, then there is what is called a *GNP gap*. If the government intervenes in the equation by increasing spending, the economy will be buoyed up and there will be a rise in employment to close the gap.

Playing the devil's advocate, a Monetarist would argue that the measures of the economy provided by government statistics are not accurate. Absent from GNP are the underground and unrecognized economies of crime, unreported earnings, and the output of mothers working at home. GNP also neglects to subtract the cost of environmental damage and add the value of leisure time produced.

The Multiplier Effect and Fiscal Policy. Keynesian theorists favor government spending to spur the economy because they believe in its positive impact. Spending by one person or by a government provides income to another individual or company. The way that such spending ripples through the economy in a repetitive cycle of spending and income is called the *multiplier effect*. How the Congress and the president decide to spend money is called the government's *fiscal policy*.

The Keynesians believe that a government's fiscal policy can "prime the pump" of a slow economy. In 1992 members of Congress raced to start public works projects to boost the economy during the recession. Road construction involves the purchase of rock, cement, steel, equipment, and labor, and the people involved in this work spend their wages and profits on food, housing, and clothes. This *multiplies* throughout the community the effect of the original government spending.

Let's see the multiplier at work for $1,000,000 of those construction salaries. The workers' impact on the economy is dependent on their *marginal propensity to consume* (MPC) or spend the money they earn. If construction workers spent 80 percent of what they earned and saved 20 percent, they are said to have an MPC of .8. The higher the MPC the greater the impact of their earnings on the economy. The effect on the economy would be calculated as follows:

$$\text{Spending Multiplier} = \frac{1}{(1 - \text{MPC})}$$
$$= \frac{1}{(1 - .8)}$$
$$= 5$$

The effect of $1 million of wages would result in $5 million ($1,000,000 × 5) of total spending in the economy. For members of Congress who win public works projects and defense contracts for their districts, their vote-buying power is also multiplied by five.

The IS/LM Curve of the Goods and Money Markets. According to Keynes, interest rates are also powerful driving forces in the economy. Higher interest rates tend to retard the investments (I) that drive economic growth. It is unlikely that consumers will buy expensive items, such as cars and houses, if high interest rates make monthly payments unaffordable. The downward-sloping curve explaining this relationship is called the *investment and spending curve* (IS).

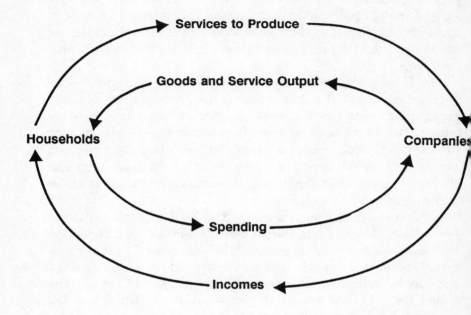

Acknowledging the power of money, Keynes noted that the higher the interest rates, the higher the *liquidity preference* for money. On December 19, 1980, interest rates reached an all-time-high of 21 percent, and people flocked to invest in money market funds. In 1992, when interest rates were hovering at 3 to 5 percent, investors rushed to shed their cash and ventured into the stock market. This relationship is illustrated by an upward-sloping curve called the *liquidity and money curve (LM)*. At some theoretical point there is an equilibrium point where the IS and LM curves meet at an equilibrium interest rate and a level of GNP.

The IS/LM curve is not fixed. It can change. If spending increases due to pump priming by the government during a recession, people will spend more in the aggregate. In this case, the entire IS curve will shift upward, resulting in higher interest rates and a higher GNP. If the money supply were also to be increased by the right proportion to accommodate the increase in spending, then interest rates could remain the same. That's in theory, of course.

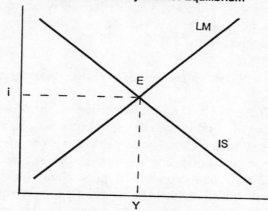

The IS / LM Curve
Goods and Money Market Equilibrium

Interest Rate (i)

Total Income, Output (Y)

Income = Output

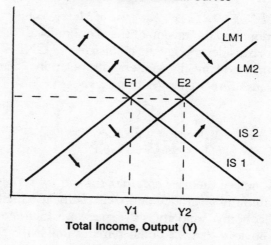

The IS / LM Curve
With a Shift in the IS and LM Curves

Interest Rate (i)

Total Income, Output (Y)

Income = Output

There is not a single interest rate for the whole economy, nor can an accurate picture of how consumer spending responds to interest rates be drawn. That's why this is economics. The IS/LM curve is not precise; it does, however, illustrate a relationship that makes logical sense.

Economic Growth and the Monetarist View

What Is Money? To begin a discussion on the Monetarists, you need to know what they are talking about when they speak of what is dearest to their hearts — *money*. Money is the medium of exchange to buy and sell goods and services. Sounds simple, but is money just cash? No. When economists speak about measuring the money supply they also include the so-called "money equivalents" such as checking account balances and money market funds.

The money supply is referred to as *M1* and *M2*. M1, the most accessible money, includes only cash, checking account balances, and nonbank traveler's checks. M2 includes M1's components plus savings and money market accounts. In 1992, M1 and M2 equaled $950 billion and $3,500 billion respectively. The government closely monitors M1 and M2 money supply to gauge the economy's demand for money, and hence, its health.

The Quantity Theory Equation of Money. Whereas Keynes addresses the monetary dimension of the economy with the LM curve, Monetarists consider money the main *driver* of GNP. The *Quantity Theory Equation* explains the Monetarists' position. Changes in money supply cause direct changes in *nominal GNP:*

$M \times V = P \times Q$
Money × Velocity = Price Level × Real GNP
Money Supply = Nominal GNP

Monetary theories consider the money supply as the product of the amount of money and the *velocity* at which it travels through the economy. Velocity is the speed at which money changes hands. It is obvious that if a dollar remains under the mattress, it has little value to the economy. Its velocity is 0. If that same dollar were to change hands many times — be spent by some and be income to others — the rate of economic growth would be increased. Nonetheless, Monetarists oddly believe that the velocity of money is constant.

The assumption of constant velocity is convenient if you look at the Quantity Theory Equation. Holding velocity constant makes the money supply the only determinant of growth in the economy. Keynesians find that proposition ludicrous. At different points in time, based on prevailing fear or euphoria, Keynesians believe there are changes in velocity. In a depression, for instance, people try to save whatever they can because they fear the next paycheck may be their last.

You might conclude from the equation that by setting the printing press on high speed, a government could send an economy into a high-growth gear. That may be true. The nominal GNP could be driven to new heights, but adjusted for inflation, the real GNP might remain the same or fall as a result.

Monetarists are most concerned about changes in price levels or inflation. If money is devalued by price increases, the real value of the economy's output is diminished. The trick is to have the wise men in Washington increase the money supply just the right amount so that there may be economic growth with little inflation.

Keynesians like a little inflation. That preference is supported by the research of A. W. Phillips of the London School of Economics, who claimed that higher inflation is accompanied by lower unemployment. The relationship between inflation and employment is shown by a graph called the *Phillips Curve*. Monetarists don't buy it. They believe that an economy with lower inflation can also have low rates of unemployment. Historical data in the United States show that the Keynesian relationship does hold. It was especially true in the period between 1950 and 1985, but it has not been consistently so over time, such as the period from 1985 to 1992.

Monetary Policy Tools. I mentioned that the supply of money can be manipulated. There is a group of seven men appointed by the president who sit on the Federal Reserve Board of Governors in Washington. The *Fed*, as it is called, has three monetary tools at its disposal to regulate the economy:

Change the discount rate

Banks borrow money from the Federal Reserve at a *discount* rate and loan it at higher rates to customers. If the discount rate is lowered, the margin between the banks' loan rate and their cost from the Fed is higher. In turn, that encourages banks to make more loans to businesses and to consumers for homes, cars, and credit cards. Banks charge their best customers their lowest loan rate, called the *prime rate*. More loans increase the money supply in the economy and the multiplier effect starts.

Trade government securities

The Fed actually trades in government securities in the financial markets. They buy and sell the government's own Treasury bonds. These trading transactions are called *open market operations*. When the Fed purchases government securities from the public it places more money in the hands of the public who sold them; the money supply increases. When investors buy government securities sold by the Fed, money is drained from their pool of cash; the money supply decreases.

Change the reserve requirement of financial institutions

The Federal Reserve requires that financial institutions, such as banks and brokers, keep a prescribed percentage of the cash deposited by customers on hand. This cash is called a *reserve*. A *reserve requirement* is needed for banks to conduct daily transactions and accommodate depositors who wish to withdraw their funds. A reserve provides a measure of security. The rest of the depositors' money is loaned to customers. When regulators require a higher level of reserves, banks cannot loan as much money; this reduces the money supply in the economy.

With these three tools, the Fed is able to change not only the money supply, but also the cost of money — interest rates. The Fed tries to gradually increase the supply of money as the economy grows. If this operation is performed correctly, inflation and interest rates can stay low and the economy can grow. If the money supply is kept too tight, a deep recession could occur, as it did in the early 1980s. If left to grow unrestrained, inflation can roar out of control, as has happened in many South American countries in the past two decades.

Which Side to Choose? If you are a conservative, you will gravitate to the Friedman camp. If you are politically liberal, Keynesian economics might be appealing since it calls for a more activist government. Regardless, the track record of both camps in keeping the economy on a steady course is not very impressive. We still have recessions in the United States.

Both monetary and spending theories play significant roles in the workings of economic systems. It is a chicken-and-egg dilemma. Who starts the process? Monetary policy determines the supply of money, which in turn affects spending and GNP. Or does the Keynesian spending "tail" wag the Monetarist "dog"? If you figure that one out, please write a book and set all the economists straight.

More Economists You Need to Know About

With Friedman and Keynes in your MBA grab bag, you need to know at least a little something about the following five economists. They are frequently mentioned as having shaped modern economics as we know it.

Adam Smith and The Wealth of Nations. Adam Smith is one of the world's earliest economists, but he is still much talked about. His book *The Wealth of Nations* (1776) described the "invisible hand" of competition as guiding an economic system based on self-interest. He saw the "wealth of nations" increase by the division of labor. Using the example of a pin factory, Smith described how productivity of a factory was enhanced when the different tasks were assigned to those workers with the appropriate skill. He observed cases in which ten people each performing a separate task turned out 48,000 pins a day in an era when individuals were still turning out but a very few pins.

Joseph Schumpeter and "Creative Destruction." This Harvard economist, long dead and forgotten, was resurrected in the 1980s.

Schumpeter has been exhumed because he saw the *entrepreneur* as the crucial figure in economic life. If you have picked up any business periodical lately, you will not have failed to notice the word "entrepreneur" or some derivation thereof used with as much frequency as an "a" and a "the."

Schumpeter considered capitalism "unruly and disconcerting, a system of flux rather than equilibrium." In *Capitalism, Socialism and Democracy* (1942) he wrote about capitalism as a process of "creative destruction." "Entrepreneurs create new industries that displace others in a painful and disquieting way." During the takeover and leveraged buyout craze of the 1980s, corporate raiders quoted Schumpeter to justify their actions and their profits as healthy activities that cleansed the capitalist system. For MBAs without the nerve to strike out on their own, theorists have created the term "intrapreneurs" as a consolation prize for those who are locked in corporations but still want to be agents of change.

John Kenneth Galbraith and a Liberal View. Galbraith, a Harvard economist, is known not for his grand theories or technical research, but for his broad policy statements. Although he is not considered a breakthrough thinker, his ability to give rousing lectures and market his books has given him a big name in economics. In 1951 Galbraith made a case for labor unions in *American Capitalism: The Concept of Countervailing Power*. In *The Affluent Society* (1958) he called for the economy to deemphasize production in favor of public services. In his 1967 *The New Industrial State*, Galbraith commented on the gradual move toward socialism in the United States. In any case, from time to time he takes a position and sells another book.

Arthur Okun and Okun's Law. Arthur Okun studied economic growth and unemployment just as A. W. Phillips did. Okun, from Yale, was one of the most influential economists on the President's Council of Economic Advisers during the Kennedy and Johnson administrations. He found that higher levels of economic growth are accompanied by lower unemployment. His historical studies indicated that for every 2.2 percentage points of real GNP growth, unemployment falls 1 point. That rule of thumb was extensively used to justify the stimulative policies pursued by Washington in the 1960s.

Arthur Laffer and the Supply-Side Economists of the 1980s. Arthur Laffer is one of the best-known supply-side economists to emerge in the 1980s. Supply-siders believe in the incentive effects of reduced taxation. Tax incentives and federal spending reductions are critical in promoting growth by causing increases in savings and investment. When individuals and businesses keep more of their earnings, they can save and invest in projects, which in turn makes the economy more productive. This increase in productivity increases the level of "supply" and produces more wealth and economic growth.

While at the University of Southern California, Laffer developed what has come to be known as the *Laffer Curve* to explain the incentive effects of tax rates. No, it's not a joke. The Laffer Curve motivated the Reagan administration and the Congress to cut taxes in 1981. His theory suggests that tax revenues are correlated to the tax rate. His curve shows that total tax revenues increase as tax rates increase, but past a certain point, increases in rates decrease total tax revenues. Higher rates encourage tax cheating. Higher tax rates discourage people from working more. If rates are too high, reducing the tax rate will encourage people to work by making it more profitable to do so. That in turn will increase gross tax receipts although the marginal tax on each dollar of income is smaller. The problem with the theory is that it is too abstract. There is, theoretically, an optimal tax rate, but nobody knows exactly what it is.

The Laffer Curve

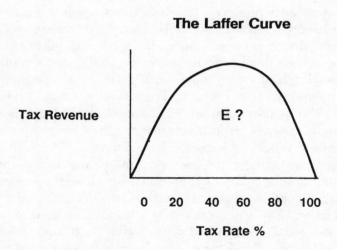

Other "radical" supply-side economists from the Reagan era who might creep into your economic conversations include George Gilder (*Wealth and Poverty*, 1981) and Jude Wanniski (*The Way the World Works*, 1978).

INTERNATIONAL MACROECONOMICS

Taking an even broader view, macroeconomics in the international arena is a favorite of business schools. With the globalization of the world's economy, international economics has become a very popular part of the MBA curriculum. The admissions departments of the top schools make special efforts to have just the "right" mix of foreign students in each entering class to add that international flavor to the classroom.

The Comparative Advantage of Nations

In 1917, David Ricardo outlined the principles of *comparative advantage* in his work *Principles of Policy, Economy and Taxation*. A comparative advantage of a nation is its ability to produce a product at a lower cost than its trading partners. Nations theoretically should maximize the production of goods that they produce most efficiently because of availability of land, labor, or good weather. Even if a country is able to produce a product at an absolute lower cost relative to another nation, that nation should maximize the output of products that it produces more efficiently than other nations. Ricardo proposed that Portugal export wine to England and import wool from England even though both products are produced at absolutely lower costs in Portugal. The rationale is that Portugal is more efficient at producing wine than wool and it has a limited productive capacity. Therefore its capacity is best utilized for wine, and thus wool should be imported from England.

In the U.S.–Japanese trading relationship, the United States should maximize its ability to produce food at a lower cost. America has plenty of good farmland, machinery, fertilizer, technical expertise, and labor. U.S. farm productivity is three times Japan's. Japan, on the other hand, is very good at producing electronics and automobiles. Theoretically, if these were the only two countries in the world, the U.S. should slash all electronics production and shift its emphasis to food production. The Japanese, conversely, should stop their inefficient food production. In reality, however, there are other national agendas and special interests at work which prompt nations to erect trade barriers. These prevent the efficiencies of comparative advantage to work. Trade barriers such as taxes on imports, import quotas, or other trading rules are governmental attempts to protect domestic industries and jobs. MBA schools consistently preach that tariffs and trade barriers are "bad," and free trade is preferred for long-term economic growth.

Balance of Payments

Just as companies keep track of their transactions with financial statements, entire nations keep track of their international transactions via *Balance of Payments* (BOP) accounting. The BOP registers the changes in a country's financial claims and obligations with all other countries. It is similar to an accountant's cash flow statement. Balance of Payments accounting shows changes in *foreign exchange* for a period of time. Foreign exchange is the balance of liquid assets such as cash and gold reserves that can be used to make international payments.

Sources of Foreign Exchange	*Uses of Foreign Exchange*
Merchandise Exports	Merchandise Imports
Travel Expenses of Foreigners Here	Travel of Citizens Abroad
Transportation Receipts of Domestic Carriers from Foreigners	Transportation Expenses by Residents Paid to Foreigners
Fees and Royalties Received	Fees and Royalties Paid Abroad
Foreign Investment Income	Interest and Dividends Paid Abroad
Government Foreign Aid Received	Government Foreign Aid Given
Private Transfers of Money into the Country	Private Transfers of Money Abroad
Increases in Foreign Liabilities	Increases in Foreign Assets

The sources and uses above show in broad terms the items that most frequently enter into a foreign exchange ledger. Excluded from the count are the international drug trade and other unreported activities. The press usually ignores the whole BOP picture and focuses only on the *merchandise trade deficit*. It is easier to say that the United States in 1991 ran a $67 billion merchandise trade deficit and make a case for gloom and doom. Journalists ignore that the U.S. ran $50 billion in surplus trading services, such as consulting and engineering, and a net surplus of investment income of $10 billion. That leaves only a net trade deficit of $7 billion in a $6 trillion economy.

Having enough foreign exchange is extremely important. The collapse of the currency in Lebanon in 1992 came as a result of insufficient foreign exchange in its central bank to make good on the purchases made by its citizens. When foreigners went to convert their Lebanese claims into dollars, marks, and yen, the central bank was emptied of its foreign exchange. Without convertibility everyone dumped their nearly worthless Lebanese pounds.

Exchange Rate and Purchase Price Parity

The *exchange rate* is the rate at which one country's currency is converted into another's. In May of 1992 one U.S. dollar could buy 130 Japanese yen, 1.6 German marks, or 55 percent of one British pound. In the early and mid-1980s the dollar was more valuable. Americans found real bargains when they traveled to Europe. In the early 1990s with a weaker U.S. dollar, traveling in Europe was very expensive for American citizens. What makes one country's currency worth more than another's? It's the old supply-and-demand relationship. International currency traders have to keep the following four factors in mind when trying to predict the gyrations of world currencies:

- **Trading Demands for Currency to Pay for Goods and Services**
  When the United States needs to buy French wine, importers sell U.S. dollars and buy French francs to make payment in French currency.
- **Demands for Currency for Attractive Investments**
  Higher relative interest rates in the United States prompt purchases of bonds by foreigners.

Higher U.S. relative rate of economic growth prompts purchases of stocks by foreigners.

- **Demands for a Safe Haven in Times of Uncertainty**

    In times of war or chaos, investors seek the currencies of stable governments. During the Gulf War in 1991, investors bought U.S. dollars believing that in an unstable climate, the United States would fare better than other countries.

- **Lower Inflation Relative to Other Countries**

    In 1987 the U.S. inflation rate was 3.6 percent versus Lebanese inflation at 723 percent, which reflected the chaos of their civil war. Lebanese investors naturally wanted to hold their investments in U.S. dollars because their pound's value was eroding quickly. The theory of *purchasing-power parity* describes the way that currencies' values adjust versus each other because of inflation. If one country's inflation is higher than another's, then its currency will be adjusted downward to compensate for the annual loss of value. During the Lebanese civil war in 1986 and 1987, their exchange rate went from 38 to 496 pounds to the dollar, a loss of 86 percent to compensate for the loss of inflation. In 1992 a dollar could buy 1,650 Lebanese pounds as a result of continued inflation.

Exchange rate movements are critical for companies involved in international trade. If exchange rates change between the time of signing a contract and its settlement, anticipated profits can be wiped out by currency fluctuations. Imagine if a farmer wanted to sell one U.S. dollar's worth of beef to Japan. At the 1992 exchange rate he would charge 130 yen, expecting a 5 percent profit. But when he got paid, he would have needed 150 yen to buy the same one dollar, because of the rate change. Although the yen payment would have remained constant at 130 yen, the currency fluctuation would have caused a 15 percent loss in U.S. dollar buying power. Companies and individuals use the futures and options markets to offset or *hedge* losses on this kind of currency transaction. This is not unlike the stock-option hedging described in the Finance chapter.

Country Analysis

B-schools teach students what to consider when trying to make predictions about a country's future. Since MBA schools aspire to turn out presidents of large multinational corporations, they must prepare these future captains of industry to evaluate investment opportunities abroad.

A *country analysis*, as developed at the Harvard Business School, is a four-step process that attempts to organize all available economic, social, political, and geographic data for close scrutiny.

1. **Analyze Past Performance**
    External Measures — Balance of Payments, Exchange Rates
    Internal Measures —
        General: GNP, Inflation, Employment
        Supply Side: Interest Rates, Investment, Capacity
        Demand Side: Consumption, Income Distribution
        Social Side: Human Migrations, Population Growth, Education
2. **Identify the Country's Strategy**
    Goals: Autonomy, Productivity, Equity
    Policies: Fiscal, Monetary, Trade, Social
3. **Analyze a Country's Context**
    Physical: Size, Population, Geography
    Political: Government Type, Stability, Corruption, Leaders
    Institutions: Government Agencies, Business, Labor, Religion, Agriculture
    Ideological: Role of Government, Family, Culture, Individualism
    International: Trade Advantages, Competitiveness
4. **Make a Prediction Based on Steps 1, 2, and 3.**

Let's take a country that is deep in debt and mired in political gridlock — as an example, the United States of America. Assume that you are in 1990 and that you are Franz Danninger, a Swiss banker at the Bank of Zurich. You are considering whether you should invest your clients' money in the United States as part of your global portfolio. What follows is — in a very broad sense — the type of analysis an MBA would do in order to make a decision.

1. Analyze the past performance of the United States
External Measures: In 1990 the U.S. trade deficit was reduced to $60 billion, down from a huge $150 billion in 1987. The U.S. dollar has shown small but consistent weakening versus the other major

currencies. Inflation has been kept steady at a low 2 to 5 percent over the past five years, with little indication of it heating up. In the same way unemployment has been kept low, between 5 and 6 percent a year.

Internal Measures: GNP increased a sluggish 1 percent in an economy of $5.4 trillion. The economy is the largest in the world, twice that of Japan, four times that of Germany, and seven times that of the United Kingdom.

Supply Side: Interest rates have been steadily falling with the prime lending rate at 8 percent to 9 percent. Because of the low level of inflation, that is considered high.

Demand Side: Personal consumption has shown small but steady growth of 6 percent in 1990. The distribution of income among the population is uneven. Minority populations are participating at a lesser percentage in the labor market than they had in the past.

Social Side: There has been no major exodus or influx of people. The birth rate is low and population growth is near zero, a sign of a prosperous industrialized nation. Public education is available to all children, but illiteracy is a problem with many students and adults.

From that collection of statistics, you conclude that the country's economy is sluggish. It has some problems, but not anything cataclysmic. With some history under your belt, the next step is to see where the American leaders want to take the nation.

2. Identify America's strategy

Goals: The United States is known for its leadership in world affairs. After the recession of 1981 and 1982, politicians and businesspeople focused on making the nation's industrial base more productive. Factory productivity has increased 3.1 percent a year since 1983 as the result of automation, new management practices, and layoffs. The Washington leadership has not made economic equity a priority. Leaders talk about "trickle down" economics; this theory suggests that if the economy is doing well, everyone will eventually participate.

Policies: The spending policies of the legislature and the executive branch continue to show little fiscal restraint in 1990. The budget deficit remains at a high $220 billion. A steady decade of overspending has added a worrisome two trillion dollars of additional debt. In 1990 fourteen cents of every federal dollar went to pay interest on that debt in 1990. Monetary policy, controlled by an independent Federal Reserve, shows great restraint by keeping a lid on the money supply, keeping inflation low but interest rates high. Because the nation considers itself a free-trading nation, the federal government does not follow a formal trade policy. Issues are dealt with on a case-by-case basis.

3. Analyze the context of the United States

Physical: The United States is one of the largest nations in the world. It is rich in natural resources, but it needs to import oil and other metals.

Political: The U.S. government is considered the world's most stable constitutional democracy. It is a federal republic with power shared between the central government and the fifty state governments. Corruption does exist, but a vigilant press keeps it to a minimum.

Institutions: The United States is an advanced industrialized nation. The infrastructure of governmental agencies, business, labor, religion, and agriculture exist and operate like most developed bureaucracies.

Ideological: The United States views the government as a servant of the people. Its constitution gives individuals an explicit Bill of Rights which the government cannot abridge. The culture of the United States is a reflection of its immigrant past and its capitalist economics. It is very diverse. A common thread of deep respect for material wealth pervades this society.

International: Being the largest consumer market in the world, the United States plays a dominant role in world trade. With a stable dollar and low inflation it continues to be a strong economy.

4. Make a prediction and an investment decision

As Franz Danninger, your analysis and prediction might be as follows: Like Switzerland, the United States is a stable industrialized country that is experiencing a sluggish patch of growth in its business cycle. I, Franz Danninger, suggest that we at the Bank of Zurich maintain our exposure to the U.S. economy. Investments should be maintained in the U.S. stock and bond markets. I do not see any better safe haven for our clients' funds. I do believe, however, that in 1990 the United States will enter into a recession for a period of two years and will experience a very slow recovery.

Isn't that MBA prediction impressive with hindsight?

If Franz were to make several forecasts of the future, MBAs would call that *scenario analysis*. The same facts supporting a recessionary prediction could also support a scenario of an economic boom or bust in the United States. An astute manager should make contingency plans in the event that one of these alternative scenarios begins to develop.

Country analysis is a multipurpose tool that provides a way to sort out all the reams of economic data that are available on a nation. As a new MBA you now have the framework that global strategists use in the boardrooms of multinational corporations and that economic analysis departments of the world's most prestigious investment firms employ.

ECONOMICS IN REVIEW

As this chapter has shown, microeconomics and macroeconomics are not that complicated if you wish to know only the MBA basics.

Microeconomics: Supply equals demand at an equilibrium price. Consumers try to minimize opportunity costs and maximize marginal profits and utility. If they respond to price changes, economists call their behavior elastic.

Macroeconomics: Keynesians like government and consumer spending. Friedman and his Monetarist friends place their faith in the control of the money supply. It looks like both camps have valid points to make but neither has a corner on explaining how economies work. In any case, supply equals demand at an equilibrium price. That much they agree on.

Global Macroeconomics: The economies of the world keep track of their activity using Balance of Payments accounting. If they are doing a good job, inflation stays low, economic growth remains steady, foreign reserves stay high, and the local currency maintains its value. If not, a country may end up in an economic quagmire like Lebanon. If you want to be a crystal ball reader and want to predict where your favorite nation is headed, use the country analysis framework to make a prediction.

KEY ECONOMICS TAKEAWAYS

Microeconomics — The study of individual, family, company, and industry economic behavior

Macroeconomics — The study of the behavior of entire economies

Equilibrium — The point at which the quantity supplied equals the quantity demanded and a mutually agreeable price is determined

Marginal Revenue and Cost — The added revenue and cost of producing and selling one additional unit

Elasticity — The change in buyers' demand as a result of price changes

Market Structures — The competitive environment in an industry determined by the number of sellers and the product's characteristics

Keynesian Theory — Spending and consumption are the main drivers of an economy.

Monetarist Theory — The size and growth of the money supply determines the growth of the economy. Money makes the world go around.

Gross National Product — The total amount of final goods and services produced by an economy over a period of time

The Spending Multiplier — The economic ripple effect of money being circulated in an economy: Spending for one person is income for another.

Fiscal Policy — A government's spending policy

Monetary Policy — A government's policy of controlling the supply of money and interest rates

Adam Smith — The economist who wrote about the "invisible hand" of capitalism in *The Wealth of Nations* in 1776

Arthur Laffer — 1980s economist who developed the Laffer Curve, which illustrated that lower tax rates would result in higher tax revenues

Balance of Payments — The accounting for the inflows and outflows of foreign exchange of a country

Country Analysis — A systematic framework to organize economic data and make predictions about the future prospects of a nation

DAY 9

STRATEGY

STRATEGY TOPICS

The Seven S Model
The Value Chain
Integration and Expansion Strategies
Industry Analysis
Competitive Strategies
Signaling
Portfolio Strategies
Globalization
Synergy
Incrementalism

Strategy is the most exciting course in the MBA curriculum because it gives you the chance to put all your new skills to work. Most professors insist that strategy be taught after completing most of the core courses, because it requires a background in all the MBA disciplines. Strategy classes place students in the chairman of the board's chair, and MBAs love that feeling. As my strategy professor told us, exposure to strategy concepts alters the way you look at businesses. Strategic thinking involves a comprehensive analysis of a business in relation to its industry, its competitors, and the business environment in both the short- and the long-term. Ultimately, strategy is a company's plan to achieve its goals.

Corporate managements often do not know clearly what they want or how they'll get there. When this is the situation, a boardroom discussion could resemble a scene from Lewis Carroll's *Alice's Adventures in Wonderland*:

ALICE: Would you tell me, please, which way ought I to go from here?
CHESHIRE CAT: That depends a good deal on where you want to get to.
ALICE: I don't much care where —.
CHESHIRE CAT: Then it doesn't matter which way you go.

Corporations need well thought-out strategic plans or inevitably they will become victims of the marketplace instead of being the victors who shape it.

STRATEGY AS PART OF AN ORGANIZATION: THE SEVEN S MODEL

Strategic plans cannot be formed in a vacuum; they must *fit* organizations, just as marketing plans must be suited to products. Two separate stages characterize strategic planning: *formation* and *implementation*. Strategists should always devise their plans with an eye toward implementation. Thomas J. Peters, of *In Search of Excellence* fame, created the *Seven S model* showing that strategy ought to be interwoven within the fabric of an organization. Actually Peters created the model with Robert H. Waterman and Julien R. Phillips, but Peters, an exceptional speaker, is usually given most of the credit. Their model provides a structure with which to consider a company as a whole, so that the organization's problems may be diagnosed and a strategy may be developed and implemented. If a strategy requires radical reorganization it's called *reengineering*. If not, it is described as "organizational tinkering." The Seven S's are:

- **Structure**
- **Systems**
- **Skills**
- **Style**
- **Staff**

- **Superordinate Goals/Shared Values**
- **Strategy**

The Seven S Model

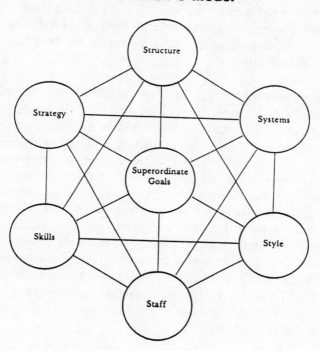

Reprinted from *Business Horizons*, June 1980. © 1980 by the Foundation for the School of Business at Indiana University. Used with permission.

The diagram illustrates the "multiplicity" and "interconnectedness" of elements that influence an organization's ability to change. The other notable feature in the diagram is that there is "no starting point or implied hierarchy." In any one organization, different factors may drive the business. In an "excellent" organization, each of the S's complements the others and consistently advances the company's goal. This is not any different from a marketing plan which should be *internally consistent* and *mutually supportive*, as explained in the first chapter. The Seven S model is a helpful tool to organize one's thoughts in order to define and effectively attack complicated problems.

If you recall the *basic organizational model* outlined in the Organizational Behavior chapter, the Seven S's should look familiar. Strategy theorists borrow ideas and concepts from other MBA disciplines and integrate them. Here the same S's appear but with some additions and deletions.

Structure. A corporation's *structure* affects its strategic planning and its ability to change. As explained in the OB chapter, a company's structure may have a customer or a geographic focus. For instance, if a company decides to alter its strategy to become more responsive to its customers, it may need to adopt a *customer* structure, which will channel all the skills of a company to meet customers' specific needs. In the case of a power tool manufacturer, the competition may demand a change from a *functional form,* which separates manufacturing, sales, and finance, to an organization with two customer divisions. One division would serve household consumers and the other industrial customers. These market segments have different needs which could most effectively be serviced by two focused divisions. In special situations, a temporary structure such as a matrix could be overlaid to form project teams skilled in developing new products.

Strategy refers to those *actions* that a company plans in response to or in anticipation of changes in its external environment, its customers, and its competitors. The spectrum of strategies a company can use is the focus of this chapter.

Style sounds like a new addition to the *basic organizational model,* but this S is more closely related to *culture.* Culture or style is the aggregate of behaviors, thoughts, beliefs, and symbols that is conveyed to people throughout an organization over time. Since it is very hard to change a company's ingrained culture, it is important to bear it in mind when developing a new strategy. If a consumer products company has a conservative bent, it will need to be convinced, beyond a shadow of a doubt, of the efficacy or viability of a new product. Historically, Procter & Gamble was in the slow-to-innovate category, but lately their behavior has been changing. P&G had test-marketed Bounce fabric softener for years before introducing it across the country. By contrast it rolled out Duncan Hines frosting nationwide after only fifteen months of development.

Staff. With no warm bodies, there's no company. By *staff* Peters means the human resource *systems*, which include appraisals, training, wages, and the intangibles, such as employee motivation, morale, and attitude. With a motivated work force, companies are able to adapt and compete. Top management often ignores this S because they feel that it is not very significant on one hand and too "touchy feelie" on the other. "Let the human resources department deal with it" is the common attitude. This soft factor is essential, however, because without employee cooperation a company will not have the ability to succeed.

Skills. Closely related to staff are the distinctive abilities and talents that a company possesses. *Skills* may range from the ability of a staff to speak Spanish, to an understanding of statistics, to computer literacy, for instance. Certain companies are strong in particular areas. Du Pont and 3M are known for their superb research and development capabilities. IBM's and General Electric's strengths lie in their ability to provide superior service support for their products. ITT, a large conglomerate, is renowned for its ability to exert tight financial controls over its subsidiaries. International companies need people with language skills and in-depth knowledge of other cultures and customs. American Express for one acquires these skills by hiring knowledgeable nationals in the markets in which it competes.

Systems. The procedures, both formal and informal, by which an organization operates and gathers information constitute the *systems* of a company. As I mentioned, Peters considers the systems relating to personnel part of *staff.* With this S, Peters is concerned with the systems that allocate and control money and materials as well as gather information.

When a company confronts a major challenge in the marketplace, management must have detailed data about its operations, customers, and competition to determine the gravity of the situation. Managerial accounting systems provide operational data about production and costs. Marketing research and sales tracking systems give information about the customers. Competitive intelligence systems provide insight as to what other companies are up to.

Superordinate Goals. This last S is at the core of an organization. According to Peters, "The word *superordinate* literally means *of higher order." Superordinate goals* are the guiding concepts — values and aspirations, often unwritten — that go beyond the conventional statements of corporate objectives. "Superordinate goals are the fundamental ideas around which a business is built." For example, Peters wrote in 1980 that Hewlett-Packard's superordinate goal was to have "innovative people at all levels in the organization." 3M's superordinate goal was to produce "new products," while IBM's was "customer service."

Mission statements are often mentioned when companies speak about their goals. A mission statement should be a short and concise statement of goals and priorities. Unfortunately they are often long, bland, and tedious documents. When senior executives return from expensive executive programs from one of the Top Ten schools, frequently they form a mission statement task force or hire a consultant for this purpose. This exercise has a large element of "keeping up with the Joneses." If a company incorporates a mission statement in its annual report, then all of its competitors go off to cook up theirs. Chrysler's and Campbell's (soup) annual reports can boast of very well-written mission statements:

> "Chrysler's primary goal is to achieve consumer satisfaction. We do it through engineering excellence, innovative products, high quality and superior service. And we do it as a team." (1988)

> "All of Campbell's activities begin with our focus on consumers. Our goals are to maximize profitability and shareholder value by marketing consumer food products that lead in quality and value; and to build and defend the first or second position in every category in which we compete." (1989)

Their goals are clear. Chrysler focused on consumer satisfaction, while Campbell's main goal was to satisfy its shareholders. The wording of the mission statement is often crafted to address the most important constituency at the time. In Chrysler's case, the company was doing well, and its price per share was high. Chrysler focused on making even more sales. Controlled by the Dorrance family, Campbell's wrote its statement at a time when the company was said to be managed for the sole benefit of the family, and not for the public shareholders. Campbell's share price lagged behind the gains of other food companies. Consequently, Campbell's sought to placate Wall Street in its mission statement by mentioning "shareholder value." Apart from the politics involved in its creation, a mission statement can be a useful surrogate for a firm's superordinate goal, if they don't have one.

A Seven S Model Example

When all of a company's S's move in concert, it can be a formidable competitor. The early success of Apple Computer can be said to have been derived from the balance of its S's. It had an entrepreneurial *style* fostered by its founders that attracted the brightest and most creative *staff*. With their cutting-edge technological *skills*, the founders organized Apple in a loose corporate matrix *structure* that fit the personalities of the people and the task of creating new products. Apple developed reinforcing *systems* to reward innovation and to track operations. Their rewards supported Apple's shared values of teamwork and fun to achieve its *superordinate goal* — placing the best user-friendly computer in every household. Apple's *strategy* was to create a proprietary, user-friendly system for the home, school, and graphics markets. All the S's fit together well and were mutually supportive of its goals.

Do your own MBA analysis of your favorite organization. List the Seven S's on a sheet of paper and dig in. A strategic consultant with an MBA would do exactly the same thing you can now do with the Seven S model. But a consulting firm would accompany the study with fancy computer graphics, put it in a binder, and charge your company a small fortune.

THE VALUE CHAIN AND INTEGRATION

When an MBA begins the strategic analysis of any company, one of the very first questions should be "What business is it in?" The value chain and integration concepts help to answer that question.

Value Chain

After the basic question has been answered, the next step for a strategic analyst is to assess the *value* a company adds to its products. The apparel industry's value chain looks like this:

Forestry ◄—*Backward Integration*◄—**International Paper**—►*Forward Integration*—► Consumer Paper

At each link in the chain, a *channel participant* adds value to the product as it makes its way to the consumer. First, the raw materials must be produced, harvested, or mined. These factors of production — wool, cotton, and chemicals — are combined to manufacture clothing. Once it is produced, marketers must promote, distributors transport, and retailers sell the clothing to the consumer.

Integration

Forward and Backward Integration. A company can perform at any link in the value chain. When a company operates in areas further down the value chain, it is said to be *forwardly integrated* toward the consumer. For example, if an orchard owner grew and sold his fruit to the public, he would be considered forwardly integrated toward the buyer. The grower could decide to sell at a lower price than the grocery store or to sell at the grocery's price and make the additional profit.

If a business operates in areas closer to the raw materials, then the company is said to be *backwardly integrated*. International Paper, which owns its own forests and paper manufacturing facilities, would be classified as being backwardly integrated.

You can see a company as either forwardly or backwardly integrated depending on the point in the value chain at which you view that company. If you consider the orchard owner primarily as a grower, then you might view his business as forwardly integrated toward the retailing end of the chain. If you believed that his main business was retailing fruit to the public, then you could say that his business is backwardly integrated because he grows what he sells. International Paper is backwardly integrated to its timberland operations and forwardly integrated to its consumer paper product manufacturing and distribution activities.

Wool/Cotton
Chemicals→ Fiber→ Yarn→ Cloth→ Clothing→ Distribution→ Retailing→ Consumer

Vertical and Horizontal Integration. Industries can also be viewed *vertically and horizontally. Vertically integrated* is a term used for companies that participate at many levels of the value chain in an industry. International Paper is vertically integrated because it owns both the trees and the paper mills. The term can describe both *forwardly* and *backwardly integrated* companies. The key is that several value-adding functions are being performed by one firm.

When Chrysler Corporation purchased American Motors/Jeep (AMC) in 1987, it acquired a competitor at the same level in the value chain. This is called *horizontal integration.* Lee Iacocca, the president of Chrysler, chose not to move to another value-adding activity. Instead Chrysler moved sideways or horizontally. If Chrysler had bought USX (formerly U.S. Steel), it would be vertically integrated. In this hypothetical case, a new value function would have been added to Chrysler's manufacturing operations in the automobile industry.

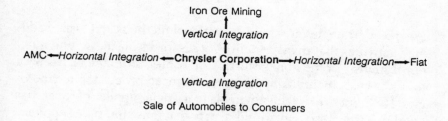

Strategic analysts review industries' value chains to identify current and future sources of competition. When chemical companies sought higher profits, they forwardly integrated into higher "value added" products such as fibers for cloth and carpet. With the likes of Du Pont, the fiber link of the chain became more competitive. Similarly, The Limited integrated the manufacturing, distribution, and retailing links in the value chain, unleashing even more competitive activity in the already cutthroat apparel industry.

Integration strategies may result in obvious benefits such as secured inputs and lower costs, but the disadvantages include a higher exposure to the downturns in a single industry. All of the corporation's eggs are in one basket. In lean times, an Exxon refinery can't squeeze concessions from its oil suppliers if the supplier is Exxon. In the same way, General Motors can't dump excess engine inventories on its customers, if the only user is the company itself.

LEVELS OF STRATEGY

Strategy is a very broad term. It commonly describes any thinking that looks at the "big picture." In fact, it is more complex. There are three levels of strategy to be considered:

Functional Strategy — The value activities engaged in
Business Strategy — How to fight the competition, tactics
Corporate Strategy — What businesses should I be in?

When putting on the strategy hat, you must ask yourself, At what level do I wish to think? Functional, Business, or Corporate?

Functional Strategy

Functional strategies are those operational methods and "value adding" activities that management chooses for its business. The functional strategy of the Philip Morris Companies, for example, has been to lower costs by utilizing the most advanced processing technologies. If Philip Morris felt vulnerable to a single supplier of tobacco, a good functional strategy would dictate that it use multiple suppliers.

Business Strategy

Business strategies are those battle plans used to fight the competition in the industry that a company *currently* participates in. They are on a higher level than functional strategies, but there is obviously an overlap between how a company operates and how it competes. Philip Morris's *business* strategy has been to beat its competition by crowding store shelves with many different brands and by spending heavily on advertising to promote its brands. Using these strategies, the large tobacco companies preserve market share and prevent new competitors from gaining a foothold in their industry.

Corporate Strategy

Corporate strategy looks at the whole gamut of business opportunities. Philip Morris's *corporate* strategy has led the company to diversify away from tobacco products and toward consumer goods. Philip Morris's executives reviewed the tobacco industry's growth potential, the legal environment, and the increased health awareness among consumers and concluded that it was wise to be in more "healthful" businesses. Its purchases of General Foods, Kraft, and Miller Brewing were made with that corporate strategy in mind. Using the same strategy, R. J. Reynolds acquired Nabisco.

EXPANSION STRATEGIES

Academics love to create diagrams to show off their theories and to make them easier to use. One of the simplest of the strategic diagrams is the *Ansoff Matrix*. H. I. Ansoff created it in 1957 as a clear way to classify routes for business expansion. What determines the strategy classification is the newness of the product to the company and the firm's experience with the intended market. The "newness" of the product or market is determined by how "new" it is to the company contemplating the strategy, not by the age of the product or market itself.

The power of the matrix lies in the fact that it can be used for any industry. Ansoff created a vocabulary to communicate a strategic direction in few words. If Hershey Foods Corporation wanted to sell more chocolate bars in the United States, that would be a *penetration* strategy (existing product, existing market). If they intended to sell chocolate in Eastern Europe, that's an *expansion* strategy (existing product, new market). Using a *related diversification*

The Ansoff Matrix

PRODUCT

	OLD	NEW
OLD	Market Penetration	Expansion (Product Development)
MARKET		
NEW	Related Diversification (Market Development)	Unrelated Diversification

strategy, Hershey could develop a new bubble gum and sell it in the United States (new product, existing market). If it wanted to sell automobiles in Eastern Europe (new product, new market), that would be *unrelated diversification*. A company always has a menu of expansion options. The catch is that there has to be enough money and management time to expand effectively. If Hershey's management were to decide to expand in all four of the directions described above, they could end up with many businesses that are managed inadequately. There are only so many hours in an executive day. Even if managers could run the new ventures, the company might lack the cash to fund them adequately.

INDUSTRY ANALYSIS

Along with the language to discuss expansion (integration and diversification), you also need tools to help develop a strategy to survive.
Michael Porter of Harvard has developed the *Five Forces Theory
of Industry Structure* to help companies survive in a competitive
environment. His books, *Competitive Strategy* and *Competitive Advantage*, are truly cornerstones of strategic thinking. If you must buy
business books (other than *this* one), they are the ones to purchase.
Porter's theories can be used to formulate survival strategies for
your current business, as well as to evaluate the "attractiveness" of
other industries for expansion. Porter offers tools for investigating
the five forces that determine the level of competition, and consequently, the level of profit in an industry.

The five forces that drive industry competition are:

- **Threat of Substitutes**
- **Threat of New Entrants**
- **Bargaining Power of Suppliers**
- **Bargaining Power of Buyers**
- **Intensity of Rivalry Among Competitors**

A Five Forces Example

Let's apply the model to the tin can industry, which would be viewed
by Porter as extremely competitive because of the array of forces at
play within the industry. The *Suppliers* of steel have many other
industries to sell their steel to. Therefore, the canning industry does
not have much leverage in the market. Porter focuses on power, the
ability of one participant in the value chain to force its will on others
in the chain.

The *Users* of cans are primarily the small group of large food
processors. Users can wield their power to force the can industry
to reduce prices by playing one competitor against another.

Processors the size of Del Monte can also threaten to *Substitute*
plastic packaging for cans. Many food processors have moved to
plastic packaging. Consequently, competition intensifies as the demand for cans shrinks.

Porter's Five Forces Theory of Industry Structure

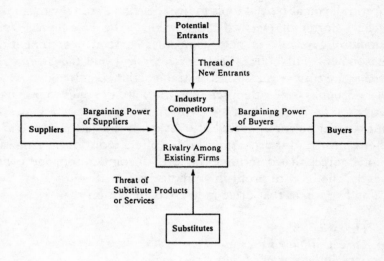

Reprinted with the permission of The Free Press, a Division of Macmillan, Inc., from *Competitive Advantage: Creating and Sustaining Superior Performance* by Michael E. Porter. Copyright © 1985 by Michael E. Porter.

Making matters worse is the fact that can-making machines can be purchased easily by *New Entrants*. Efficient can production can be accomplished at low cost and at relatively low volumes. This opens the industry up to new competitors if profit margins are at an attractive level. Del Monte, if it wished, could buy packaging equipment and produce for itself. Because the manufacturing technology is widely available and reasonably priced, the *Barriers to Entry* are low. Ease of entry increases the level of potential competition.

Because these four forces make the industry highly competitive, the fifth force, *Rivalry Among Existing Firms*, is equally intense. Salespeople know their competition very well because they compete for orders from a shrinking group of customers. This competitive force includes the possibility of bitter price wars. Under certain

DETAILED
Porter's Five Forces Theory of Industry Structure

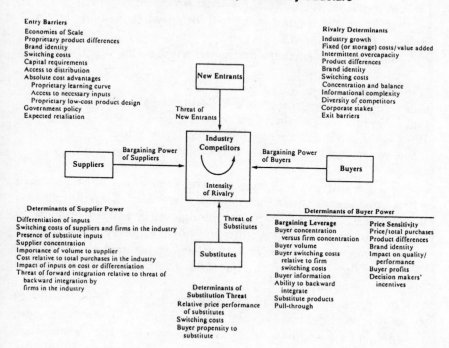

Entry Barriers
Economies of Scale
Proprietary product differences
Brand identity
Switching costs
Capital requirements
Access to distribution
Absolute cost advantages
  Proprietary learning curve
  Access to necessary inputs
  Proprietary low-cost product design
Government policy
Expected retaliation

Rivalry Determinants
Industry growth
Fixed (or storage) costs/value added
Intermittent overcapacity
Product differences
Brand identity
Switching costs
Concentration and balance
Informational complexity
Diversity of competitors
Corporate stakes
Exit barriers

New Entrants

Threat of
New Entrants

Industry
Competitors

Bargaining Power
of Suppliers

Suppliers

Intensity
of Rivalry

Bargaining Power
of Buyers

Buyers

Determinants of Supplier Power
Differentiation of inputs
Switching costs of suppliers and firms in the industry
Presence of substitute inputs
Supplier concentration
Importance of volume to supplier
Cost relative to total purchases in the industry
Impact of inputs on cost or differentiation
Threat of forward integration relative to threat of
  backward integration by
  firms in the industry

Threat of
Substitutes

Substitutes

Determinants of Buyer Power

Bargaining Leverage	**Price Sensitivity**
Buyer concentration	Price/total purchases
versus firm concentration	Product differences
Buyer volume	Brand identity
Buyer switching costs	Impact on quality/
relative to firm	performance
switching costs	Buyer profits
Buyer information	Decision makers'
Ability to backward	incentives
integrate	
Substitute products	
Pull-through	

**Determinants of
Substitution Threat**
Relative price performance
of substitutes
Switching costs
Buyer propensity to
substitute

circumstances, competitors will adopt artificially low prices regardless of the impact on profit because they want to win the account at all cost. The industry's competitive intensity results from all five forces exerting their pressures on the industry as seen in Porter's model.

What's a company to do in this sort of competitive environment? Crown Cork & Seal of Philadelphia has pursued a strategy of adding *value* to its product. It offers expert consulting services to solve clients' packaging problems, quick delivery to lower clients'

inventory costs, and customized and innovative packaging modifi-
cations to meet specific clients' needs. On the cost side, Crown
Cork & Seal has focused on low-cost production, which allows it
to price its products competitively. Not only has the company sur-
vived, it has prospered.

As a prospective entrant into the tin can industry, one should ask:

Is this an attractive industry for me to be in?
Can I duplicate the Crown Cork & Seal strategy?
Can I win in a price battle if I choose to enter?
What is the profit potential for me, if I choose to enter?
Could my money be better invested elsewhere?

Regardless of the industry, the same questions must be asked
when a manager wishes to expand into a new field. Even if expansion
is not contemplated, the Porter model offers insight on how to
compete more effectively within one's own industry. Please review
the *determinants* of the Five Forces in the detailed Porter model
very carefully. Those are the questions that MBAs ponder to gain
competitive advantage.

The forces at play in an industry are dynamic. The essence of
strategy is to understand the current forces and to use them to your
advantage. In waste disposal, Waste Management Inc. lobbies hard
for enactment of stringent environmental regulations. Why? Because only a few companies are able to comply with them. In that
way, regulation simultaneously assists Waste Management and hin-
ders its competitors. Stringent regulation creates *barriers to entry*
for *new entrants*, and most important increases the profits of the
remaining waste disposal players.

GENERIC STRATEGIES

There are many ways for a company to analyze its competitive
challenges. One such way is the Five Forces framework outlined by
Porter which we have just discussed. But most options for action
fall into what are called *generic strategies*. A generic strategy is one
that can be used across many industries, from dish towels to comput-

ers. Porter has aptly captured the three major strategies in a matrix of functional and business strategic possibilities:

Cost Leadership
Differentiation
Focus

Three Generic Strategies

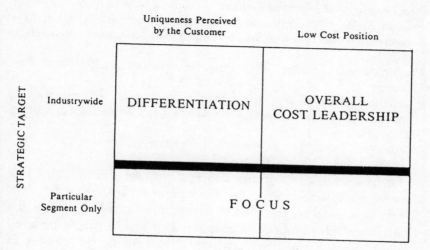

STRATEGIC ADVANTAGE

Reprinted with the permission of The Fress Press, a division of Macmillan, Inc., from *Competitive Strategy: Techniques for Analyzing Industries and Competitors* by Michael E. Porter. Copyright © 1980 by The Free Press.

Cost Leadership and the Learning Curve

The simplest strategy is *cost leadership*. By achieving the lowest cost of production in an industry, a company can either reduce its prices or keep the increased profits to invest in research to develop new and better products. *Low Cost Producers* (LCPs) can also choose to use their profits to advertise and market their products more vigorously.

An operations concept related to cost leadership is *economies of scale*. This means that as one produces more, costs per unit fall. As factories produce more, they learn and become more efficient in several ways.

These "learning" efficiencies can come from six sources:

Labor Efficiency — learning through repetition or automation. Tremendous progress has been made in factory automation by using robots and computer-aided manufacturing (CAM)

New Processes and Improved Methods — less costly ways to do the same task

Product Redesign — redesign to lower costs of materials and labor. If a computer is used to design the product it is called computer-aided design (CAD)

Product Standardization — decreasing the variations of a product's components

Efficiencies of Scale — doubling factory capacity does not cost twice as much. Adding machines or additional space is not as expensive as starting from scratch

Substitution — using less expensive but adequate materials

To be useful, the learning concept must be quantifiable. The *learning curve*, sometimes called the *experience curve*, does just that. It was developed by the Boston Consulting Group (BCG) in the 1960s to attach numbers to economies of scale benefits believed to exist. They found that each time the "cumulative" volume of production doubled, the cost of manufacturing fell by a constant and predictable percentage.

For example, a consultant's investigation of a manufacturing task could identify an "80 percent learning curve." This means that for every doubling of accumulated production, the next unit produced would cost 80 percent of the first unit, or 20 percent less. Computer spreadsheet models exist to perform the mathematics. The important point to remember is that "accumulated production" starts with unit one, not the first unit produced that month or year, but the very first one off the assembly line using that manufacturing method.

To demonstrate the math involved, I have hypothesized what the effects of an 80 percent learning curve would have been on the cost of producing disposable razors for Gillette.

The Learning Curve Effect
Cost of Production of Razor Blades

Units Produced	Unit Cost	Math Per Unit	Production Method
1	$10.00		By Hand
2	8.00	$10 \times .8$	
4	6.40	$8 \times .8$	Manual Assembly Line
1,048,576	.12	$10 \times (.80)^{20}$	
2,097,152	.09	$10 \times (.80)^{21}$	Fully Automated

The math demonstrates that after the razor production doubles twenty-one times, the cost per unit decreases 20 percent each time from a cost of $10.00 to $.09. A simple learning curve can also be seen graphically as shown:

Razor Blade Learning Curve

80% Learning

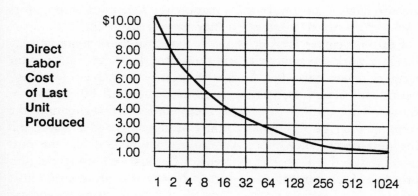

Direct Labor Cost of Last Unit Produced

Total Units Produced

The strategic implications of the learning curve lie in *moving down the learning curve* before competitors do. A firm wishing to maintain cost leadership will strive to produce more units than its competition. That way its production costs will be decreased more quickly.

The concept of "dumping" products below cost is a tactic the Japanese have used in the electronics industry while pursuing a cost leadership strategy. These forward-thinking companies sold video recorders at low prices, expecting to realize profits as they increased production at a lower cost. Japanese manufacturers calculated their profits using a five-year rather than a one-year time horizon. Therefore, they planned losses for their first year, so that larger profits could be realized in years three and four. The Japanese gained market share and squeezed out American competitors as a result of their learning curve strategy. American competitors saw the industry as unattractive and plagued by irrational pricing, while the strategic-minded Japanese companies walked away with the market. As the older products matured, the Japanese used the profits from their sale to develop new products like laser discs, a technology passed over by RCA.

As a product matures in its *product life cycle* and becomes widely adopted, as described in the marketing chapter, the curve becomes less useful. To double accumulated production would require tremendous increases in volume that are simply not realistic. Profits are also likely to be low. In this situation, the remaining competitors have the chance to catch up, if they haven't given up.

Learning curves are not static. A new process or material may increase worker productivity and thus alter the curve. In the razor instance, a new curve may be at work at, say, "75 percent learning" because of a new assembling machine instead of 80 percent as shown. That is called *jumping to a new curve*. In this situation, the running total of accumulated units produced is set to zero, and the new curve takes effect. When production doubles, the next unit produced will cost 75 percent of the first one using the new process, or 25 percent less. With products that are continuously innovated, the learning curve is of little use. New curves are formed all the time, and there is not much time to "move down" any of them.

Differentiation

As discussed earlier, *differentiation* is a prime marketing objective. It involves making your product or service appear different in the mind of the consumer. With products, this means offering better design, reliability, service, and delivery. With services, a point of differentiation can be employee courtesy, availability, expertise, and location. Products and services can be differentiated via advertising, even if they are virtually the same. A media campaign can convince the consumer that one is better. For instance, consumers could be persuaded that Nike shoes are better than Converse because of a celebrity endorsement.

Focus

Using a *focus* strategy, a company concentrates on either a market area, a market segment, or a product. The strength of a focus strategy is derived from knowing the customer and the product category very well. Companies establish a "franchise" in the marketplace. In the beer market, dominated by titans such as Anheuser-Busch, Coors, and Miller, little Hudepohl Beer ("Hudy") holds its own in Ohio. The giants can boast lower costs and slick marketing, but they do not enjoy the local "cult" following. Hudy pursued a loyal following over the years through local exposure and community involvement. Hudy *focuses* on Ohio.

COMPETITIVE TACTICS: SIGNALING

Signaling is a key strategic tool. It involves letting your competitors know what's on your mind. Combatants signal what they plan to do or what steps they will take in response to a competitor's move. Of course, a company can also bluff. Signaling is used to prevent disastrous (and costly) price wars. Direct contact with the competition to set prices or allocate markets is illegal! There are antitrust laws that forbid this behavior. But by judiciously signaling, companies can achieve the desired outcome without time behind bars.

In the airline industry signaling is commonplace. On reservation screens across the country, a daily cat-and-mouse game goes on. For example, Delta may briefly lower fares significantly on its prized routes from Atlanta to Los Angeles in response to American Airlines' price cuts along the same route. The Delta price move says, "American, if you want to play games on this route, it'll be bloody." If American responds by raising prices, in effect they are signaling, "Let's call a truce." If American keeps the low fare, it is signaling its intention to do battle. It's just like poker.

Six common types of *legal* signals are:

Price Movements — to signal intentions and to penalize unacceptable behavior.

Prior Announcements — to threaten, to test competitors' resolve, and to avoid surprises. In 1991 when IBM announced its alliance with Apple Computer, it signaled its resolve to keep its share of the computer hardware (machines) market. At the same time IBM and Apple also made known their intention to expand aggressively into computer software (programs). Microsoft, the leading software company in 1991, could not help but see this alliance as a strong indication of its determination to challenge Microsoft's dominance of the software industry.

Media Discussions — to communicate your rationale for actions and to convey your thoughts to the competition. Because executives of competing companies are barred from communicating with each other directly, they do it indirectly via the media. A Mobil executive, for example, could express his weariness with fruitless price wars and his hope that "marketing messages" would constitute the basis of competition. In this way, Texaco, Chevron, and Amoco would be put on notice to observe Mobil's price climb and act accordingly.

Counterattack — to hit your competitor's home market with a price cut or promotion in retaliation for their encroachment on your turf. Say New York was Maxwell House coffee's best market, and Folger's best was California. If the Maxwell House brand manager attacked Folger's turf with aggressive pricing and promotion, his counterpart at Folger's would be up in arms, to put it mildly. He would have two options: one, to defend California aggressively; or two, to take the offensive and attack Maxwell House's New York market. If he were to choose the second option, he would be signaling his anger and suggesting that a truce might benefit them both.

Announce Results — to communicate clearly to the competition the results of an action to avoid a costly misunderstanding. In test-market situations a manufacturer could clearly announce a failure in hopes of dissuading a competitor from counterattacking other established products. In pricing battles, a competitor could announce that the price cut is for only a limited time in an effort to avoid signaling a long-term intention to keep prices low.

Litigation — to tie up a competitor in court. When Kodak entered the instant photography business, Polaroid made it clear through the courts that it considered Kodak's camera and film as a patent infringement. Polaroid also announced publicly that it would pursue its claims with all the resources at its disposal. Eventually Kodak withdrew from the market, and in 1991, the company agreed to pay Polaroid a $1 billion settlement and abandon instant photography.

Signaling and the Prisoner's Dilemma

A related signaling concept is the *prisoner's dilemma*, as it is frequently referred to in corporate battles. As the story goes, two people are arrested for a murder and separated so that they cannot communicate. The police do not have enough evidence to convict either man, but if they can convince either man to confess and testify against the other, they will then have a strong case against one of them. The police promise each a lighter sentence if he turns state's evidence against the other. If they both refuse to confess and implicate the other, they will go free for lack of evidence. But what each prisoner does not know is how the other will act. Can one trust the other to keep quiet?

In competitive situations such as prevail in the airline industry, this scenario is similar to two companies that maintain high prices, each trusting the other to do the same. It is always tempting to break this silent pact, because a price war could result in the elimination of the other carrier. If they decide to cooperate in this unstable arrangement, they are both caught in a prisoner's dilemma.

All forms of signaling will be doomed if a competitor acts "irrationally." In that case, any attempt to call a competitive truce would go unheeded because in an irrationally competitive mind, winning, rather than maximizing profits, is the goal.

The Prisoner's Dilemma

	Silence	Confess
Silence	Freedom for Both	Light Sentence/ Tough Sentence
Confess	Tough Sentence/ Light Sentence	Moderate Sentence for Both

(In the case where the two prisoners act differently, the confessing prisoner gets a lighter sentence)

PORTFOLIO STRATEGIES

If signaling sounds like fun, its enjoyment is eclipsed by the pleasure MBAs take in playing portfolio games. *Portfolio strategy* is considered the highbrow area of *corporate level* strategic planning. It is the dominion of MBAs and of the elite management consulting firms headquartered in Boston and New York. In the 1960s, many academics and executives believed that if a corporation could put together the right *portfolio* of unrelated and countercyclical businesses, it would be immune to economic downturns. Accordingly, the concept of diversification became the craze of the decade. A prime example is General Electric, a company that was involved in 160 businesses during the sixties.

But in the 1970s, when profits declined and Wall Street became dissatisfied with *unrelated diversification*, boards of directors ran to consultants for help. They wanted to know what businesses they should be in, which they should continue in, and which they should sell. Cash was scarce and a strategy had to be found that would help funnel their limited capital to the best prospects.

As you might expect, each consulting firm developed its own theory and matrix model to answer the portfolio management problem. Knowledgeable MBAs are familiar with the four major portfolio models, and you should be too.

The Boston Consulting Group's Growth/Share Matrix

The Boston Consulting Group's (BCG) model uses market growth rates and relative market share to classify companies into four categories. Their studies showed that high market share was highly correlated with higher ROI (return on investment) and lower costs because of *learning curve effects*. Therefore, the theory suggests that it is best to have a stable, high market share in some businesses to fund the cash needs of other businesses. There are four classifications that rest on that premise.

The BCG Business Portfolio Chart

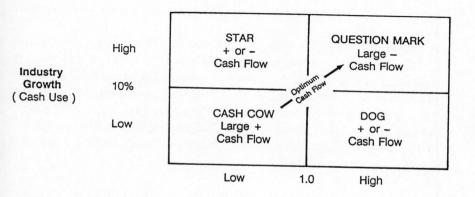

Relative Market Share
(Cash Generation)

   The *Star* is a high-market-share business in a high-growth industry. Stars grow and finance themselves. King World Productions, the syndicator of *Wheel of Fortune, Jeopardy!* and *The Oprah Winfrey Show*, is a good example of a self-financing growth company. Its profit margin of 19.6 percent on sales of $476 million in 1991 was ample to meet its cash needs for new and existing projects. Characteristically, these types of companies exist in competitive markets and they require vigilant managements in order to maintain their enviable positions on the BCG matrix.
   Cash Cows are high-market-share businesses in low-growth indus-

tries. These gems provide the cash to fund other businesses. Yesterday's stars, tobacco companies, are today's cows. In Philip Morris's case, the money generated from Marlboro is used to buy food companies and pay dividends. Needless to say, Philip Morris's goal is to keep its dominant share in the low-growth tobacco industry in the United States and keep "milking the cow" if it can.

Dogs are small-market-share businesses in low-growth industries. These businesses are going nowhere and consume corporate cash and management's time in an attempt to stay competitive. In the steel industry many companies are dogs. Their plant and equipment need expensive modernization, but with softer demand and increased foreign competition, they do not warrant additional investment by their parent companies. As a consequence, boards of directors that agree with this assessment have let their steel plants rust.

Question Marks are small-market-share businesses in high-growth industries. To grow they need cash. Some strategists call them "problem children." If they become successful, they will become stars, and later, cash cows. If they fail, they either die or become dogs as their industries mature. Start-up biotechnology firms such as Immunex, Enzo Biochem, and Calgene fall into the question mark category. Expensive research has to be funded in the hope of producing a miracle drug.

All this animal talk is fun until it is *your* business that the consultants label a dog. Dogs are not necessarily bad businesses. They just aren't the type of businesses that large corporations want in their *portfolio*. Wall Street investors demand a level of sales growth and cash generation that dogs cannot provide. Many millionaires have been minted as the dogs' management and buyout artists have taken these companies off larger corporations' hands. My Acquisitions course was taught by a number of visiting "professors" who had profited nicely from the housecleaning of large corporations' troublesome critters.

Portfolio strategies have their drawbacks. They assume that businesses in a portfolio have no significant *linkages*, which is often not the case. Many collections of businesses share technical, marketing, and support functions. Using shared resources is difficult when using portfolio concepts because they dictate a continual juggling act of companies to maximize growth and cash. Historically, with few exceptions, only investment bankers and advising consultants have profited from the juggling transactions of trading the BCG *animals*. The other beneficiaries of company juggling are the managements of these portfolio companies. If a business is not working out, there is no need to fix it. Just sell it to them!

McKinsey & Company's Multifactor Analysis

McKinsey & Co. takes a different approach to portfolio juggling. In response to dissatisfaction at General Electric in 1970 with the BCG's two-variable model, McKinsey developed its own. The guidance is the same from both models: Sell, hold, or invest in a business in the portfolio. In McKinsey's vocabulary, you *harvest* a cash cow and *divest* a dog.

The model has two general variables that govern a business evaluation: *industry attractiveness* and *business strength*. McKinsey's model is not a simple one. Each variable is determined by a number of industry factors. In any given industry, some factors will be of greater importance than others.

The McKinsey model has nine quadrants versus BCG's four. The six generic courses of action dictated by the model are:

- **Invest and Hold**
- **Invest to Grow**
- **Invest to Rebuild**
- **Selectively Invest in Promising Areas of the Business**
- **Harvest, Milk the Cow**
- **Divest, Sell the Dog**

Although the McKinsey model is attractive because it takes into account many factors, nonetheless the evaluation is subjective. As shown by the matrix, the individual factors culminate in a "high," "medium," or "low" assessment. For example, Wal-Mart's sales growth is accessible through its published annual report, but how can one objectively quantify Wal-Mart's "image"? It is a component that McKinsey uses in evaluating a business's position in their matrix. It's all very subjective.

The McKinsey Company Position / Industry Attractiveness Screen

		Low	Medium	High
Business Position	High	S	I	I
	Medium	H	S	I
	Low	H	H	S

Low   Medium   High

Industry Attractiveness

I = Invest / Grow   S = Selectivity / Earnings   H = Harvest / Divest

Arthur D. Little's SBU System

Arthur D. Little (ADL) is another bastion of MBA portfolio experts. ADL has cooked up a system that revolves around the SBU, the *strategic business unit*. When similar businesses of a corporation are grouped into SBUs, portfolio strategies become less complicated because there are fewer units to worry about. Businesses in different SBUs have little association with one another other than the financial ties imposed on them by the parent corporation.

The ADL portfolio process has four steps:

1. Classify all the businesses of a corporation into SBUs.
2. Place the SBUs into a matrix.
3. Evaluate the conditions of the industries in which each SBU operates.
4. Make a decision.

ADL's matrix has twenty-four quadrants compared to McKinsey's nine. The two variables that are operative in ADL's model are *industry maturity level* and *competitive position*. Needless to say, these are very similar to McKinsey's and BCG's. However, ADL vocabulary derives its inspiration from traffic signals rather than the animal world. SBUs either with high market share or in an attractive market are classified as *green*. Those caught in the middle are *yellow*. And the poor prospects with low market shares or in mature markets are branded *red*, as shown:

The ADL Strategic Business Unit Model

	Embryonic	Growth	Maturity	Aging
Leading	G	G	G	G
Strong	G	G	G	Y
Favorable	G	G	Y	R
Tenable	G	Y	R	R
Weak	Y	R	R	R
Nonviable	R	R	R	R

Competitive Position (rows: Leading, Strong, Favorable, Tenable, Weak, Nonviable)

Industry Maturity (columns: Embryonic, Growth, Maturity, Aging)

G = Green   Y = Yellow   R = Red

Based on their traffic light classification, the consultants devise appropriate strategies for each SBU owned: *Build, Maintain*, or *Liquidate*. For green SBUs there are many different strategies available. For the red ones, the options available are constrained by the poor "conditions" in which they find themselves. Once the SBU is classified, the consultants turn to their palette of generic strategies such as *focus, penetration*, or *diversification* to construct appropriate tactical plans.

The PIMS Data Base

A related portfolio tool available in academia is the PIMS data base, *Profit Impact of Market Strategies*. While BCG was researching the learning curve in the 1960s, Harvard University and General Electric collaborated to form the Strategic Planning Institute. The Institute's mission was to determine the "economic success factors" that lead to superior business performances across different industries. Eighty-seven variables were identified and a data base containing information on two thousand companies was established in an effort to discover the "magic formula" for success. Corroborating BCG's findings, market share was determined to be the key to higher returns on investment.

The original data base is updated periodically and a report service is available. An interested company can enter information on thirty key variables into the PIMS model and an Invest/Divest recommendation will be issued after comparing the business to the historical performances of other businesses in the same industry. PIMS is yet another MBA tool to be aware of and to incorporate in the portfolio planning process. Theories and tools give MBAs the power to anoint the best companies as stars, and cast out the unworthy as dogs.

GLOBALIZATION AND STRATEGY

The world is becoming increasingly economically interdependent. The West is trying to integrate the former Soviet empire and Europe is attempting some form of unification. Thus strategic planning on a global scale has become a timely concern. The MBA buzzword is *globalization*. It is a rather nebulous term, but it is a "hot" topic and efforts are made to interject the word "global" into all MBA courses and writings.

The possibility of globalization depends on the classification of the industry in which a business operates. If an industry is *national* in nature, it can operate successfully without being threatened by large *multinational corporations* (MNCs) swooping in and either trying a hostile takeover or competing in some sense. Baking and trucking are two examples of national industries. Automobiles and computers on the other hand are examples of global industries. The necessity of heavy research spending and significant learning curve effects tend to favor large MNCs. Whatever the industry, there are forces at work that either facilitate or impede globalization.

Forces encouraging globalization:

Improved Communications and Transportation — Fax, cable, satellite, supersonics

Fewer Trade Restrictions — Lower tariffs, duties, uniform regulations

Convergence of Consumer Needs — People everywhere are beginning to have the same tastes.

Technological Complexity and Change — Emerging high-tech industries require larger investments and worldwide efforts to keep pace with rapid change.

MNC Rivalries — MNCs fight for world domination of their particular industries.

Sony and Matsushita have been battling for world dominance in the electronics industry. The rivalry is said to be a personal one between the two chairmen, Akio Morita of Sony and Masaharu Matsushita of Matsushita. When Sony bought Columbia Pictures in 1989 for $3.4 billion, Matsushita bought MCA, Inc., in 1990 for $6.1 billion. One man could not be outshined by the other.

Forces hindering globalization:

Cost of Coordination — more managers, communication costs

Geographic Restraints — transportation constraints and logistical barriers of operating over wider areas

National Differences — taste preferences, usage, media, language, distribution channel differences

Protectionism — tariffs, government subsidies, regulatory approvals

The debate over which classification, global or national, an industry belongs to is not as important as investigating the forces that do or don't make it so. If a company finds itself in an emerging global industry, it must take action or it will be overtaken by others. Because the classification lies on a spectrum that ranges from national to global, the courses of action available are also in that range. A threatened automaker could lobby government to close its market to foreigners to make an industry national. On the other hand, in the same situation the automaker may choose to pursue an aggressive expansion strategy as Ford Motor Company and General Motors have done.

SYNERGY AND STRATEGY

Synergy is the benefit derived from combining two or more businesses so that the performance of the combination is higher than that of the sum of the individual businesses. When you are making portfolio acquisitions and divestitures, synergy becomes a key issue. Mistakes are often made when the synergistic effects of combining businesses are not explicitly defined and quantified. There may be possibilities for shared production, distribution, and markets, but these *linkages* or *interrelationships* must be scrutinized before including them in the price of an acquisition or merger target. In a merger, the target company has to be valued so that the appropriate number of shares of the parent's stock is exchanged for the target's.

For example, the impetus for the merger of Marion Pharmaceutical and Merrell Dow Pharmaceutical in 1989 may have included the benefit of a consolidated corporate staff. Marion's new headquarters were located in Kansas City while Merrell's old headquarters were in Cincinnati. Surely analysts would have investigated the costs of the duplication of efforts of the two corporate staffs against the benefits of merging the staffs, and the potential synergy derived by combining the best elements of the two. The company did find some savings in the merger but still maintains both facilities.

The four types of business linkages are:

Market Linkages:
  Customer Bases — same buyers
  Distribution Channels — same path to the consumer
  Brand Identifications — transference of a brand's name and equity to
    other products
Technological Linkages:
  Operations Technologies — factory processes
  New Product Technologies — research
  Information Technologies — data collection, data bases
Product Linkages:
  Product Line Extension Possibilities
  Excess Production Capacity — to be used for other products
  Materials Procurement — buyer power with suppliers enhanced
  Staff Functions — the same accountants and personnel staff can provide
    services across product categories.

Intangible Linkages:
   Shared Managerial Know-how:
      Experience with same type of buyer
      Similar configuration of the value chain
      Similar generic strategies used

Examine a recent episode in the life of Hallmark Cards, Inc., the premier greeting card company. It controlled over 40 percent of the U.S. market and enjoyed large cash flows but limited opportunities for further growth, so the company logically sought to diversify. In 1988, Hallmark purchased Univision, the operator of the largest Hispanic television network in the United States. The rapidly growing Hispanic population made Univision a real growth opportunity.

In the words of an employee, Hallmark was really in the "entertainment" business, as was Univision. "There's synergy in our acquisition," he said. But did real linkages exist between Hallmark and Univision? That is the question a strategist would have asked. Although Hallmark's investment may eventually pay off, *synergy* does not seem to be a factor in Univision's prospects for success.

Even when synergy does exist, there are often significant costs associated with making two organizations work together. Decision making may be hampered by lengthier processes of approval. Increased organizational inflexibility may be the byproduct of a larger organization. In rapidly changing markets, this inflexibility could be a strategic disadvantage.

STRATEGIC SKEPTICISM

The preceding discussion may have given the impression that corporations are successful as a result of expert strategic planning. In the area that I call *strategic skepticism*, strategic planning is not quite the analytical process preached by academics.

According to James Brian Quinn of MIT's Sloan School, strategy is considered to be a process of *logical incrementalism*. In his view, strategy is the result of many smaller decisions taken over a long period of time. Other theorists also hold that strategy is not as formal a process as that presented in the preceding pages. Strategy can take five forms, all starting with "P":

- **Plan**
- **Ploy**
- **Pattern**
- **Process**
- **Perspective**

In one company, strategy is the result of a formal *plan*. General Electric buys and sells its divisions using McKinsey's portfolio techniques. In another strategy is the execution of a successful tactical *ploy*. Instead of marketing coffee only in the grocery stores, Kraft General Foods uses mail order to sell its Gevalia brand.

Strategy can also be just a *pattern*, a *process*, or *perspective* of conducting business and making decisions. In my own experience in a small jewelry business, we followed a simple philosophy. We treated our customers well, gave them the best prices, and were completely honest about the merchandise. It was a consciously chosen way of conducting business and it was a successful *strategy*.

Strategy can be the product of an entrepreneur's insight as a result of being hit with the boom of his sailboat, or it can be a series of ad hoc plans that develop over time. Either way, the formal planning processes sold by consultants are not always the answer.

History is often rewritten to suit the theories of strategic planners. One version of the success of Honda motorcycles described Sochiro Honda as a free spirit driven by will and a dream. He had no grand plan. The success of the company was the product of his burning desire to build a winning racing motorcycle and his slow, step-by-step introduction of his motorcycle into the U.S. market in 1958. Luckily for Sochiro, the United States placed few restrictions on his "inconsequential" Japanese import.

Consultants at BCG told a much different story about Honda to their British motorcycle industry clients. In their view, Honda had calculated to *go down the learning curve* in order to achieve lower costs and build world market share through low pricing. The company's dominant market share allowed for large investments in research and advanced manufacturing techniques. BCG reported that Honda's market leadership also allowed the company to advertise and promote Honda at lower costs per bike. Which version of history is true? Personally, I gravitate toward the more colorful story, but the cost leadership principle obviously played a large role in Honda's success, planned or not. In fact, if theory is used in conjunction with a manager's own good judgment and common sense, strategy can be a winning mix of art and science.

STRATEGY AND CHINESE WARFARE

No lesson on strategy would be complete without mentioning Sun-tzu, a Chinese military strategist of the fourth century B.C. Somehow his maxims have entered into many an MBA conversation about strategy. I imagine the irascible Mr. Honda quoting him quite often. Sun-tzu's book *The Art of War* even sat on my former boss's desk. Quoting Sun-tzu is sure to make you either sound terribly smart or appear like the ruthless insider trader Gordon Gekko in the movie *Wall Street*. Here are a few choice quotes for your next business meeting, if you dare use them:

> "All warfare is based on deception."
> "Offer the enemy a bait to lure him; feign disorder and strike him."
> "For to win 100 victories in 100 battles is not the acme of skill. To subdue the enemy without fighting is the acme of skill."
> "In war, numbers alone confer no advantage. Do not advance relying on sheer military power."
> "Thus, what is of supreme importance in war is to attack the enemy's strategy."

STRATEGIC IMPLEMENTATION

As I indicated at the beginning of this chapter, strategy development without an eye toward implementation is a waste of time. Strategic changes are an easy topic for MBAs to talk about, but are not easy to accomplish. A clever quote won't cut it. I cannot possibly tell you how to turn around a failing business in a chapter, but I can put strategic thinking into perspective. Contrary to what some academics would lead you to believe, no one tactic or trick constitutes strategy; rather, strategy is how the "totality" of a company works together to achieve goals.

Executives do not think up or implement strategy in one day.

Leaders have to discern which factors are within their control and which are not. MBAs call those factors within their control the *action levers*. Strategists must also deal with the reality of human resistance to change. They must set tangible goals, formulate their action plan, and develop contingency plans if things do not go as intended. This is the same action planning sequence outlined in the Organizational Behavior chapter.

Strategy is dynamic. Executives must review their strategy continuously to ensure that it reflects the changes in the business environment, the company, and its goals. *The source of competitive advantage is the pursuit of an evolving strategy that cannot be easily duplicated by competitors.*

KEY STRATEGY TAKEAWAYS

The Seven S model — Strategy is how all of a company's S's work together.
The Value Chain — The process of producing and delivering goods and services
Integration — Ways to expand a business: backward, forward, vertically, horizontally
Ansoff Matrix — Four strategies for business expansion
Porter's Five Forces Theory — Five forces that determine the competitive intensity of an industry
The Learning Curve — The more units produced the lower the cost per unit falls due to production efficiencies.
Signaling — Indirectly communicating with competitors
The Prisoner's Dilemma — The captive nature of competitive relationships within an industry
Portfolio Strategies — The theories large multibusiness corporations use to decide which companies they should buy, sell, or hold
Globalization — The worldwide competition inherent in certain industries due to a variety of globalizing factors
Synergy — The incremental profits generated by the combination of two companies that share resources
Incrementalism — The concept that strategy is not a grand scheme but is developed over a period of time, step-by-step

DAY 10

MBA MINI-COURSES

RESEARCH
PUBLIC SPEAKING
NEGOTIATING
INTERNATIONAL BUSINESS

THE MINI-COURSE ON RESEARCH

It is said that information is power. That is why MBA schools teach students research skills. The key to efficient and productive research is to know where to seek information. By putting a little more effort into your job, you as a *Ten-Day MBA* may get that brilliant insight or fact that may elude your less industrious colleagues. Of all the sections in this book, this one may be the most valuable to you, so I finish with it. Suppose you need facts about a competitor, a person, or an industry, the following are some of the *right* places to look. Your local university library is your best resource.

Compact Disk Data Bases Available on Library Computers

There are several services that read all major publications and make them accessible without the hassle of rummaging through many books of indexes. Here are two:

ABI/Inform — This data base on compact disks contains the articles and abstracts from more than eight hundred major business publications. By using key words it makes quick work of magazine research. Each article is summarized. Most often, the abstract is complete enough that you won't need to see the full article.

Infotrac Computer Systems — In addition to the information provided by ABI, Infotrac offers information on companies and products. Brokerage house industry and company reports are available in their entirety. The limitation is that this system, in most cases, gives only citations of articles. However, these citations will often lead you to trade magazines. Trade magazines give you the best data about industries, competitors, and products.

Books

Standard & Poor's Industry Surveys — This two-volume set provide excellent, timely, in-depth research of twenty major industries.

Value Line Investment Surveys — This source provides detailed up-to-date company information for investors in seventy-six industries.

U.S. Industrial Outlook — This government publication provides industry profiles and forecasts of 350 industries.

Million Dollar Directory, Dun & Bradstreet — This five-volume corporate directory lists both public and private companies.

Gale Research — Gale Research publishes a series of books that are the cornerstones of all good business libraries:

* *Market Share Reporter* — This book presents market share data that appear in public sources. It's a time saver! ($170)
* *Business Rankings Annual* — This book gives business ranking data that appears in public sources. It is a good industry source. ($155)
* *Ward's Business Directory: U.S. Private and Public Companies* — a corporate atlas. ($1,150)
* *Encyclopedia of Associations* — Most industries and products have associations, trade groups, and clubs. These organizations are happy to assist people to learn about them, their membership, or their interests. Many publish research studies, membership directories, and newsletters. Their people can also lead you to other sources of information. Do not overlook the *Encyclopedia of Associations*. I own a set myself. ($320, 800-877-GALE)

Encyclopedias — Probably the most overlooked source of quick, predigested information. You're never too old to look at the *World Book* or the *Encyclopedia Britannica*.

The Lifestyle Market Analyst — This annual study published by National Demographics and Lifestyles is one of the best sources of marketing information. It combines demographics, life-styles, and media habits. They also publish the *Zip Code Analyst*. ($288 each, 708-256-6067)

Congressional Quarterly's Washington Information Directory — This book puts all the resources of the Washington bureaucracy at your fingertips. The entries about the Commerce Department are helpful for international trade. If you pay your income taxes, you have paid for this service. Why not use it? ($90, 800-638-1719)

International Business

Country Profiles — These quarterly magazines dedicated to individual nations are published by the Economist Intelligence Unit, 40 Duke Street, London. They provide much of the economic, social, and historical information that you need to perform the country analyses described in the Economics chapter. They are available only at the best-stocked libraries.

Doing Business in . . . This series published by Price Waterhouse is an excellent source of information for the international business person. It discusses the customs and a variety of the finer points of international business that *Country Profiles* misses. (Contact your local Price Waterhouse accounting and consulting office.)

Expensive Research

The Nexis research data base, **Mead Data Central** — This expensive on-line computer service is available at some libraries and businesses. It has access to whole libraries of news, financial, and marketing data. Nexis is not as user-friendly as the compact disk sources listed above. Key word searches must be carefully defined because so much data are available. Nexis also requires knowledge of special commands. It costs $40 to $50 per hour plus charges for access to specific data libraries. Seek free sources of information first if you are cost-conscious. If not, this is one of the most powerful data bases that exist. It will save you a lot of time.

BRS and *Dialog* — Other well-known research data bases.

Find/SVP — Provides off-the-shelf studies of most product categories. Their well-written reports range in price from a few hundred to several thousand dollars. Their studies contain much of the information that is available for free from other sources, as well as some proprietary research. (Catalog, 800-346-3787)

Interviews

Information can always be gathered by talking to people. The biggest mistake is to finish an interview and neglect to ask for referrals to other sources. After networking with several company or industry insiders, you can name-drop your way to other people. By mentioning the name of someone they already know, you make interviewees feel more at ease, and they become more generous with their information.

Keeping Current

There are a few newspapers and magazines that MBAs must make time for. MBAs must be informed, and these publications give them the information edge. How can they expect to talk and think intelligently if they do not know what is going on in the world? To succeed, you must read.

The Wall Street Journal — If you don't have time, just read the front page. It gives you the business news that you need to know.

Forbes, Business Week, and *Fortune* — These are the best business magazines. For news, there is the *Journal,* but these magazines give you the trends and the types of stories and analysis that are written for the intelligent business reader.

Advertising Age — Most business magazines have a financial bent, but *Advertising Age* comes at business from a pure marketing perspective. It is the trade magazine of the advertising world. It gives a person a well-rounded business outlook. Since most products are advertised, it is a good source of competitive information.

Local paper/local business journals — If you don't know the business players in your community, they probably will never know you.

THE MINI-COURSE ON PUBLIC SPEAKING

1. Know your audience.
    Their interests, attention span

2. Know your own capabilities.
   Can you deliver a joke?
3. Keep it simple.
   Detailed information is best delivered in print.
   Speeches should deliver concept and motivate.

KISS — Keep it Short and Simple.

THE MINI-COURSE ON NEGOTIATING

1. Know your opponent.
   Temperament, history, capabilities, resources.
2. Know yourself.
   Temperament, history, capabilities, resources.
   When the desires of two individuals clash, there is a tension in that some people handle conflict better than others. It's best not to fool yourself about your own temperament. Try to work either to improve your ability to handle conflict, or to learn to compensate for it.
3. Do your homework.
   Understand the impact of possible settlement scenarios.
4. Determine your strategy and limits ahead of time.
   Do not get caught up in the "need to win" at all costs.
5. Review each negotiation afterward to gain knowledge for the next negotiation.
   What can I improve on? What can I learn from my opponent?

THE MINI-COURSE ON CONDUCTING INTERNATIONAL BUSINESS

1. Understand the host's culture, values, customs, and beliefs. Don't assume that your values are shared.
2. When you are in a foreign country, you are a guest. They are the host and they have the power.
3. You are a foreigner and you will never *really* understand them.
4. Multinational corporations get their competitive advantage from their ability to transfer their experience across borders and avoid mistakes.
5. International investment is a long-term investment. The measure of its return should also be a long-term one.

6. You will have little success without true respect for the host country and its people. If you do not respect them, they'll know it.
7. In international business there is a lot of room for ethical decision making. Act as your own policeman.

By the authority of the author,
this diploma confers upon

the degree of Ten-Day MBA
and herewith all the rights and privileges of
a Master of Business Administration
from the University of the Self Taught

Ten-Day
MBA

Steven Alan Silbiger

Author

These notes on international business were taken from a case discussion led by Professor Neil H. Borden, Jr., at the Darden Graduate School of Business at the University of Virginia, used with permission.

APPENDIX

QUANTITATIVE ANALYSIS TABLES

Present Value of $1

PRESENT VALUE FACTOR OF $1 = $(1 + r)^{-n}$

r = discount rate   n = number of periods until payment

PERIODS = N	1%	2%	3%	4%	5%	6%	7%	8%	9%	10%	12%	14%	15%	16%	18%	20%	25%
1	0.9901	0.98039	0.97087	0.96154	0.95238	0.9434	0.93458	0.92593	0.91743	0.90909	0.89286	0.87719	0.86957	0.86207	0.84746	0.83333	0.8
2	0.9803	0.96117	0.9426	0.92456	0.90703	0.89	0.87344	0.85734	0.84168	0.82645	0.79719	0.76947	0.75614	0.74316	0.71818	0.69444	0.64
3	0.97059	0.94232	0.91514	0.889	0.86384	0.83962	0.8163	0.79383	0.77218	0.75131	0.71178	0.67497	0.65752	0.64066	0.60863	0.5787	0.512
4	0.96098	0.92385	0.88849	0.8548	0.8227	0.79209	0.7629	0.73503	0.70843	0.68301	0.63552	0.59208	0.57175	0.55229	0.51579	0.48225	0.4096
5	0.95147	0.90573	0.86261	0.82193	0.78353	0.74726	0.71299	0.68058	0.64993	0.62092	0.56743	0.51937	0.49718	0.47611	0.43711	0.40188	0.32768
6	0.94205	0.88797	0.83748	0.79031	0.74622	0.70496	0.66634	0.63017	0.59627	0.56447	0.50663	0.45559	0.43233	0.41044	0.37043	0.3349	0.26214
7	0.93272	0.87056	0.81309	0.75992	0.71068	0.66506	0.62275	0.58349	0.54703	0.51316	0.45235	0.39964	0.37594	0.35383	0.31393	0.27908	0.20972
8	0.92348	0.85349	0.7841	0.73069	0.67684	0.62741	0.58201	0.54027	0.50187	0.46651	0.40388	0.35056	0.3269	0.30503	0.26604	0.23257	0.16777
9	0.91434	0.83676	0.76642	0.70259	0.64461	0.5919	0.5493	0.5025	0.46043	0.4241	0.36061	0.30751	0.28426	0.26295	0.22546	0.1938	0.13422
10	0.90529	0.82035	0.74409	0.67556	0.61391	0.55839	0.50835	0.46319	0.4241	0.38554	0.32197	0.26974	0.24718	0.22668	0.19106	0.16151	0.10737
11	0.89632	0.80426	0.72242	0.64958	0.58468	0.52679	0.47509	0.42888	0.38753	0.35049	0.28748	0.23662	0.21494	0.19542	0.16192	0.13459	0.0859
12	0.88745	0.78849	0.70138	0.6246	0.55684	0.49697	0.44401	0.39711	0.35553	0.31863	0.25668	0.20756	0.18691	0.16846	0.13722	0.11216	0.06872
13	0.87866	0.77303	0.68095	0.60057	0.53032	0.46884	0.41496	0.3677	0.32618	0.28966	0.22917	0.18207	0.16253	0.14523	0.11629	0.09346	0.05498
14	0.86996	0.75788	0.66112	0.57748	0.50507	0.4423	0.38782	0.34046	0.29925	0.26333	0.20462	0.15971	0.14133	0.1252	0.09855	0.07789	0.04398
15	0.86135	0.74301	0.64186	0.55526	0.48102	0.41727	0.36245	0.31524	0.27454	0.23939	0.1827	0.1401	0.12289	0.10793	0.08352	0.06491	0.03518
16	0.85282	0.72845	0.62317	0.53391	0.45811	0.39365	0.33873	0.29189	0.25187	0.21763	0.16312	0.12289	0.10686	0.09304	0.07078	0.05409	0.02815
17	0.84438	0.71416	0.60502	0.51337	0.4363	0.37136	0.31657	0.27027	0.23107	0.19784	0.14564	0.1078	0.09293	0.08021	0.05998	0.04507	0.02252
18	0.83602	0.70016	0.58739	0.49363	0.41552	0.35034	0.29586	0.25025	0.21199	0.17986	0.13004	0.09456	0.08081	0.06914	0.05083	0.03756	0.01801
19	0.82774	0.68643	0.57029	0.47464	0.39573	0.33051	0.27651	0.23171	0.19449	0.16351	0.11611	0.08295	0.07027	0.05961	0.04308	0.0313	0.01441
20	0.81954	0.67297	0.55368	0.45639	0.37689	0.3118	0.25842	0.21455	0.17843	0.14864	0.10367	0.07276	0.0611	0.05139	0.03651	0.02608	0.01153
21	0.81143	0.65978	0.53755	0.43883	0.35894	0.29416	0.24151	0.19866	0.1637	0.13513	0.09256	0.06383	0.05313	0.0443	0.03094	0.02174	0.00922
22	0.8034	0.64684	0.52189	0.42196	0.34185	0.27751	0.22571	0.18394	0.15018	0.12285	0.08264	0.05599	0.0462	0.03819	0.02622	0.01811	0.00738
23	0.79544	0.63416	0.50669	0.40573	0.32557	0.2618	0.21095	0.17032	0.13778	0.11168	0.07379	0.04911	0.04017	0.03292	0.02222	0.01509	0.0059
24	0.78757	0.62172	0.49193	0.39012	0.31007	0.24698	0.19715	0.1577	0.1264	0.10153	0.06588	0.04308	0.03493	0.02838	0.01883	0.01258	0.00472
25	0.77977	0.60953	0.47761	0.37512	0.2953	0.233	0.18425	0.14602	0.11597	0.0923	0.05882	0.03779	0.03038	0.02447	0.01596	0.01048	0.00378
26	0.77205	0.59758	0.46369	0.36069	0.28124	0.21981	0.1722	0.1352	0.10639	0.08391	0.05252	0.03315	0.02642	0.02109	0.01352	0.00874	0.00302
27	0.7644	0.58586	0.45019	0.34682	0.26785	0.20737	0.16093	0.12519	0.09761	0.07628	0.04689	0.02908	0.02297	0.01818	0.01146	0.00728	0.00242
28	0.75684	0.57437	0.43708	0.33348	0.25509	0.19563	0.1504	0.11591	0.08955	0.06934	0.04187	0.02551	0.01997	0.01567	0.00971	0.00607	0.00193
29	0.74934	0.56311	0.42435	0.32065	0.24295	0.18456	0.14056	0.10733	0.08215	0.06304	0.03738	0.02237	0.01737	0.01351	0.00823	0.00506	0.00155
30	0.74192	0.55207	0.41199	0.30832	0.23138	0.17411	0.13137	0.09938	0.07537	0.05731	0.03338	0.01963	0.0151	0.01165	0.00697	0.00421	0.00124

Future Value of $1

FUTURE VALUE FACTOR OF $1 $= (1 + r)^n$

r = discount rate n = number of periods until payment

PERIODS =N	1%	2%	3%	4%	5%	6%	7%	8%	9%	10%	12%	14%	15%	16%	18%	20%	25%
	1.01	1.02	1.03	1.04	1.05	1.06	1.07	1.08	1.09	1.1	1.12	1.14	1.15	1.16	1.18	1.2	1.25
1	1.0201	1.0404	1.0609	1.0816	1.1025	1.1236	1.1449	1.1664	1.1881	1.21	1.2544	1.2996	1.3225	1.3456	1.3924	1.44	1.5625
2	1.0303	1.06121	1.09273	1.12486	1.15763	1.19102	1.22504	1.25971	1.29503	1.331	1.40493	1.48154	1.52088	1.5609	1.64303	1.728	1.95313
3	1.0406	1.08243	1.12551	1.16986	1.21551	1.26248	1.3108	1.36049	1.41158	1.4641	1.57352	1.68896	1.74901	1.81064	1.93878	2.0736	2.44141
4	1.05101	1.10408	1.15927	1.21665	1.27628	1.33823	1.40255	1.46933	1.53862	1.61051	1.76234	1.92541	2.01136	2.10034	2.28776	2.48832	3.05176
5	1.06152	1.12616	1.19405	1.26532	1.3401	1.41852	1.50073	1.5687	1.6771	1.77156	1.97382	2.19497	2.31306	2.4364	2.69955	2.98598	3.8147
6	1.07214	1.14869	1.22987	1.31593	1.4071	1.50363	1.60578	1.71382	1.82804	1.94872	2.21068	2.50227	2.66002	2.82622	3.18547	3.58318	4.76837
7	1.08286	1.17166	1.26677	1.36857	1.47746	1.59385	1.71819	1.85093	1.99256	2.14359	2.47596	2.85259	3.05902	3.27841	3.75886	4.29982	5.96046
8	1.09369	1.19509	1.30477	1.42331	1.55133	1.68948	1.83846	1.999	2.17189	2.35795	2.77308	3.25195	3.51788	3.80296	4.43545	5.15978	7.45058
9	1.10462	1.21899	1.34392	1.48024	1.62889	1.79085	1.96715	2.15892	2.36736	2.59374	3.10585	3.70722	4.04556	4.41144	5.23384	6.19174	9.31323
11	1.11567	1.24337	1.38423	1.53945	1.71034	1.8983	2.10485	2.33164	2.58043	2.85312	3.47855	4.22623	4.65239	5.11726	6.17593	7.43008	11.64153
12	1.12683	1.26824	1.42576	1.60103	1.79586	2.0122	2.25219	2.51817	2.81266	3.13843	3.89598	4.8179	5.35025	5.93603	7.28759	8.9161	14.55192
13	1.13809	1.29361	1.46853	1.66507	1.88565	2.13293	2.40985	2.71962	3.0658	3.45227	4.36349	5.49241	6.15279	6.88579	8.59936	10.69932	18.18989
14	1.14947	1.31948	1.51259	1.73168	1.97993	2.2609	2.57853	2.93719	3.34173	3.7975	4.88711	6.26135	7.07571	7.98752	10.14724	12.83918	22.73737
15	1.16097	1.34587	1.55797	1.80094	2.07893	2.39656	2.75903	3.17217	3.64248	4.17725	5.47357	7.13794	8.13706	9.26552	11.97375	15.40702	28.42171
16	1.17258	1.37279	1.6047	1.87298	2.18287	2.54035	2.95216	3.42594	3.97031	4.59497	6.13039	8.13725	9.35762	10.748	14.12902	18.48843	35.52714
17	1.1843	1.40024	1.65285	1.9479	2.29202	2.69277	3.15882	3.70002	4.32763	5.05447	6.86604	9.27646	10.76126	12.46768	16.67325	22.18611	44.40892
18	1.19615	1.42825	1.70243	2.02582	2.40662	2.85434	3.37993	3.99602	4.71712	5.55992	7.68997	10.57517	12.37545	14.46251	19.67325	26.62333	55.5115
19	1.20811	1.45681	1.75351	2.10685	2.52695	3.0256	3.61653	4.3157	5.14166	6.11591	8.61276	12.05569	14.23177	16.77652	23.21444	31.948	69.38894
20	1.22019	1.48595	1.80611	2.19112	2.6533	3.20714	3.86968	4.66096	5.60441	6.7275	9.64629	13.74349	16.36654	19.46076	27.39303	38.3376	86.73617
21	1.23239	1.51567	1.86029	2.27877	2.78596	3.39956	4.14056	5.03383	6.10881	7.40025	10.80385	15.66758	18.82152	22.57448	32.32378	46.00512	108.4202
22	1.24472	1.54598	1.9161	2.36992	2.92526	3.60354	4.4304	5.43654	6.6586	8.14027	12.10031	17.86104	21.64475	26.1864	38.14206	55.20614	135.52527
23	1.25716	1.5769	1.97359	2.46472	3.07152	3.81975	4.74053	5.87146	7.25787	8.9543	13.55235	20.36158	24.89146	30.37622	45.00763	66.24737	169.40659
24	1.26973	1.60844	2.03279	2.5633	3.2251	4.04893	5.07237	6.34118	7.91108	9.84973	15.17863	23.21221	28.62518	35.23642	53.10901	79.49685	211.75824
25	1.28243	1.64061	2.09378	2.66584	3.38635	4.29187	5.42743	6.84848	8.62308	10.8347	17.00006	26.46192	32.91895	40.87424	62.66863	95.39622	264.6978
26	1.29526	1.67342	2.15659	2.77247	3.55567	4.54938	5.80735	7.39635	9.39916	11.91818	19.04007	30.16658	37.8568	47.41412	73.94898	114.47546	330.87225
27	1.30821	1.70689	2.22129	2.88337	3.73346	4.82335	6.21387	7.98806	10.24508	13.10999	21.32488	34.38991	43.53531	55.00038	87.2598	137.37055	413.59031
28	1.32129	1.74102	2.28793	2.9987	3.92013	5.11169	6.64884	8.62711	11.16714	14.42099	23.8837	39.20449	50.06561	63.80044	102.96656	164.84466	516.98781
29	1.3345	1.77584	2.35657	3.11865	4.11614	5.41838	7.11426	9.31727	12.17218	15.86309	26.74993	44.69312	57.57545	74.00851	121.50054	197.81339	646.23452
30	1.34785	1.81136	2.42726	3.2434	4.32194	5.74349	7.61226	10.06266	13.26768	17.4494	29.95992	50.95016	66.21177	85.84988	143.37064	237.37631	807.79357

Table of the Normal Distribution

Each number in the table is the area under the normal density curve which lies between the mean and "Z" standard deviation units from the mean.

Z = (x − mean) / Standard Deviation

Z	0.00	0.01	0.02	0.03	0.04	0.05	0.06	0.07	0.08	
0.0	0.000	0.004	0.008	0.012	0.016	0.0199	0.0239	0.0279	0.0319	0.
0.1	0.0398	0.0438	0.0478	0.0517	0.0557	0.0596	0.0636	0.0675	0.0714	0
0.2	0.0793	0.0832	0.0871	0.091	0.0948	0.0987	0.1026	0.1064	0.1103	0
0.3	0.1179	0.1217	0.1255	0.1293	0.1334	0.1368	0.1406	0.1143	0.148	0.
0.4	0.1534	0.1591	0.1628	0.1664	0.17	0.1726	0.1772	0.1808	0.1844	0.
0.5	0.1915	0.195	0.1985	0.2019	0.2054	0.2088	0.2123	0.2157	0.219	•
0.6	0.2257	0.2291	0.2324	0.2357	0.2389	0.2422	0.2454	0.2486	0.2518	0
0.7	0.258	0.2612	0.2642	0.2673	0.2704	0.2734	0.2764	0.2794	0.2823	0
0.8	0.2881	0.291	0.2939	0.2967	0.2995	0.3023	0.3051	0.3078	0.3106	0.
0.9	0.3159	0.3186	0.3212	0.3238	0.3264	0.3289	0.3315	0.334	0.3365	0
1.0	0.3413	0.3438	0.3461	0.3485	0.3508	0.531	0.3554	0.3577	0.3599	0.
1.1	0.3643	0.3665	0.368	0.3708	0.3729	0.3749	0.377	0.379	0.381	•
1.2	0.3849	0.3869	0.3888	0.3907	0.3925	0.3944	0.3962	0.398	0.3997	0.
1.3	0.4032	0.4049	0.4066	0.4082	0.4099	0.4115	0.4131	0.4147	0.4162	0.
1.4	0.4192	0.4207	0.4222	0.4236	0.4251	0.4265	0.4279	0.4292	0.4306	0
1.5	0.4332	0.4345	0.4357	0.437	0.4382	0.4394	0.4406	0.4418	0.4429	0.
1.6	0.4452	0.4463	0.4474	0.4484	0.4495	0.4505	0.4515	0.4525	0.4535	0.
1.7	0.4554	0.4564	0.4573	0.4582	0.4591	0.4599	0.4608	0.4616	0.4625	0.
1.8	0.4641	0.4649	0.4656	0.4664	0.4671	0.4673	0.4686	0.4693	0.4699	0.
1.9	0.4713	0.4719	0.4726	0.4732	0.4738	0.4744	0.475	0.4756	0.4761	0
2.0	0.4772	0.4778	0.4783	0.4788	0.4793	0.4798	0.4803	0.4808	0.4812	0
2.1	0.4821	0.4826	0.483	0.4834	0.4838	0.4842	0.4846	0.485	0.4854	0
2.2	0.4861	0.4864	0.4868	0.4871	0.4875	0.4878	0.4881	0.4884	0.4887	•
2.3	0.4893	0.4896	0.4898	0.4901	0.4904	0.4906	0.4909	0.4911	0.4913	0.
2.4	0.4918	0.492	0.4922	0.4925	0.4927	0.4929	0.4931	0.4932	0.4934	0.
2.5	0.4938	0.494	0.4941	0.4943	0.4945	0.4946	0.4948	0.4949	0.4951	0.
2.6	0.4953	0.4955	0.4956	0.4957	0.4959	0.496	0.4961	0.4962	0.4963	0.
2.7	0.4965	0.4966	0.4967	0.4968	0.4969	0.497	0.4971	0.4972	0.4973	0.
2.8	0.4974	0.4975	0.4976	0.4977	0.4977	0.4978	0.4979	0.4979	0.498	0
2.9	0.4981	0.4982	0.4982	0.4983	0.4984	0.4984	0.4985	0.4985	0.4986	0.
3.0	0.49865	0.4987	0.4987	0.4988	0.4988	0.4989	0.4989	0.4989	0.499	•
3.1	0.49903	0.4991	0.4991	0.4991	0.4992	0.4992	0.4992	0.4992	0.4993	0.
3.2	0.4993129	0.4993	0.4994	0.4994	0.4994	0.4994	0.4994	0.4995	0.4995	0.
3.3	0.4995166	0.4995	0.4995	0.4996	0.4996	0.4996	0.4996	0.4996	0.4996	0.
3.4	0.4996631	0.4997	0.4997	0.4997	0.4997	0.4997	0.4997	0.4997	0.4998	0.
3.5	0.4997674	0.4998	0.4998	0.4998	0.4998	0.4998	0.4998	0.4998	0.4998	0.
3.6	0.4998409	0.4998	0.4999	0.4999	0.4999	0.4999	0.4999	0.4999	0.4999	0.
3.7	0.4998922	0.4999	0.4999	0.4999	0.4999	0.4999	0.4999	0.4999	0.4999	0.
3.8	0.4999277	0.4999	0.4999	0.4999	0.4999	0.4999	0.4999	0.5	0.5	
3.9	0.4999519	0.5	0.5	0.5	0.5	0.5	0.5	0.5	0.5	
4.0	0.4999683	0.5	0.5	0.5	0.5	0.5	0.5	0.5	0.5	
4.5	0.4999966	0.5	0.5	0.5	0.5	0.5	0.5	0.5	0.5	
5.0	0.4999997133	0.5	0.5	0.5	0.5	0.5	0.5	0.5	0.5	

BIBLIOGRAPHY

DAY 1: MARKETING

Assael, Henry. *Consumer Behavior & Marketing Action.* Boston: Kent Publishing, 1981, p. 471 (paper towel perceptual mapping).

"The Deal Maker." *U.S. News & World Report,* February 8, 1988, p. 78 (Ralph Lauren).

Koselka, Rita. "How to Print Money." *Forbes,* December 24, 1990, p. 118 (Vlassis).

Kotler, Philip (Northwestern). *Marketing Management Analysis, Planning and Control.* Englewood Cliffs, N.J.: Prentice-Hall, 1984.

Maxwell, John C., Jr. "Coffee Sales Climb in '89." *Advertising Age,* April 16, 1990, p. 64 (coffee market shares).

Morgensen, Gretchen. "The Trend Is Not Their Friend." *Forbes,* September 16, 1991, p. 118 (brand extensions).

Newton, Derek A. *Sales Force Management: Text and Cases.* Boston: Irwin, 1990, pp. 7–9 (salesman historical periods).

Paley, Norton. *Manager's Guide to Competitive Marketing Strategies.* New York: American Marketing Association, 1989, pp. 18–19 (Xerox), pp. 46–47 (segmentation selection).

Schifrin, Matthew. "Mom's Cooking Was Never Like This." *Forbes,* August 19, 1991, pp. 50, 54 (premium dog food sales).

Silbiger, Steven. "Study of the General and Gourmet Coffee Markets." Sponsored by Westway Merkuria, Inc., Englewood Cliffs, N.J., July 1989.

———, and Mark Parry. "Cafe Blason," Case UVA-M-369, copyright © 1990 by the Darden Graduate Business School Foundation, Charlottesville, Virginia.

Willoughby, Jack. "The Last Iceman." *Forbes*, July 13, 1987, p. 196 (vacuum tubes).

DAY 2: ETHICS

Freeman, R. Edward, and Daniel R. Gilbert, Jr. "The Problem of Relativism: When in Rome ..." Chapter 2, *Corporate Strategy and the Search for Ethics*. Englewood Cliffs, N.J.: Prentice-Hall, 1988, pp. 24–41. Adapted by permission of Prentice-Hall.

Friedman, Milton (Chicago). "The Social Responsibility Is to Increase Profits." *The New York Times*, September 13, 1970.

DAY 3: ACCOUNTING

Stern, Richard I. "McDonnell Douglas' Make-or-Break Year." *Forbes*, January 7, 1991, p. 37 (McDonnell Douglas income statement).

DAY 4: ORGANIZATIONAL BEHAVIOR

"Active Listening," Case UVA-OB-341, copyright © 1986 by the Darden Graduate Business School Foundation, Charlottesville, Virginia.

Beer, Michael. "Note on Performance Appraisal," Case 478-019, College, copyright © 1977 by the President and Fellows of Harvard College; all rights reserved.

Byrne, John A. "Business Fads: What's In — and Out." *Business Week*, January 20, 1986, p. 55 (MBA buzzwords).

Edwards, Jeffrey R. "Assessing Your Behavior Pattern," Case UVA-OB-360, copyright © 1987 by the Darden Graduate Business

School Foundation, Charlottesville, Virginia, p. 3 (Types A and B).

French, John R. P., and Bertram Raven. "The Bases of Social Power," *Group Dynamics*, ed. Darwin Cartwright. Evanston, Il.: Row, Peterson, 1960, pp. 607–623 (power).

Gabarro, John J., and John P. Kotter. "Managing Your Boss." *Harvard Business Review*, Vol. 57, No. 1 (January/February 1980), pp. 92–100. Copyright © 1980 by the President and Fellows of Harvard College; all rights reserved.

Hackman, J. Richard, and Greg R. Oldham. "Development of Job Diagnostic Surveys." *Journal of Applied Psychology*, Vol. 60, 1975, pp. 159–170.

Hogan, Eileen A. "One Model for Action Planning," Case UVA-OB-261R. Copyright © 1983 by the Darden Graduate Business School Foundation, Charlottesville, Virginia.

Kepner, Charles H., and Benjamin B. Tregoe. *The Rational Manager: A Systematic Approach to Problem Solving and Decision Making*. New York: McGraw-Hill, 1965, p. 55 (deviations, want got gaps).

Kotter, John P., and Leonard A. Schlesinger. "Choosing Strategies for Change." *Harvard Business Review*, Vol. 57, No. 2 (March/April 1980), pp. 106–114. Copyright © 1980 by the President and Fellows of Harvard College; all rights reserved (strategies for change).

Levine, Joshua. "*Dare e togliere* (give and take away)." *Forbes*, October 28, 1991, p. 115 (Armani).

Tannenbaum, Robert, and Warren H. Schmidt. "How to Choose a Leadership Pattern." *Harvard Business Review*, Vol. 51, No. 3 (May/June 1973), pp. 162–173. Copyright © 1973 by the President and Fellows of Harvard College; all rights reserved.

Zierden, William E. "A Framework for Understanding Organizations," Darden School Case UVA-OB-187, copyright © 1982 by the Darden Graduate Business School Foundation, Charlottesville, Virginia (the basic organization model).

DAY 5: QUANTITATIVE ANALYSIS

"Cash Flow and the Time Value of Money," Case 9-177-012, copyright © 1976 by the President and Fellows of Harvard College; all rights reserved.

Frey, Sherwood C. "Assessment and Use of Probability Distributions," Case UVA-Q-294, copyright © 1983 by the Darden Graduate Business School Foundation, Charlottesville, Virginia.

————. "Probability Assessment with the Aid of Historical Data," Case UVA-Q-288, copyright © 1983 by the Darden Graduate Business School Foundation, Charlottesville, Virginia.

"An Introduction to Decision Analysis," Case 181-046, copyright © 1980 by the President and Fellows of Harvard College; all rights reserved.

"Notes on Decision Diagrams," Case 9-171-035, copyright © 1970 by the President and Fellows of Harvard College; all rights reserved.

Oksman, Warren, and Sherwood C. Frey. "Introduction to Analytical Probability Distributions," Case UVA-Q-205, copyright © 1980 by the Darden Graduate Business School Foundation, Charlottesville, Virginia.

Pfeifer, Phillip E. "Forecasting Using Data," Case UVA-QA-381, copyright © 1988 by the Darden Graduate Business School Foundation, Charlottesville, Virginia.

Que Corporation, *Using 1-2-3*, Carmel, Ind.: Que Corporation, 1987, p. 514 (regression).

DAY 6: FINANCE

Cooper, Carol. "The Forbes 500." *Forbes*, April 27, 1992, p. 193 (Chemical Bank layoffs).

Dreman, David. "Bye-bye to Beta." *Forbes*, March 30, 1992, p. 148 (beta).

"Japanese Firms Pull Southland Corp. from Chapter 11." *Los Angeles Times*, March 6, 1991, p. D2 (Ito-Yokado Group buys 7-Eleven).

Ross, Stephen A. (Yale), and Randolph W. Westerfield (Wharton). *Corporate Finance*. St. Louis: Times Mirror/Mosby College Publishing, 1988.

The Value Line Survey. "Caterpillar Inc." May 15, 1992, p. 1346.

DAY 7: OPERATIONS

Byrne, John A. "Business Fads: What's In—and Out." *Business Week*, January 20, 1986, p. 54 (CPM).

"Constructing and Using Process Control Charts," Case 9-686-118, copyright © 1986 by the President and Fellows of Harvard College; all rights reserved (SPC).

Davis, Edward W. "Material Requirements Planning," Case UVA-OM-279, copyright © 1980 by the Darden Graduate Business School Foundation, Charlottesville, Virginia.

Freeland, James R. "Managing Inventories," Case UVA-OM-623, copyright © 1987 by the Darden Graduate Business School Foundation, Charlottesville, Virginia.

Landel, Robert D. *Managing Productivity Through People: An Operations Perspective*, Chapter 3. Englewood Cliffs, N.J.: Prentice-Hall, 1986; and Case UVA-OM-528, copyright © 1984 by the Darden Graduate Business School Foundation, Charlottesville, Virginia (queuing theory).

"A Note on Quality: The Views of Deming, Juran and Crosby," Case 9-687-011, copyright © 1986 by the President and Fellows of Harvard College; all rights reserved.

Savage, Sam L. *The ABC's of Optimization Using What's Best!* Oakland, Calif.: Holden-Day, Inc., 1986, p. I-17 (linear programming example).

Smitka, Michael J. *Competitive Ties: Subcontracting in the Japanese Automotive Industry*. New York: Columbia University Press, 1991, p. 145 (JIT in Japan).

DAY 8: ECONOMICS

Baldwin, William. "Creative Destruction." *Forbes*, July 13, 1987, p. 49 (Schumpeter).

Banks, Howard. "The World's Most Competitive Economy." *Forbes*, March 30, 1992, pp. 84, 85 (U.S. trade deficits and productivity).

Country Profiles 1991–1992, United States and Lebanon. The Economic Intelligence Unit, London (economic statistics).

Dornbusch, Rudiger (MIT/Chicago), and Stanley Fischer (MIT/ Chicago). *Macroeconomics.* New York: McGraw-Hill, 1987.

Linden, Dana Wechsler. "Dreary Days in the Dismal Science." *Forbes,* January 21, 1991, p. 68 (chapter lead).

McConnell, Campbell R. *Economics.* New York: McGraw-Hill, 1981, pp. 453–455 (elasticity).

Rosenblum, John. "Country Analysis and General Managers," Case 9-379-050, copyright © 1987 by the President and Fellows of Harvard College; all rights reserved.

Samuelson, Paul A. (MIT). *Economics.* New York: McGraw-Hill, 1980.

Sowell, Dr. Thomas. "Galbraith Strikes Again." *Forbes,* May 25, 1992, p. 140.

Stern, Richard L., "The Graying Wild Ones." *Forbes,* January 6, 1992, p. 40 (Harley-Davidson).

DAY 9: STRATEGY

Allan, Gerald B., and John S. Hammond III. "Note on the Use of Experience Curves in Competitive Decision Making," Case 175-174, copyright © 1975 by the President and Fellows of Harvard College; all rights reserved.

Bartlett, Christopher A. "Global Competition and MNC Managers," Case 9-385-287, copyright © 1985 by the President and Fellows of Harvard College; all rights reserved.

Bourgeois, L. J. "Note on Portfolio Techniques for Corporate Strategic Planning," Case UVA-BP-292, copyright © 1988 by the Darden Graduate Business School Foundation, Charlottesville, Virginia.

Germane, Gayton E. (Stanford). *The Executive Course.* Reading, Mass.: Addison-Wesley Publishing, 1987, pp. 367–70 (linkages).

Montana, Patrick, and Bruce Charnov. *Management.* New York: Barron's, 1987, p. 97 (Alice).

Paley, Norton. *Manager's Guide to Competitive Marketing Strategies.* New York: American Management Association, 1989, p. 6 (P&G Bounce).

Pascale, Richard T., and E. Tatum Christiansen. "Honda (A), (B)," Cases 9-384-049, 050, copyright © 1983 by the President and

Fellows of Harvard College; all rights reserved (two versions of Honda).

Porter, Michael E. *Competitive Strategy: Techniques for Analyzing Industries and Competitors*. New York: The Free Press, 1980, pp. 39, 75–82 (signaling).

Quinn, James Brian. "Strategic Change: Logical Incrementalism." *Sloan Management Review*, MIT, Fall 1978, pp. 7–22.

Romm, Joseph, J. "The Gospel According to Sun Tzu." *Forbes*, December 9, 1991, p. 162.

"The World's Billionaires." *Forbes*, July 22, 1991, pp. 138–139 (Sony rivalry).

Case Sources:

Darden Graduate School of Business
Educational Materials Service
University of Virginia, Box 6550
Charlottesville, VA 22906-6550
Attn: Ann Morris, Director
804-924-3009, FAX 804-924-4859

Harvard Business School Case Services
Harvard Business Review
Publishing Division
Boston, MA 02163
617-495-6117

INDEX

D

Q

T

Gabarro, John J., and John P. Kotter. "Managing Your Boss." *Harvard Business Review* (January/February 1980), Exhibit, "Managing the Relationship with Your Boss," p. 99. Copyright © 1979 by the President and Fellows of Harvard College; all rights reserved. Reprinted by permission.

Greiner, Larry E. "Evolution and Revolution as Organizations Grow." *Harvard Business Review* (July/August 1972), Exhibit II, "The Five Phases of Growth," p. 41. Copyright © 1972 by the President and Fellows of Harvard College; all rights reserved. Reprinted by permission.

Zierden, William E. "A Framework for Understanding Organizations," Darden School Case UVA-OB-187, Figure 1, p. 5. Copyright © 1982 by the Darden Graduate Business School Foundation, Charlottesville, Virginia.

Zierden, William E. "Introduction to Job Design," Darden School Case UVA-OB-91R, Figure 1, p. 2. Copyright © 1975 by the Darden Graduate Business School Foundation, Charlottesville, Virginia.

"Why People Behave the Way They Do," Darden School Case UVA-OB-183, Figure 5, p. 16. Copyright © 1986 by the Darden Graduate Business School Foundation, Charlottesville, Virginia.

Day 5: Quantitative Analysis

Cullum, Leo. Cartoon, "Meaningless Statistics."

Oksman, Warren, and Sherwood C. Frey. "Introduction to Analytical Probability Distributions," Case UVA-Q-205, pp. 5, 6, 14. Copyright © 1980 by the Darden Graduate Business School Foundation, Charlottesville, Virginia.

Day 6: Finance

"An Introduction to Debt Policy and Value," Case UVA-F-811, p. 1. Copyright © 1989 by the Darden Graduate Busienss School Foundation, Charlottesville, Virginia.

Cullum, Leo. Cartoon, "It's Not a Takeover."

Cullum, Leo. Cartoon, "Limited Partners."

Day 7: Operations

Cullum, Leo. Cartoon, "We're Stuck with 700,000 Bushels."

Day 8: Economics
Cullum, Leo. Cartoon, "I Have No Idea What It Means."

Day 9: Strategy
Ansoff, H. Igor. "Strategies for Diversification." *Harvard Business Review* (September/October 1957), Exhibit I, "Product Market Strategies for Business Growth Alternatives," p. 114. Copyright © 1957 by the President and Fellows of Harvard College; all rights reserved. Reprinted by permission.

Porter, Michael E. *Competitive Strategy: Techniques for Analyzing Industries and Competitors*, Figure 2-1, p. 39. Reprinted with the permission of The Free Press, a Division of Macmillan, Inc. Copyright © 1980 by The Free Press.

Porter, Michael E. *Competitive Advantage: Creating and Sustaining Superior Performance*, Figure 1-1, p. 5, Figure 1-2, p. 6. Reprinted with the permission of The Free Press, a Division of Macmillan, Inc. Copyright © 1985 by Michael E. Porter.

Waterman, Robert H., Thomas J. Peters, and Julien R. Phillips. "Structure Is Not Organization." *Business Horizons*, June 1980, Figure, p. 18. Copyright © 1980 by the Foundation for the School of Business at Indiana University. Used with permission.

Day 10: Mini-Courses
Borden, Neil H., Jr. "Class Notes on Conducting International Business," Darden Graduate School of Business, Charlottesville, Virginia, used with permission.

Piatkus Business Books

Piatkus Business Books have been created for people who need expert knowledge readily available in a clear and easy-to-follow format. All the books are written by specialists in their field. They will help you improve your skills quickly and effortlessly in the workplace and on a personal level.

Titles include:

General Management and Business Skills
Best Person for the Job, The Malcolm Bird
Beware the Naked Man Who Offers You His Shirt Harvey Mackay
Be Your Own PR Expert: the complete guide to publicity and public relations Bill Penn
Brain Power: the 12-week mental training programme Marilyn vos Savant and Leonore Fleischer
Complete Conference Organiser's Handbook, The Robin O'Connor
Complete Time Management System, The Christian H Godefroy and John Clark
Confident Decision Making J Edward Russo and Paul J H Schoemaker
Creating Abundance Andrew Ferguson
Creative Thinking Michael LeBoeuf
Dealing with Difficult People Roberta Cava
Energy Factor, The: how to motivate your workforce Art McNeil
Firing On All Cylinders: the quality management system for high-powered corporate performance Jim Clemmer with Barry Sheehy
Great Boom Ahead, The Harry Dent
How to Choose Stockmarket Winners Raymond Caley
How to Implement Corporate Change John Spencer and Adrian Pruss
How to Run a Part-Time Business Barrie Hawkins
Influential Manager, The: how to develop a powerful management style Lee Bryce

Making Profits: a six-month plan for the small business
Malcolm Bird

Sales Power: the Silva mind method for sales
professionals José Silva and Ed Bernd Jr

Selling Edge, The Patrick Forsyth

Telephone Selling Techniques That Really Work Bill Good

Winning Edge, The Charles Templeton

Winning New Business: a practical guide to successful
sales presentations Dr David Lewis

Presentation and Communication

Better Business Writing Maryann V Piotrowski

Complete Book of Business Etiquette, The Lynne Brennan
and David Block

Confident Conversation Dr Lillian Glass

Confident Speaking: how to communicate effectively using
the Power Talk System Christian H Godefroy and
Stephanie Barrat

He Says, She Says: closing the communication gap
between the sexes Dr Lillian Glass

Marketing Yourself: how to sell yourself and get the jobs
you've always wanted Dorothy Leeds

Networking and Mentoring: a woman's guide Dr Lily M
Segerman-Peck

Outstanding Negotiator, The Christian H Godefroy and Luis
Robert

Personal Power Philippa Davies

Powerspeak: the complete guide to public speaking and
presentation Dorothy Leeds

Presenting Yourself: a personal image guide for men Mary
Spillane

Presenting Yourself: a personal image guide for women
Mary Spillane

Say What You Mean and Get What You Want George R.
Walther

Secrets of Successful Interviews Dorothy Leeds

Your Total Image Philippa Davies

Careers

How to Find the Perfect Job Tom Jackson

Perfect CV, The Tom Jackson

Perfect Job Search Strategies Tom Jackson

Ten Steps To The Top Marie Jennings

**Which Way Now? – how to plan and develop a successful
career** Bridget Wright

**For a free brochure with further information on our
complete range of business titles, please write to:**

**Piatkus Books
Freepost 7 (WD 4505)
London W1E 4EZ**

PIATKUS

POWERSPEAK:
THE COMPLETE GUIDE TO PUBLIC
SPEAKING AND COMMUNICATION
by Dorothy Leeds

Excellent speaking and presentation skills are the key to success. In *Powerspeak*, Dorothy Leeds shows you how to:

- Control fear – and use it to your advantage
- Get attention and hold it
- Learn techniques and strategies known only to top professional speakers
- Avoid being boring
- Handle difficult questions confidently
- Make every presentation a winner

Dorothy Leeds runs a management consultancy firm in the United States. She is an experienced public speaker and runs seminars and workshops on public speaking and communication skills.

LEADERSHIP SKILLS FOR EVERY MANAGER
by Jim Clemmer and Art McNeil

Leadership Skills for Every Manager offers the key to organisational effectiveness. It shows you how to:

- Develop leadership skills throughout your company
- Examine the four leadership elements – vision, values, environment and behaviour – that exist in every organisation
- Build powerful and effective teams
- Align organisational culture
- Train people towards higher personal performance
- Transform good intentions into concrete results

Executives, managers and supervisors will find *Leadership Skills for Every Manager* an invaluable catalyst for action.

Jim Clemmer and Art McNeil are founders and operating executives of The Achieve Group, which specialises in leadership development and organisational effectiveness.

CONFIDENT DECISION MAKING
by J. Edward Russo and Paul J.H. Schoemaker

This is the decision-making programme that executives have been waiting for. Buying this book could be among the best decisions you've ever made!

- Avoid the common decision traps of self-taught amateurs
- Learn how to 'frame' a problem correctly
- Recognise and make use of all relevant information
- Follow a scientific decision-making process
- Improve your management skills by making better and more confident decisions

J. Edward Russo is Associate Professor of Marketing and Behavioural Science at Cornell University's Johnson Graduate School of Management and Paul J.H. Schoemaker is Associate Professor of Decision Sciences and Policy in the Graduate School of Business at the University of Chicago.

THE COMPLETE TIME MANAGEMENT SYSTEM
by Christian H. Godefroy and John Clark

The Complete Time Management System will change the way you work and think. It will increase your enjoyment of life and your chances of success. It will show you:

- How to do in 2 hours what you usually need 4 hours to do
- How to revive your concentration
- How to read 240 pages an hour – with better understanding and memorisation
- How to make an important decision faster
- How to delegate
- How to organise your office
- How to shorten meetings
- And much, much more

Learn the secrets of time management and you will profit from them all your life.

Christian Godefroy is a training specialist, founder of a publishing company in France, and best-selling author.